OF CANOES AND CROCODILES

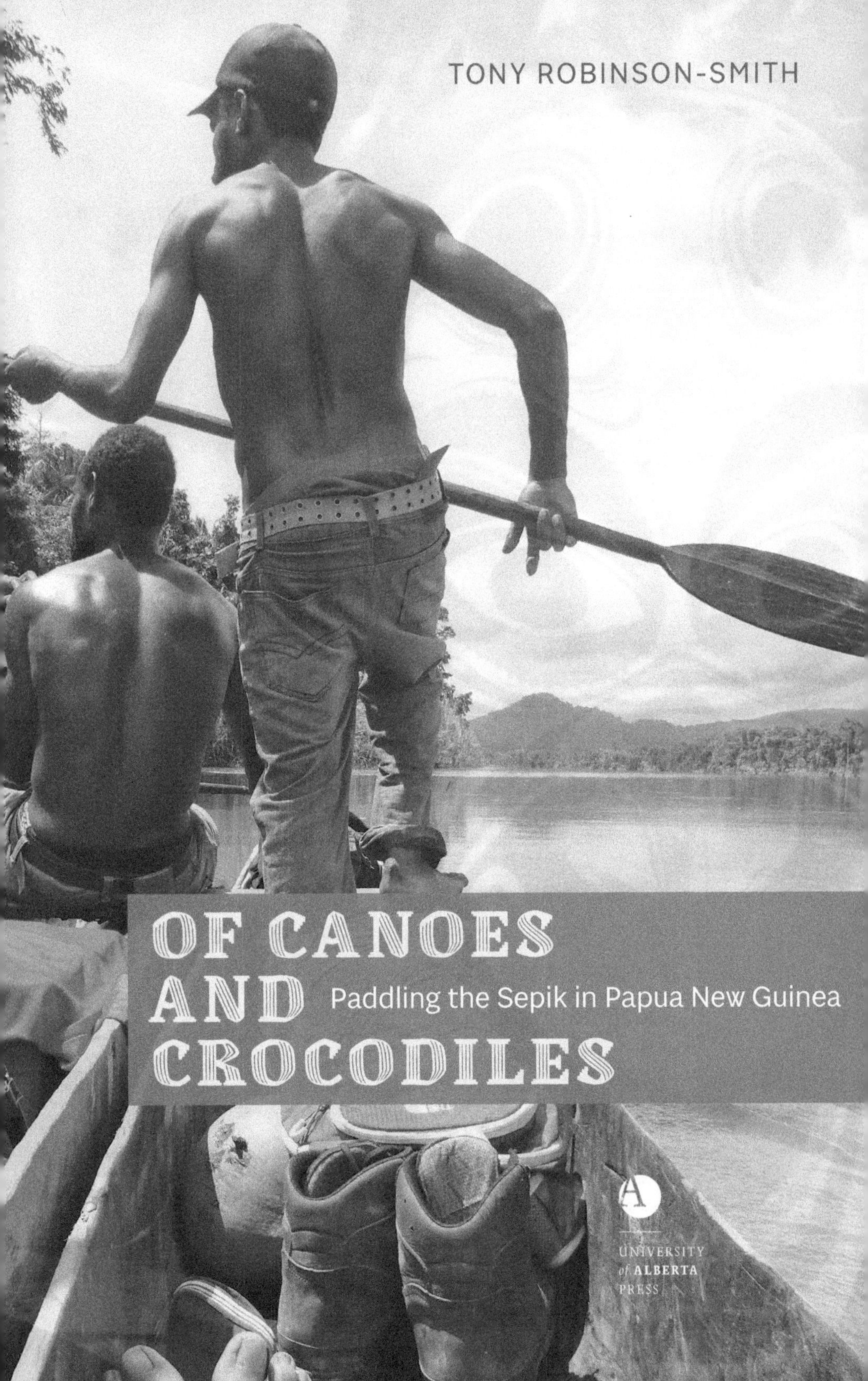
TONY ROBINSON-SMITH
OF CANOES AND CROCODILES
Paddling the Sepik in Papua New Guinea
UNIVERSITY of ALBERTA PRESS

Published by

University of Alberta Press
1–16 Rutherford Library South
11204 89 Avenue NW
Edmonton, Alberta, Canada T6G 2J4
amiskwaciwâskahikan | Treaty 6 |
Métis Territory
ualbertapress.ca | uapress@ualberta.ca

LIBRARY AND ARCHIVES CANADA CATALOGUING IN PUBLICATION

Title: Of canoes and crocodiles : paddling the Sepik in Papua New Guinea / Tony Robinson-Smith.
Names: Robinson-Smith, Tony, 1964– author.
Series: Wayfarer (Edmonton, Alta.)
Description: Series statement: Wayfarer
Identifiers: Canadiana (print) 20230553737 | Canadiana (ebook) 20230553850 | ISBN 9781772127348 (softcover) | ISBN 9781772127508 (EPUB) | ISBN 9781772127515 (PDF)
Subjects: LCSH: Robinson-Smith, Tony, 1964– —Travel—Sepik River (Indonesia and Papua New Guinea) | LCSH: Ladouceur, Nadya—Travel—Sepik River (Indonesia and Papua New Guinea) | LCSH: Sepik River (Indonesia and Papua New Guinea)—Description and travel. | LCSH: Papua New Guinea—Description and travel. | LCSH: Papua New Guinea—Social life and customs—21st century. | LCGFT: Travel writing.
Classification: LCC DU740.2 .R63 2024 | DDC 919.57/5045—dc23

First edition, first printing, 2024.
First printed and bound in Canada by Friesens, Altona, Manitoba.
Copyediting and proofreading by Kirsten Craven.
Map by Tony Robinson-Smith and Alan Brownoff.

University of Alberta Press gratefully acknowledges the support received for its publishing program from the Government of Canada, the Canada Council for the Arts, and the Government of Alberta through the Alberta Media Fund.

Canadä

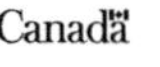

Alberta
Government

To Nadya, who helps me understand more deeply.

&

To my late father, naturalist and birdwatcher.

It is curious how quickly and with what little effort one can slip from one world into another.

—P.G. DOWNES, *Sleeping Island*

I think everyone can benefit by becoming a little more attuned to wild places—even if it's just for a day, or merely an hour to "unplug." I'm asked how I deal with the stress of my journeys, but in reality that's easy. What's hard is dealing with the stress of a modern, hyper-connected world—traffic, emails, texts, social media, 24/7 connectivity, paperwork, asphalt, concrete, noise. That's stressful. But there's a tonic to it—take a stroll in a nature park, or sit and watch the birds.

—ADAM SHOALTS, *Beyond the Trees*

CONTENTS

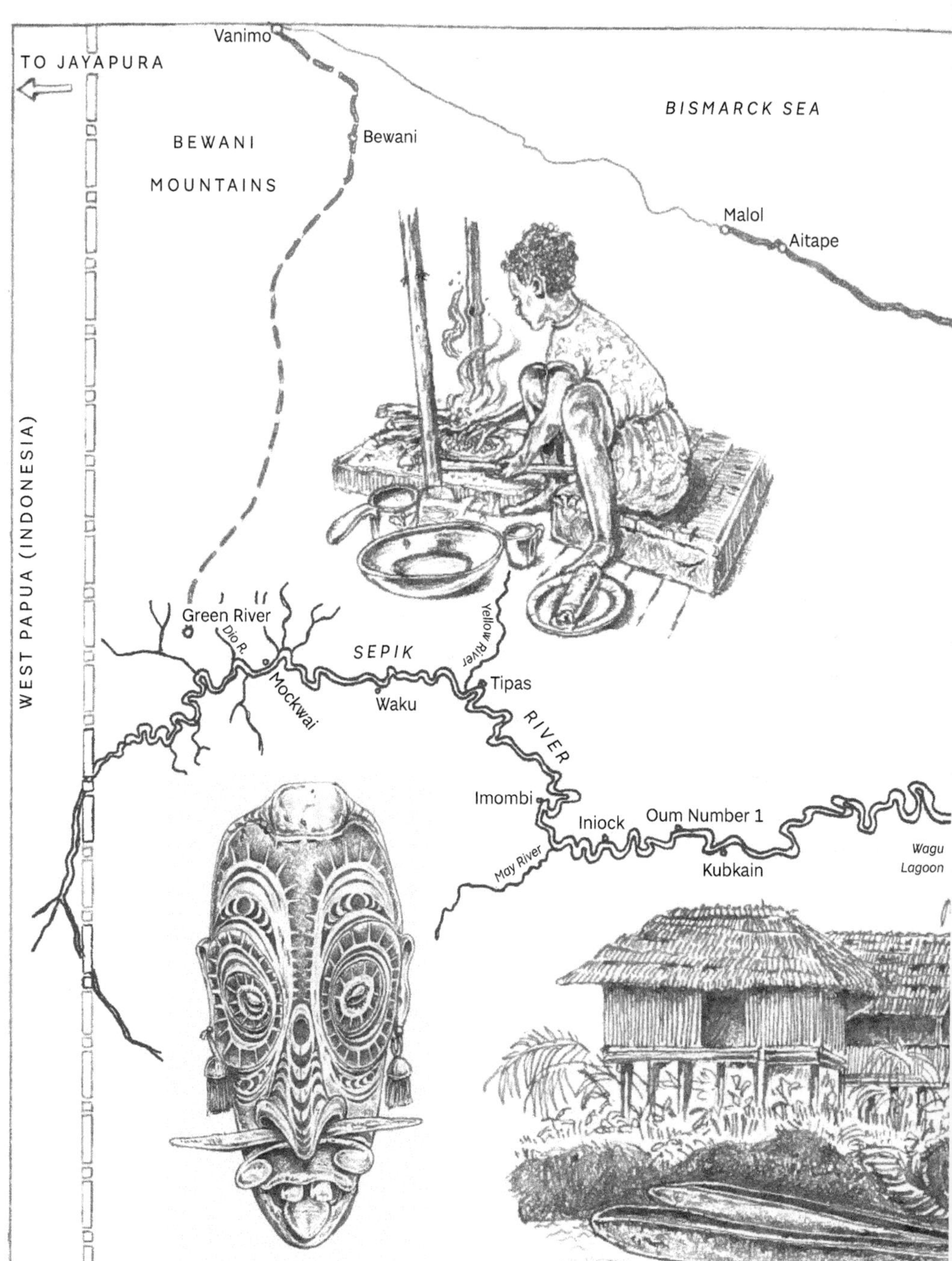

TO JAYAPURA
Vanimo
BISMARCK SEA
Bewani
BEWANI
MOUNTAINS
Malol
Aitape
WEST PAPUA (INDONESIA)
Green River
Dio R.
Yellow River
SEPIK
Mockwai
Waku
Tipas
RIVER
Imombi
Iniock
Oum Number 1
May River
Kubkain
Wagu
Lagoon

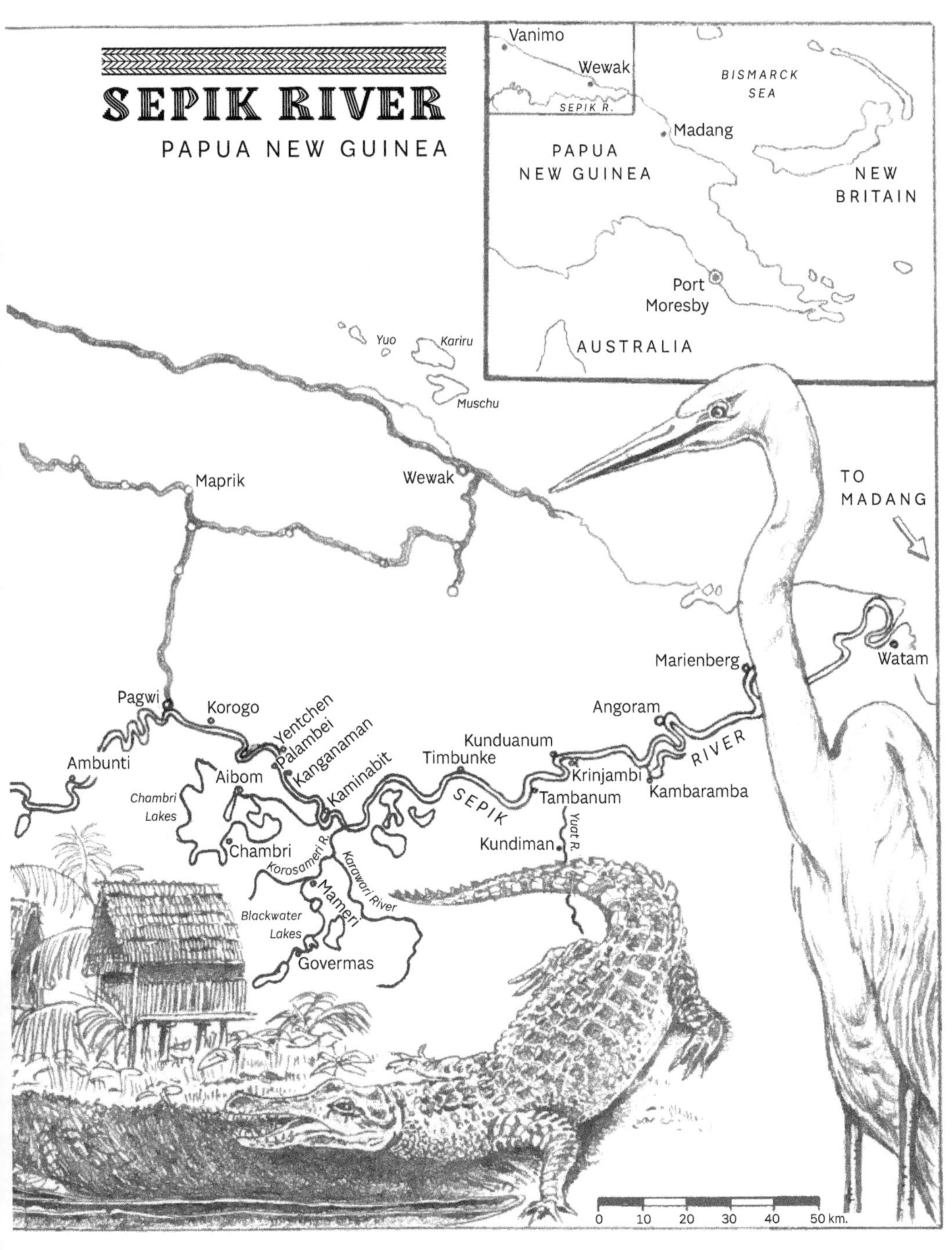

SEPIK RIVER
PAPUA NEW GUINEA
Vanimo
Wewak
SEPIK R.
BISMARCK SEA
Madang
PAPUA NEW GUINEA
NEW BRITAIN
Port Moresby
AUSTRALIA
Yuo
Kariru
Muschu
Maprik
Wewak
TO MADANG
Marienberg
Watam
Pagwi
Korogo
Yentchen
Palambei
Kanganaman
Angoram
Kunduanum
Timbunke
RIVER
Ambunti
Aibom
Kaminabit
Krinjambi
Kambaramba
Chambri Lakes
SEPIK
Tambanum
Yuat R.
Kundiman
Chambri
Korosameri R.
Karawari River
Mameri
Blackwater Lakes
Govermas
0
10
20
30
40
50 km.

1 INTO THE JUNGLE

The mighty Sepik is one of the great rivers of the world. In serpentine fashion it flows for 1126 km through swamplands, tropical rainforests and mountains. However, the Sepik is more than just a river—it's also a repository of complex cultures, a place where some men have crocodile skin while others place masks on yams in celebration, where mysterious rituals live on in haus tambarans (spirit houses) and master carvers still create the most potent art in the Pacific.

As you make your way around one of the endless river bends, the scale of the river, the bird life, the eerie lagoons and the traditional stilt villages make it easy to believe that you've travelled clean out of the 21st century and into a timeless, wondrous place.

—LONELY PLANET, *Papua New Guinea & Solomon Islands*

"And *why* do you want to do this?" Jeffrey Waino asks.

Nadya and I are sitting on rattan chairs in the living room of the CBC Guesthouse in Vanimo, a town on the north coast of Papua New Guinea. Our new acquaintance, a lean, woolly bearded man in his late thirties with milk-chocolate skin and an unfaltering gaze, is the principal of Green River Christian Secondary, a school buried deep in the jungle two hundred kilometres south of town. He is in Vanimo to buy supplies and pick up an electrician to rewire the staff quarters. Green River, a village and tributary of the Sepik, is where Nadya and I wish to go.

"That...is a very good question," I reply.

I feel my wife and I should have some worthy anthropological motive for what we intend to do: "Our purpose is to conduct an in-depth study of the communities living along the banks of the river to gain insight into their cultural practices and spiritual beliefs..." Or to track down an endangered marsupial perhaps: "Our goal is to observe the black-spotted cuscus in its natural habitat and study its mating behaviour..." Actually, I didn't expect to be having this conversation on our second day in the country. We haven't been to PNG before, and our plan was to use our two-month visa to explore the coast, get to know the people, and practise speaking Tok Pisin. Once we'd found our feet, *then* we could get another visa, head for the interior, and buy a canoe.

"We think it would be a good way to learn about village life," Nadya supplies helpfully.

"And to see the wildlife," I add.

The principal exchanges a look with the electrician, a bear of a man with hulking shoulders and a spreading stomach, slumped in an armchair chewing betel nut. Like Jeffrey, John Mariati has a beard, but his is grizzled and erupts from his chin in twin forks. The hair on his head he has wound into finger-length dreadlocks. The four of us, and the school accountant, are the only guests at CBC, a plank bungalow with half a dozen rooms and iron grills covering the windows. A notice on the wall forbids "suspicious behaviours," such as "Coming with a partner who is not your legal spouse," or "Causing problem outside and chased after by your enemies." CBC stands for "Christian Brethren Church," but everyone here uses the acronym. A fan spins frantically over our heads, rattling and whining.

"How far do you want to go?" Jeffrey asks.

The east-flowing Sepik is the longest river on the island of New Guinea. It meets the sea about a thousand kilometres from Green River.

"All the way," I reply.

The two Papuans nod thoughtfully and stroke their beards. I wipe sweat from my eyebrows with my palm. The fan seems more to stir the air than send a refreshing breeze. If it is this hot on the coast, what is it like in the interior?

"Is that possible, do you think?" Nadya asks Jeffrey. Good question. Papua New Guinea is just emerging from the rainy season. Is the water level too high at this time of year?

Jeffrey looks at us carefully for several moments. "It is possible, but, without a motor, it will take a long time. A month, maybe two."

"And," John says, leaning forward, "it will be dangerous. There are *pukpuk* in the river, and sometimes *raskol* raid other boat. West Sepik is peaceful. We know the tribes there. But the ones after that, well."

"Yes," says Jeffrey. "You should not go alone."

I nod. We had suspected as much. Yet I still cling to the notion we can simply get a canoe and paddle into an idyll, fishing for our meals, trading with villagers along the way, and riding up on the riverbank each night to pitch our tent. Who would wish to drop everything and go with us as a guide? We know nobody here. Besides, we aren't ready to leave for the jungle. We have almost no kina, only the little we got at the border in exchange for our remaining Indonesian rupiah, and we have no food (there are no stores in Green River, Jeffrey says, indeed none along the Upper Sepik). We should do the sensible thing. Bide our time on the coast, find out more about the Sepik, and prepare ourselves properly.

"Do you have room in the back of your truck for two Canadians?" I ask.

Jeffrey laughs and shakes his head. "Right now, no. My car is *bagarap*. I have to get a man to fix it. Also, I have rations to bring back to my school. And one more passenger to pick up. I'll see."

|| *"Sori, mi laikim kumin plis,"* I say as we thread our way through the crowd gathered in front of the supermarket the following morning. It is the second full sentence of Tok Pisin I have uttered since crossing the border, the first being *"Apinun, yu stap gut?"* (Hello, how are you?) The national language is a creole of Indigenous languages, German, and English, and many of the words are recognizable. *Sori* means "excuse me," *mi* means "I" or "me," *laikim* is "like," *kumin*, "come in," *plis*, "please." Nadya and I have brought a pocket-size

Tok Pisin phrase book (*tok*, "talk," *pisin*, "Pidgin") with us, but it only has thirty pages and doesn't contain a dictionary. The first phrases it presents are *kar i hariap* (the car was speeding or, literally, car he hurry up) and *pukpuk i lukim sutman* (the crocodile saw the hunter).

An armed guard in a black uniform waves us through a stile into the supermarket. With his shaved head, broad brow, and flat nose, he reminds me of a young Mike Tyson. I look over at his equally brawny counterpart at the exit, gun and baton at his waist, digging through the contents of a woman's cloth shoulder bag and comparing what he finds with her receipt.

Like the bank, the supermarket is busy. We have arrived at Easter, and people are stocking up. Women in brightly coloured cotton dresses, bandanas on their heads, flip-flops on their feet, wander the aisles, trailing their kids behind. A shoeless man with a rolled-up cigarette tucked behind his ear weighs a bag of rice in the palm of his hand. The supermarket appears to be owned by—or run by—Chinese merchants. Papuan women take the cash at the tills, but Chinese men hover behind them supervising, or else they sit, like umpires at Wimbledon, on tall stools at strategic points around the store, surveying the activity. Signs on the walls read *"Digicel top up hia"* and "Cash Only." If you want pens, batteries, or razor blades, you must go to a counter and ask for them.

"Let's start by getting a plastic bin," Nadya suggests. We figure that if Jeffrey can't give us a lift to the Sepik, someone must be going.

We find a bin the size of a microwave oven that comes with a clip-on lid. Whether it will fit in a Papuan canoe, we cannot say. What to fill it with is also guesswork. Jeffrey told us we could expect to get sago and fish at the villages, but that we shouldn't count on them. We must buy food to last at least two weeks, enough to get us to Pagwi, the first village that has a road link to a town. In our bin go twenty tins of Diana brand tuna, ten of luncheon meat, eight kilogram bags of Hamamas rice, instant noodles, ten 250-gram bags of salt and ten of sugar, a jar of peanut butter, a bottle of cooking oil, toilet rolls, teabags, and some sachets of Nescafé. Rather than Australian Bush Biscuits, which look about as palatable as our passports, we choose Papuan Em Nau (literally, Him Now) crackers, which are thinner and come in different flavours. To satisfy my sweet tooth, I add Mint-choc Creams, Arnott's Classic Assorted, and Paradise Foods' Nambawan (Number One) biscuits.

"We are going to need more money," I say when we emerge, the guard waving us through the exit without checking our bin or receipt. We need enough to buy a canoe, pay for our night stays in villages, and possibly hire guides. We need an extra stash for emergencies.

Nadya sighs. The automated tellers at BSP (Bank South Pacific) were fickle when we tried them earlier. The banking hall closed, we had had to join a long queue for the three ATMs. Most people were leaving empty-handed. Those yet to try their luck were visibly nervous, gripping their debit cards tightly, their eyes evaluating the machines like they were Vegas slots. Plumping for the middle of the three, as it seemed to glow the brightest, I punched in a request for K1,000 (Can$400). Out shot my card like a tongue. "Insufficient funds." I stared at the display. How could that be? I had plenty in my account. Five hundred kina, then. Back in went the card. Out it came. "Insufficient funds." I dug out my other bank card, yet to be used on the trip. "Insufficient funds." I stepped back and let Nadya have a go. Two K500 withdrawals without difficulty (*what?*), although not a third. So a thousand was the daily limit. I looked appealingly at the guard, who was chopping the air idly with his baton. "You try that machine," he said, pointing to the one on the left. "That is lucky one today."

Only John is at the guest house when we stagger in with our bin, shirts stuck to our skins, and collapse into chairs on the verandah. Everyone has gone to church, he says, adding a mustard stalk coated in lime powder to the betel nut in his mouth so as to get a high. "Only us sinners left."

We invite him to take a look in our bin and remark on the contents. Have we bought enough? He extracts a six-pack of Paradise pineapple creams I had managed to squeeze in at the last moment.

"I think you better give this biscuit to *pukpuk* so he get fat and leave you alone. Otherwise, he eat tasty Canadian for dinner."

John is from Yellow River, another tributary of the Sepik and a two- or three-day paddle downstream from Green River. We get out our map, and he shows us his village. Near Tipas, where his uncle John Youpa lives. The exact locations of the villages are difficult to make out as much of the Upper Sepik region is flecked with blue dashes. Swampland.

"Can you swim at all in the Sepik?" I ask, mopping my brow and imagining the relief that would be in the tropical heat.

"Yes. But only where the villagers go."

|| Easter Monday, the stores and banks are closed, so Nadya and I head for the beach. Vanimo is situated on the handle of a frying pan of land sticking out into the Bismarck Sea. The protected bay on the west side shelters the port, a terminus for cargo vessels with tall cranes and barges stacked high with timber. No movement there today, and we pause for a while to watch women fishing—twenty-two of them, I count—standing waist-deep, side by side in the sea, rods held high, bags for their catch tied about their heads. Then we cross the handle to the corresponding bay on the east side, passing through the empty streets of the town. There's a helmeted friarbird hooting in a coconut palm and a flock of red-eyed shining starlings as twittery as their European equivalents. After the frantic pace of Jayapura in West Papua, our last port of call with its buzzing scooters and bustling *bemos*, we are glad of some peace. Vanimo has no motorbikes or scooters; apparently, registering them is expensive. People get around on foot or take PMVs (public motor vehicles), minibuses larger than Indonesian bemos.

We are not sure whether it is culturally acceptable to strip off and swim, but there are a few Papuan families cooling their ankles. It is good to see how clean the beach is. Some of the ones in West Papua were awash in fishing nets and plastic. Here, all I see are coconut husks and some empty SR beer bottles beside an outrigger canoe. Maybe Papua New Guineans are more responsible regarding litter.

We wallow and snorkel around coral heads, Nadya keeping her capri pants and T-shirt on, and then stretch out on the beach.

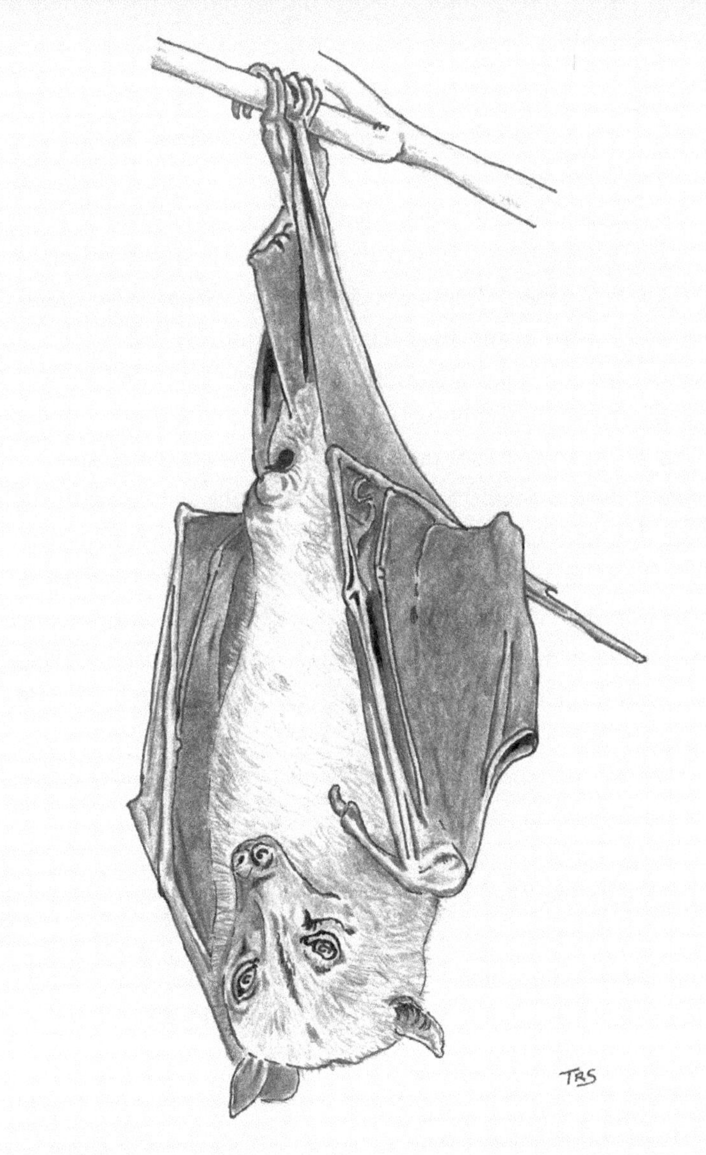

Flying fox.

"Good of Jeffrey to give us some tips last night on where to stay on the river," I say, fishing some Em Nau crackers out of my bag.

"And what costs to expect. He seems genuinely interested in our trip. I think he would like us to see his school too. He is clearly devoted to it. He was telling me last night how he hopes to encourage teachers to stay for longer by building new staff quarters, bringing in solar panels, and getting internet. There are over three hundred kids at the school but only thirteen teachers. He aims to have twenty-three."

"He is a man with a vision. What do you make of John?"

"Teddy bear with a growl. It would be good to spend more time with these two men." Nadya sits up suddenly. "What is that sound?"

A tree farther up the beach has exploded into life. I see umbrellas hanging from the tallest branches and hear excited twittering. We put our clothes on and investigate.

As we draw near, I see inverted heads with long snouts and beady eyes. A triangular panel unfolds from one and then retracts. A hundred bats, each the size of a cat, their wings shiny and black, their chests furry and orange. Some are asleep, their bodies wrapped in their leathery wings; others compete for roosting space with their neighbours, baring their teeth and screeching. Those displaced edge their way further along the branches, reaching out with black hooks that serve as their hands.

"We are not permit to shoot flying fox in town," says a man also gazing at the spectacle.

"If you could, would you eat them?"

"Yes, but they are not very tasty."

|| We leave Vanimo in Principal Waino's Toyota pickup on Tuesday afternoon. Nadya and I squeeze into the cab with Jeffrey. John, the school accountant Samuel, and two members of staff take the benches in the open back, their legs buried under sacks of rice and boxes of rations. According to our map, there isn't a road going to Green River, but our guidebook assures us one exists. It starts out well, asphalted and smooth, when we turn onto it from the coast road, but, creeping up into the Bewani Mountains, it soon deteriorates into rutted dirt and rocks. Where streams cross it, we must mount large boulders or rattle over gappy log bridges.

As the vehicle bounces along, I peer out the smeared side window at the towering forest. Flocks of parakeets or perhaps lorikeets hurtle by overhead, alarmed by our intrusion. We disturb a pair of pheasant coucal, large black birds resembling grackles but with

Jeffrey Waino with author and Nadya.

broader tails and vulturine heads, picking through debris and regrowth after logging. At one point, an oversized rat dashes across the road in front of us.

"What's that, Jeffrey?"

"Bandicoot."

Busy texting his school while driving, the principal offers only brief answers to our questions. The term is winding down at Green River Christian Secondary, and the students are soon to go home for the holidays. They must sit their exams and clean up the dormitories. The teachers must mark the exams, submit their grades, and write reports. He is more forthcoming when Nadya asks him about his faith, though. He is a follower of Pastor David Dii, he tells us, a Papuan "who heard the word of the Lord and took Jesus into his heart" and built many churches. But Jesus was not fully satisfied with the pastor's work, apparently, and bid him travel around the country to spread the *gut nius* personally. Jeffrey also wishes to spread the good news and actively does so with his students. Suspicious of institutionalized religion, he is building a sanctuary ("not a church, a shelter") at the school where students can gather and share their faith.

Before leaving Canada, I had read about Kay Liddle, a missionary from New Zealand who brought the gospel to Green River in the 1950s. In his memoir, he wrote, "The call the Lord gave to the Apostle Paul became personalised to me: 'I am sending you to them to open their eyes and turn them from darkness to light and from the power of Satan to God, so that they may receive forgiveness of sins and a place among those who are sanctified by faith in me.'" The assumption that Papua New Guineans were satanic and sinful had made me wince, the arrogance that said they should look to a Christian god for salvation. Given the name of our guest house in Vanimo and now Jeffrey's statements, it would seem that Christian missionaries have left their mark here. I ask our driver whether his parents knew Pastor Liddle. His wife Gwen taught them, he replies.

We arrive at the "no-go zone" at dusk. Jeffrey warned us about this section of the road earlier but mischievously refused to say more. John and the others jump down with spades and a bush knife. Samuel begins chopping down brush, but no branches will bridge the yawning, mud-filled crater ahead. I haven't seen a pothole this size since Land Rovering through the Democratic Republic of the Congo in the 1990s. Large enough to swallow a car, such goop-filled potholes the Africans renamed "bogholes."

"Sometimes, we spend many hours here, sometimes the whole night," Jeffrey says, rubbing his eyes. He has been driving for eight hours.

The Toyota, I notice when I roll down the window, is in a green tunnel. On all sides, moss-clad trees reach for a dense canopy seventy or eighty metres above us. Lianas the thickness of fire hose spill down from this roof, some curling like snapped guitar strings, others resembling record-breaking fingernails. They lend the forest an eerie, surreal quality. Broad palm fronds arch over the road, extending their fingers and casting more shade. Beside the road, there are skid marks, smashed ferns, and a ditch. In the Democratic Republic of the Congo, jeeps or trucks would rarely travel long distances alone. In pairs or threes, one or two vehicles could tow the stranded one out of bogholes or ditches. What happens if we don't emerge from this monster pothole? But for a single wheezy logging truck coming in the opposite direction, we've seen no traffic on the road today.

"You should fasten your seatbelts," Jeffrey says and asks me to close the window. "God willing, we will arrive safely on the other side."

Our chauffeur grips the steering wheel firmly with both hands and pumps the accelerator. He waits a moment longer for John and Samuel to finish digging divots out of the far bank: traction for the front wheels. Fireflies spark in the headlights. Crossing his heart, Jeffrey lets rip. The truck shoots forward and then abruptly plunges down. Curtains of mud rise on either side, and mud rains down on the windshield. I jerk back and cling to my seat.

"Ouf!" Nadya blurts as her head smacks the roof.

Up the other side of the pothole we go, wheels spinning manically. We all lean forward. Jeffrey breaths out as we arrive dripping on level ground, the radiator hissing. God, it would seem, was willing. Thankfully, the exhaust pipe is of the type that trails up the side of the windshield.

"We carry spades in our cars too," Nadya remarks, rubbing her head. "To shovel snow off the road in wintertime."

We arrive at a clearing in the forest at one in the morning. All I can see of the school by the headlamps of the Toyota are rectangular stilt huts with tin roofs. We pull up in front of a bungalow beside a cylindrical water tank. John lowers himself falteringly from the back of the pickup, his clothes streaked with mud, cakes of it in his beard, and stretches. He rakes his beard with his fingers, digs a betel nut out of his pocket, and chuckles.

"I must do no-go zone two times more!"

He is here only to assess the electrical needs of the school. He must return to Vanimo to get the materials he requires for the job.

Nadya and I trail Jeffrey to a guest room in the bungalow. It contains a single bed with a bare mattress.

|| Neither Jeffrey nor John is about in the morning when we heave ourselves stiffly out of bed, so we wander around the school on our own. Students fly out of the huts, astonished. What are we doing here? Where have we come from? Have we come to teach? They are wearing brightly coloured T-shirts, baggy shorts or jeans rolled to the knee, and thongs. We get out our map and say what we hope to do. One dashes off to fetch a school map. Printed in Australia, it is called "Animals of PNG" and has pictures with captions. For the Sepik region, I see "Death Adder. *Acanthophis antarcticus.* Nocturnal and very venomous," "Bird-eating Spider. *Selenocosmia crassipes.* Fangs of over 1 cm deliver a very strong digestive enzyme which liquefies the prey so it can be digested," and "Anopheles Mosquito. *Anopheles sp.* Causes disease in humans, especially malaria and dengue fever." Are there birds of paradise in this part of Papua, I ask, seeing "Raggiana bird of paradise," the national bird, superimposed over the Highlands. Yes, yes, chorus the students, the villagers shoot them for their feathers.

Jeffrey told us on the way here that some of the students could accompany us on our voyage as their villages are downstream. They seem full of beans and speak good English, but the oldest are in Grade 10, meaning they are probably fifteen or sixteen years old. Would teenagers be able to negotiate a fair price for a canoe? Could they repair one if it sprang a leak? Would they be good ambassadors when it comes to befriending a tribe? What of fending off *raskols*?

The students head for their classes, and we continue our tour. At the school shop, a shed with rusty tins of tuna and cans of Sprite on the shelves, we meet an English language teacher called Ruth. She tells us that some villagers on the Sepik may mistake us for the ghosts of their ancestors, returning to their village.

"They will give you lots of food and ask you to stay for good!"

"That could be awkward," I reply, assuming she is joking. "Our visas only last for two months."

But I also know that tribes in the interior reacted similarly to the arrival of whites back in the 1930s when Australia governed Papua New Guinea. Leading an expedition across the Great Papuan Plateau in 1934 and 1935, patrol officers Jack Hides and Jim

O'Malley caught the Etoro by surprise. A tribesman who had been a boy at the time reported later how the village Elders had reacted. "When they saw the clothes on the *sowelo*...they thought they were like people you see in a dream; 'these must be spirit people...coming openly in plain sight.'" Surely, eight decades later, the tribes of the Sepik have seen enough white visitors not to mistake us for ghosts or spirits.

After two days at the school, I am beginning to get itchy feet. The principal's guest room is the size of a broom cupboard, and his two infants make exhausting daytime companions. We are unable to take a look at the river or at a canoe as Green River isn't near the school and the Sepik further away. The word is we must get to the Dio, another tributary of the Sepik, but we have no idea where that is. Some say Ibru village is the place to go. They have canoes at Ibru. Is that on the Dio? No, it's on a river that flows into Green River. I go in search of John, reminding myself not to be impatient. A lot is going on at the school.

"My white brother from a white mother!"

I discover him, feet up, on the verandah of a hut. He has yet to begin his assessment of the electrics, he tells me, as many of the classrooms are still in use. He has been busy fixing the school generator after yesterday's power outage.

"I have a proposition for you, John."

Nadya and I think this Falstaffian character would make good company on our voyage. Would he be interested in paddling with us as far as Yellow River where his home village is? Naturally, we would pay his way and feed him. He could spend some of the Easter vacation with his family. I expect him to decline. He has only just arrived at the school, and he is on contract. But he surprises me. If Jeffrey doesn't mind, yes, he could join us. We walk immediately to the principal's office. Another yes—provided John is gone no more than a week. Jeffrey also tells us that a car would leave for the Dio in the afternoon.

I give Nadya the good news and pack my bag. John is fifty, imposing, obviously capable with his hands, and a good communicator. If we get into a fix, I can imagine him being an invaluable ally. Things are starting to come together. But an hour later, I see John striding over, looking serious.

"My Black brother from a Black mother, what means that frown?"

He explains that going to Yellow River with us is no problem, but his return would be. He has made some enquiries. Because there are few motor-canoes this high on the Sepik, we would need to buy a 44-gallon drum of petrol so he could motor back to Green River, a three-day journey at this time of year. That would cost K1,000, even K1,500. Our luck on the BSP slots in Vanimo went no further than K5,000. We can't afford that.

Shouldering our backpacks, Nadya and I hug Jeffrey's wife, Fiona, and thank her for putting us up, say bye to their kids, and, with a bin of food knocking our knees, march over to the main office. John trails behind. Any last advice from my Black brother?

"The mosquitoes with malaria are last ones to come out at night," he says with a wink. He reminds us to look up his uncle when we get to Tipas.

Today is the last for students at Green River Christian Secondary, and about a hundred have lined up on the grass in front of the main office. Principal Waino is delivering his closing address when we arrive.

"Praise the Lord, the term has been a great success. God sent us here with a mission, and, together, we have fulfilled that mission..." He ends with the words, "Any students living on the Sepik, please stay behind."

Seven students remain, baffled expressions on their faces, as the rest scatter. They look at their principal, then at us, and again at their principal. With their athletic bodies and shaggy chins, they seem more like army cadets soon to go on leave than high school kids breaking up for Easter. Each has a *bilum*, a string pouch with a strap going over one shoulder, to carry food and betel nuts. At Jeffrey's bidding, they introduce themselves.

Fice seems the most amenable. He nods and smiles at us in a relaxed way, and I get the impression we could rely on him. To his right are Alex and Lurijawe, who mumble their names and don't crack smiles. Lurijawe seems suspicious of us. Alex has a sixty-centimetre bush knife sticking out of his *bilum*. To Fice's left is Tom, who has a slighter build than the others and regards us furtively. Donald has sloped shoulders and an impish grin. With his shirt collar turned up and his ball cap on back-to-front, he looks like the class wise guy. The two at the back are Kingston and Towei, whom I recognize from the end-of-term soccer tournament Nadya and I watched yesterday. Both are strapping, Kingston with a square jaw and high cheekbones. On the football pitch, they defended their goal with brutal tackles. In traditional dress, they would make fearsome warriors.

Twenty minutes later, Nadya and I are bumping along in the cab of a pickup truck like Jeffrey's heading south, and our new companions are in the back. The road deteriorates until it is so eroded the driver can no longer negotiate its craters. He halts before a steep decline and points. Somewhere down there, hidden in the jungle, is a village and a river. Nadya and I shoulder our bags and the lads their *bilums*, and we start walking.

2 A WILD PLACE

You will come to a place where the streets are not marked.
Some windows are lighted. But mostly they're darked.
A place you could sprain both your elbow and chin!
Do you dare to stay out? Do you dare to go in?

—DR. SEUSS, *Oh, the Places You'll Go!*

The idea of buying a local canoe and paddling down one of the great tropical rivers of the world had been in the back of our minds since Nadya and I canoed through Indonesia in 1997. Wishing to get off the beaten track in a highly touristed country, we went to a village on the sparsely populated south coast of Java, and, with the help of locals, bought a *prahu kecil*, a traditional fishing canoe with outriggers and a 5cc tuk-tuk engine, and travelled along the coastlines of Java, Bali, Lombok, Sumbawa, Rinca, and Komodo. We quickly realized that having our own boat gave us great freedom: it meant we could go where we pleased and stop whenever we wished. It also threw us into the company of local people. We met fishermen on the water and stayed in their villages. They taught us how to count waves before launching into the surf, how to negotiate whirlpools when crossing between islands, and how to take tuk-tuk apart and clean out the salt water. In our conical straw hats and with our basic Indonesian, we discovered during our four-month voyage that, to some extent, we could share their way of life. Our treasured memories were of heading out to sea with the fishermen at sunrise, of meeting people on shore at the end of each day, and of standing on a beach at sunset watching hundreds of fruit bats pass overhead.

The only problem with our *prahu* was the incessant clatter of its engine. The dugout with its outriggers was so heavy and the waves so wild for much of our voyage that we motored more than we paddled.

Travelling downstream on a river, you don't need a motor. Choose a long enough river, and we might spend months riding the current, fishing for our lunch, training our binoculars on kingfishers, and staying with villagers living along the banks. Inclined to return to Southeast Asia, we dug out a map. Where might we mount such a voyage? Borneo? The world's third-largest island might be the ticket. There were several long rivers there, and we could resurrect our Indonesian. I had read Redmond O'Hanlon's 1984 memoir of his canoe journey along the Rajang and Baleh rivers in Sarawak, Malaysia. Nadya and I shared the Englishman's interest in birds. Borneo was home to such brightly painted rarities as the rhinoceros hornbill, the stork-billed kingfisher, Whitehead's trogon, and the Bornean bristlehead.

I looked for other memoirs on Borneo and found *Stranger in the Forest* by Eric Hansen. Guided by nomadic Penan tribesmen, he had travelled on foot and by boat into the interior about the same time as O'Hanlon. He formed close relations with his guides and learned about their uncanny sense of direction in the forest, their superstitions, birthing rituals, and hunter's concept of time. But the book's epilogue described the destruction of the forests. There was a photograph of five Penan warriors standing on a logging road looking at smashed trees on either side. It seemed that logging companies had ravaged much of the island. Was this true? I ordered an up-to-date guidebook, and this confirmed the sad fact. Similar devastation had occurred in Sumatra where commercial palm oil plantations had replaced large tracts of primary rainforest.

We looked again at our map, our eyes wandering east of Borneo to the world's second-largest island. New Guinea also had some long rivers: the Mamberamo and Baliem on the Indonesian side (known as West Papua), the Fly and Sepik on the Papua New Guinean side. I could find practically no contemporary accounts of voyages either in print or online until I chanced upon a book by an intrepid

Englishwoman. Christina Dodwell spent four months in the early 1980s paddling a dugout down the Sepik in PNG and exploring its tributaries and adjoining lakes. She had a hard time. Thieves twice stole her canoe, she collapsed with high fever in one mosquito-infested village, and she was taken for an Indonesian spy and arrested. Travelling alone in a male-dominated society at times meant fending off the advances of men. Yet she also met with extraordinary kindness. Papuans gave her wood carvings, fish, sago grubs, sugar cane, water-melons, and a mosquito swat as gifts, and invited her to their ceremonies; they taught her how to skin a crocodile and carve a canoe prow. Hers sounded like the kind of immersive experience we were after.

I bought a detailed relief map of Papua New Guinea. Dodwell had flown in a four-seater plane from the coastal town of Wewak to a tiny village called Ama in the interior and begun her voyage on the May River, a tributary of the Sepik. I traced my finger east from the confluence of the two rivers back to the source of the Sepik in the Victor Emanuel Range. The river had already flowed about a third of its total length by the time it met the May, and I wondered from what point the Upper Sepik was navigable. I learned from reading that, when PNG was an Australian territory in the 1920s, two colonial patrol officers and their Papuan porters had tried to descend the Sepik from its upper reaches on log rafts. Unable to find buoyant duduye logs to lash together, they settled for a heavier wood. Five of their six rafts hit snags and disintegrated. Against his companion's advice, Ivan Champion persisted with the slightly more buoyant sixth and described his experience in his journal afterwards:

> *There was another and greater crash; one corner had hit a submerged snag and this time the craft did not swing clear. In a moment we had turned sideways on. I saw one side of the raft rise up; instinctively I flung myself across in a puny effort to bring it down but found myself under the water hanging on with both hands.*

Perhaps dugout canoes of the sort Dodwell had used would prove more manoeuvrable. But I could see from the map that there was another snag. The Upper Sepik snaked into West Papua and remained there for a good fifty kilometres before curling back into PNG. That would likely mean visa problems, as both countries required them. Not only this, Indonesian immigration also typically demanded a *surat jalan*, a travel permit, to visit remote areas of the country. Maybe we could join the river a hundred kilometres or so downstream from its source, near to where it returned to PNG. I looked for a village on the Sepik close to the border and saw Green River. The nearest town was Vanimo on the north coast, but no road seemed to connect the two.

I ordered a guidebook and discovered in the opening pages that Papua New Guinea was home to the birds of paradise, one of the most outlandish species of birds on Earth. In my head were images from a wildlife documentary of one with pink and orange plumage hanging upside down from a branch and chuckling, another with a skirt of feathers dancing in a forest glade like a ballerina. I got a bird book and was surprised to learn how different they looked from one another. Some were small as finches, with antennae sprouting from their crowns or coiled springs jutting from their rears, others large as crows with extravagant plumes trailing along their backs that they chucked forward in display. They were united as a family, it seemed, only in their peculiarity. Apparently, the males were endowed with these unlikely appendages for the sole purpose of attracting females, and they performed complex dance manoeuvres to impress them. These birds lived deep in the forest, and would, no doubt, be a sight to behold.

Wanting to learn more about the colonial history of the country, I visited the library. According to John Dademo Waiko, PNG has a dark past. The Papuan historian described Germany's occupation of the northern half of his country in the late 1800s and grim working conditions for local labourers on cocoa, tobacco, and copra plantations, and of Britain's occupation of the south and punitive patrols sent to villages that resisted white administration. After the First World War, Australia took control of the country and apartheid prevailed: racial segregation at the workplace and on public transport, local men forbidden to wear shirts or smile at a white woman in public.

During the Second World War, both the invading Japanese and occupying Australian forces recruited Papuans as carriers, labourers, police, and soldiers, and discrimination persisted. In a "New Deal" thereafter, the Australian government promised compensation for war damages and financial aid to boost economic development and expand educational and health services, but most Papuans did not appear to benefit as they lived outside the cash economy, remained unconnected to the towns by road, and continued to depend mainly on subsistence agriculture.

PNG gained independence in 1975 but had to rely heavily in the years that followed on Australia for aid because wealth was not staying in the country. Export income derived from cash crops, especially coffee, the largest plantations still owned by foreigners, and from mining operations, especially gold and copper, run by transnational companies. Wishing for greater access to Western goods, many villagers with little or no education migrated to the towns but, unable to find work or housing, built shanties and resorted to crime to survive. Waiko spoke of "growing lawlessness" on the streets at this time and traditional social order breaking down, of an undisciplined and underpaid police force, of corrupt politicians engaging in illicit financial deals, and parliamentarians courting local businesses to fund their parties. But wishing perhaps not to paint too bleak a picture, he concluded by identifying some stabilizing influences evident in the 1990s. PNG had a wealth of natural resources (fertile growing land, fish, precious minerals, oil, and timber), a robust subsistence sector, family ties that tended to be strong, two widely spoken languages (Tok Pisin and English, the language of instruction in schools), and Christian churches that were playing an important role in promoting peace.

Recent news reports revealed, however, that Papua New Guinea was still a volatile and at times violent place. Tribal fighting erupted from time to time in the Highlands, and the guidebook recommended staying out of some provinces (one a prime location for seeing birds of paradise). *Raskol* gangs frequented Port Moresby, Lae, Wewak, and Mount Hagen. The word "*raskol*" is Tok Pisin for "rascal," and I imagined street kids picking pockets and snatching tourists' cameras until I called up some images online. *Raskols*, in fact, resembled urban guerillas and carried bush knives the length of a cricket bat and jerry-rigged pistols or shotguns held together with tape. There were neighbourhoods in town, especially in the capital, to avoid day or night, and the book suggested putting fifty kina "*raskol* money" in your pocket before going out on the street and keeping the rest in your shoe. Violence was also a product of an enduring belief in sorcery. Villagers still turned to sorcerers to determine who was responsible for a family member's sudden illness or death so they might take revenge. Women were accused of practising the dark arts and tortured to death.

Wanting to get a first-hand impression of Papua New Guinea, Nadya and I tried to find someone who had been. It seemed no one had. Then a couple living on the New Brunswick coast got in touch. Volunteers for CUSO International in the late 1970s, Steve and Barbara Pierce had served as schoolteachers there for two years. Over beers with us, they shared memories of *sing-sings* and extravagant bird of paradise feather headdresses, of tribal wars and the system of "pay-back," of sorcerers and Christian missionaries. The Pierces were in the country just after independence, a time when Papuans were "proud and welcoming."

"Has the country been ruined by deforestation?" I asked Steve. I had seen one documentary that told of illegal logging operations.

"Not that I remember. Mining polluted the Fly River, I think... but that was after our time. You will see ruin, Tony, if you want to see it—anywhere. Then you go around the corner, and someone invites you into their home."

Nadya and I bought a stormproof tent, a UV lamp water purifier, a mosquito bed net, an eight-month supply of malaria tabs, broad-brimmed hats, long-sleeved shirts treated with permethrin insecticide, binoculars, and other gear suitable for a long voyage on a tropical river. We bought a string of airline tickets that would get us from our hometown Fredericton in Atlantic Canada to Jayapura, the capital of West Papua.

Gear for a voyage on a tropical river.

|| We arrived in New Guinea in February 2018, and spent two months in West Papua birdwatching, snorkelling on coral reefs, and hiking in the mountains. As we moved about, we tried to get an impression from Indonesians of their neighbour to the east. Don't go there, they said. It's expensive. It's dangerous. It's backward. Had they been? No. An elderly Norwegian we met while touring the Highlands said he had once visited Port Moresby but would never go back. "They all eat betel nut and spit. The cost is very high, and there are gangs on the streets with machetes. There is no tourism developed like here." In Jayapura, we asked the German pastor running our homestay if he had been over the border. It was only fifty kilometres away.

“I have been invited to church meetings there many times, but I never went,” Pastor Scheunemann replied. “My wife doesn’t want me to go. Too violent. You couldn’t go out at night. There are *raskols* in the town. In the country, the tribes are always fighting. It is a wild place!”

A Belgian anthropologist we met on a bus one day said she had travelled down the Sepik in a dugout in 1999. She had taken spectacles, cigarettes, and biscuits with her to give as gifts. The village guest houses she stayed in were in ruins, she recalled; she had pitched her tent inside them. We should watch out in Wewak. *Raskols* had chased her on the streets there. She had to dive into someone’s house to escape.

“Il faut suivre les conseils.” When we hear about danger from locals, heed their advice.

Such warnings worried us, but they came from people who either hadn’t been to PNG or hadn’t been recently. Even our guidebook was two years old. What was PNG like now, in March 2018? It was important to heed warnings, but let these come from people we meet on the other side of the border. Nadya and I would, no doubt, attract attention, and Papua New Guineans, given their long, troubled history of colonial intrusion, may be suspicious of our intentions. It was up to us to shake hands, listen to their stories, and learn about their lives in the way Christina Dodwell had. I felt privileged to have a visa for PNG in my passport. A blazing yellow rectangle with a bird of paradise in the middle, it had taken five days to get from the consulate. Why did we wish to visit, the official had wondered. “Because we want to find out about your people, about your culture...” Nadya replied.

“Do you know anyone in Vanimo we can look up?” Nadya asked Pastor Scheunemann on our final night in Indonesia.

“Nay, but Yuli might.”

Yuli was a Papuan employed at the homestay who helped visitors apply for *surat jalans* to visit remote areas of West Papua and fill out visa application forms for PNG. We told her about our plans to buy a local canoe and paddle down the Sepik. No, she knew no one in Vanimo, but she had referred the occasional travellers going there to the CBC Guesthouse. She would tell Dorothy, the manager, we were coming. She might know of someone travelling to the river. Nadya and I would remember Yuli as the first link in a chain of associations.

3 UPPER SEPIK

At ground level the heat was oppressive, but I knew that I would have to get used to it. Step one, I decided, was to get acclimatised and to absorb my surroundings...I went to visit the officer in charge. He was a black kiap, and he was helpful and efficient. I explained that I was planning to buy a canoe and paddle down the Sepik; the idea startled him at first but he agreed that a canoe was essential for travelling in this area since the streams and rivers were used as "roads" and even his men went on patrol by canoe.

—CHRISTINA DODWELL, *Travels in Papua New Guinea*

"Apinun, yu stap gut?"

An hour's walk downhill on a rutted dirt road ends at a hut with stilt legs and a roof thatched with palm leaves. Nadya and I peel off our packs, wipe the sweat from our faces, and shake the hand of a fierce-looking man with piercing eyes, a shaved head, and a spiked beard. His name is Solomon. The students from Green River Christian Secondary accompanying us have already told him what we want. Yanking a long-shafted paddle out of the ground, he signals us to follow him down a dirt path.

Naked boys are flinging themselves off the two-metre riverbank and shrieking as their bodies smack the churning, muddy waters below. One plasters himself from head to foot in mud before coming to look us over. The Dio, a tributary of the Upper Sepik, is about thirty metres wide and bordered by tall grasses and a rich tangle of vine-throttled trees. I see a pair of ten-metre dugouts with outboard engines nestled against the near bank. Not what we are after. Solomon points to a log, and we lean our bags down against it and sit. He disappears into the bush. Young women in flowery dresses, carrying babies on their hips, join us; they are also looking to go downstream.

"Oscar, *em kamap nau*," Solomon announces when he returns.

A rangy man with coal-black skin is pumping a skinny, six-metre pirogue down the river toward us. He angles the boat to shore. Nadya suggests I go for a spin. I slide down the riverbank and almost lose balance as I climb in. The boat is nothing more than a hollowed-out tree trunk. I sit down quickly and brace my knees against the sides. Oscar stabs the bank with his paddle and shoves us out into the current. The pirogue rocks dangerously from side to side, and I cling nervously to the gunwales. How can he paddle while standing and keep his balance? I try to turn around to observe his technique, but turning means lifting my butt and the shift in weight threatens to tip us over. I face forward again and hunch over. With each thrust from Oscar's paddle, I find I need to lean on the opposite side to compensate.

Back on dry land, Oscar hands over his paddle and urges me to have a go. It is heavy and has a crocodile head carved into the end of the shaft. Nadya hops in the front of the dugout with a short paddle she got from someone. We push off, and she puts to use her considerable paddling skills while I, firmly seated in the stern, manhandle the oversized paddle. We manage a loop: into the current, upstream a bit, across to the far bank, into the current again, and back to where we started, the pirogue dancing about, barely under control and taking on water. We are both relieved to get out. I look at the river coursing by and shake my head. No way I could stand and propel this craft a thousand kilometres to the sea. It would capsize on the first day; the muddy soup would swallow our belongings. We'd be crocodile food. There must be wider-hulled, medium-sized canoes around for sale. Perhaps at Mockwai, the first village on the Sepik. Maybe we should ride with the mothers and their babies in a motor-canoe and make further enquiries there.

Another man turns up in a dugout like Oscar's. Would we be interested in buying two canoes perhaps? One student could travel with Nadya, another with me. The remaining five could ride in the

Two dugout canoes become a raft.

motor-canoe with the mothers. If one dugout isn't going to work, how can two be better? Tom, the student wishing to travel furthest with us, has the answer. We should buy both and bind them together to make a raft. With what? The students disappear into the forest with their bush knife and return with two sticks the thickness of my forearm. I shake my head again. How on earth are they going to make a raft without any nails or rope or planks? Off they go into the tall grasses at the waterside and return dragging a dozen two-metre canes. Puzzled, Nadya and I sit on the log and watch.

Holding the bush knife by the blade rather than by the handle, Fice peels each stalk and teases out the fibres from within. They are like string and clearly tough as Alex can wind one around his hand. Kingston extracts another and does the same. Tom fetches one of the sticks. While he and Fice hold the dugouts steady, Alex and Kingston lay it across the two bows. Kingston ties the end of the cane fibre to one end of the stick and loops the loose end under one hull. He passes it up between the boats to Alex, who takes it, wraps it twice around the stick, and pulls it taut. Under the second hull it goes and back to Kingston. Kingston tugs hard and ties a knot. They get another cane fibre and repeat the process in reverse. I expect the fibre to snap at any moment, but it doesn't, despite getting repeated dunkings in the river. Next, the sterns. It is Tom and Fice's turn to string them together. Alex peels more cane.

When they are done, they call us over. We climb aboard and test the new accessories. Solid. We can even sit on these sticks to paddle or, now that we have a twin-hulled vessel, stand to do so. And our improvised raft is sturdy enough to give four students a ride home (the remaining three will take the motor-canoe). We pay K200 (Can$80) for each canoe and K20 for the tall paddle. I have no idea what the going rate is for a scooped-out tree trunk, and it doesn't occur to me to bargain. The villagers only have one paddle to sell, so Tom lops off a branch to serve as a second.

We load up and set off in the last of the light. Two hours to find canoes, buy them, make a raft, and set sail. I am amazed. In 1997, it had taken us days to get hold of a canoe to explore Indonesia and six weeks to accustom ourselves to handling it at sea. There was a bill of sale to sign and a travel permit to get from the police. Nadya and I know nothing about dugout canoes and have no idea whether foreigners are permitted to paddle one down the Sepik. Tom plunges the branch into the brown water and leans on it gondolier-fashion. The current seizes us.

"*Tenkyu tru!*" we call to the villagers. Thank you kindly. Some wave, but most just stare. "*Lukim yu.*" So long.

I look downstream and wonder if we are wise setting off at dusk. Half of the river is in shadow, and I see branches poking up from the surface: fallen trees, uprooted by a swollen river that is dismantling its banks after the rainy season. We must avoid these obstructions. We are soon travelling at speed, Alex at the stern steering with the tall paddle. When Kingston points at a submerged trunk, Tom raises his pole and shoves us away at the critical moment. This happens again and again. Our raft twists and spins, even travelling backwards down the Dio until Alex corrects.

My doubts about high school kids making good pirogue partners are beginning to dissolve. I thought they might go their own ways once liberated from school; instead, they seem committed to helping us and capable of doing so. I wonder whether they feel a sense of duty to the principal of their school. He has assigned them the task of escorting the two visiting Canadians down the Sepik, and I recall their earnest nods when he outlined our plans this morning. They clearly hold this man in high regard. I watch the students working hard to get us downriver and smile. For the first time since arriving in the country, I feel that our project has shifted out of the realm of fantasy and into one of possibility.

Parrots, their bright colours now dull in the fading light, bullet by low overhead in bands of three or four, screeching uproariously. I scan the banks nervously for crocodiles. After an hour and a half, and just as the sun is dipping behind the trees, we round a bend and join the Sepik. Ah. The fast water from the tributary splays into boils and eddies. We bump over these and turn east, tracking the north bank of the wider river. Then, suddenly, it is dark, and the forest erupts into song: a thousand eerie chirruping, trilling, and peeping sounds, some close, others far, some droning and repetitive, others explosive and high-pitched. Nadya and I put on our headlamps, and we all listen for the telltale sloshing sounds that say a submerged log is near. We hit a few but don't get snagged, which seems to me remarkable, given that our twin-hull vessel is like a big fork with two tines. Crane flies smack their heads on our lamps, and mosquitoes whine about our ears. Now we're committed. Drifting down a jungle river, our fate uncertain. No turning back. But how far is Mockwai and what will it be like? There seems little point in asking. There are no landmarks, no lights except ours, no watches on the wrists of our crew, and who is to say how slow or fast two strapped-together tree trunks travel? Clock time will be of no relevance over the next month.

We arrive at the village in pitch dark. Mockwai appears to be ten huts on stilts lining the riverbank. We ride up on the mud below them, gather our belongings, and scramble up. Our headlamps illuminate twenty faces staring down at us in disbelief. Where on earth have

Mockwai guest house.

we materialized from? Where are we going at this hour? What do we want? A flood of Tok Pisin or perhaps tribal language. I have no idea what these people are saying and wonder for a while whether we are welcome as their voices are shrill and agitated. Are they just shocked, or do they think we mean harm? Custom says that voyageurs on the Sepik stay at village guest houses or with a family. When we arrive, Jeffrey Waino told us, we should present ourselves to the Chief. He would be able to make arrangements. Fice, the most composed of our escort, explains the situation to the villagers, who now gather around us in a ring. There is a moment of uncertainty as they debate among themselves. Then we find ourselves trailing three silhouettes through a banana grove, papery leaves smacking our faces, to a hut standing away from the others.

Up the four-rung ladder we should go, says Fice. The entire village seems to follow us, and the structure trembles in protest. The two rooms at the top contain no furniture and have springy floors—made of bark?—that sink under our weight. Our lights discover a fireplace in the back corner of one: some half-burnt logs, two sooty billycans, and a cracked plastic basin. Alex and Tom heave our bin of food up the ladder while Kingston fetches kindling and Fice goes in search of water. The Mockwaians retreat, leaving an old man in charge of us. I am not sure if he lives here or is just our host for the night, but Fice says he isn't the Chief. He sits down cross-legged, puffing a homemade cigarette, and watches Nadya dig rice and luncheon meat out of our bin.

The evening is short. All of us are whacked. We eat, sharing our food with our host, unroll our sleeping mats in the adjacent room, hoist our mosquito nets, and crash out. When Nadya and I switch off our lamps, there is only one thing to see: the winking orange tip of our host's stogy.

|| I begin the new day in the swamp behind the hut, tossing water over my head. I expected an audience, but there is no one about. A cloud of gnats rolls over the stagnant water, and mosquitos try to breakfast on my back.

It doesn't take us long to eat and be on our way. A hundred kina goes to our host, the amount Jeffrey Waino had suggested we pay for lodging. Nadya supplements this with some teabags, and I hand the old man a packet of cigarettes I bought in Indonesia as a thank you. He seems jubilant and seizes our hands and pumps them, chuckling. As we load, a boy races over with two short (lady) paddles for sale, ten kina apiece. The blade of one looks like it got chewed by a crocodile. Still, better that than a shaved branch.

It is a cloudless morning, and the sun is dazzling. We shove off, Fice, Kingston, and Nadya taking the paddles. Ours is the only vessel on the river, but our presence, I see, does not go unobserved. I dig out my binoculars. Tall, white storks—a good metre tall—with serpentine necks and beaks resembling marlin spikes line the riverbank, fishing. They freeze when they see us, their unblinking yellow eyes trained, their wings twitching. I sense surveillance, too, from above. A pair of fishing eagles, perched on a dead branch twenty metres up, one about the size of our northern harrier but with a striated, fawn breast, the other much larger and brawnier. This one has a beak like a rose thorn, broad shoulders, and, rather amusingly, shaggy white trousers. How either stork or eagle can catch fish in the river at this time of year is a mystery. The water is grainy with silt and thick with debris. Cakes of mud keep sliding from the riverbank, dissolving and making it muddier.

An hour passes, two, and the heat of the day builds. I tuck away the binoculars and take the tall paddle from Kingston. I must get used to using this. I have never paddled standing up in a canoe before, but then I cannot say I have paddled sitting down in a canoe much either. An immigrant to Canada from England, I went on my first canoe trip in 2010 when I was forty-five: a week with Nadya on a backcountry river in Quebec. It was just the two of us. The outfitter who rented us the canoe drove us a hundred and fifty kilometres upriver on a logging road, unloaded the canoe from his trailer, and waved *au revoir*. Nadya taught me the basics of paddling en route.

"To get in, you put your paddle across the canoe, place your two hands on it, and then step in."

"When you're in the stern, to keep the canoe straight, pull back with the paddle and then twist it at the end of the stroke and push out. That's called a J-stroke."

"To turn the canoe, you can do a wide stroke, like this, away from the side."

"To get the canoe close to the dock, you reach over and draw the water toward the canoe, like this."

The trip was in August and the water level low. The only real obstacles in the river were submerged boulders. We had to keep an eye out ahead for spots of smooth water with chop and froth to either side. Avoid these, and we would be okay. I don't remember us hitting a single boulder, and I know we didn't capsize. The weather was also fine the entire time. Over the years, I have improved my skills, but we rarely rent canoes and, when we do, it is always on placid lakes or amiable rivers. I wondered before coming to PNG whether my rudimentary paddling skills and our lack of whitewater experience might be our undoing. Surely the Sepik would have wild stretches, steep-walled canyons, unexpected waterfalls. I look down at our raft.

Who knows what's ahead. If we can't paddle a stretch of this river, there will be no portaging two tree trunks, even if we separate them. Not that I know anything about doing that. I have never once portaged a canoe in Canada.

I pump hard for two hours, plunging Oscar's tall paddle deep into the oxtail soup and drawing it back, panting and wiping sweat from my eyes. The paddle has a thick shaft—thicker than a yard broom—and it is heavy. Sometimes I need to rest it on the gunwale after a stroke and catch my breath. It would help if it had a handle I could grip, but the shaft just continues way above my head. I look round at Nadya, sitting in the stern and hiding from the sun under her Tilley hat. Is she using the J-stroke? Seems not. Just dipping her short, croc-chewed paddle into the water, drawing it back, and, at the end of every third stroke, letting the blade linger in the water to act as a rudder.

It puzzles me that our shipmates aren't keen to do more of the paddling. They are all clearly in fine trim and appear untroubled by the heat. Aren't they impatient to return to their families? Perhaps they are humouring us: Have these *waitpela* even been in a canoe before? The big one looks like he's digging a hole. Carry on like that and he's gonna have a heart attack. Instead, they chat, chew betel nut, or snooze. I found out last night that Tom and Fice are nineteen years old, Alex and Kingston twenty, the age of college students back home. This discovery makes me less anxious about travelling with them. It would be good to get to know them better, but, when I ask questions, they only give curt replies. Hardly a surprise. Only the boldest students at their school talked to us. We were a novelty. None had seen foreigners at Green River before.

Tom suddenly seizes the third paddle and starts digging at the water vigorously. Though the shortest and skinniest of our crew, he seems to have the most vigour. Kingston relieves Nadya and follows suit. Continuing my slow, deliberate sweeps, I look at them, baffled. Did they see a crocodile slide off the bank? Our raft has drawn close to land as we round a bend in the river. I look about for other boats. Hostile territory? The pair continues pumping hard, their muscles bulging with the effort. I look ahead. They appear to be making for a line of half-submerged branches and bobbing coconut husks midstream. I try to match their pace but fail. When we reach the floating debris, they lay down their paddles, and, as if nothing were amiss, sink back into reverie. This happens several times, and it takes me the day to figure out their strategy. To save energy, paddle only when the boat has slipped out of the current.

We say *lukim yu* to Kingston in Biwei, another tiny community living precariously close to the river. I can see now why all the houses are built on stilts. The timing of our arrival is fortuitous. Light rain turns to heavy as we claw our way up the gluey bank and find shelter under a palm awning. As at Mockwai, everyone comes out of the houses to inspect us. The children are the boldest, ganging around, shoving each other forward, touching our arms. The smallest have nothing on, their older siblings only outsized T-shirts that reach below their knees and look like dresses. Most appear healthy, but there are exceptions: two skinny lads with flaking skin that is curiously patterned. It appears as though someone has drawn a maze in chalk on their bodies or that some insect has left behind an elaborate system of trails. Kingston calls the condition "sipoma" when I ask—probably what missionaries referred to as "grille," a tropical fungal infection. Beyond the kids are the adults: a knot of women to the left, talking excitedly, and a band of men to the right, regarding us warily. Breaking through the cordon of children, Nadya and I go over to the men and greet them, offering our hands and smiling. The rain eases off, and a man holding a bush knife the length of a baguette steps forward and introduces himself as Joseph. Would we like some coconuts?

"Oh, yes, yes," we chorus, already feeling giddy from the heat. When we left Canada in January, it was minus 32 degrees Celsius in the wind; here in April it is more like plus 32.

While we wait for two boys to shin up a palm tree and get the fruit, I ask Joseph what else they grow in the village. Bananas, paw-paw, watermelons, and sago, he replies. Vanilla and cocoa to sell at market. They can get eight kina for a kilo of cocoa in Vanimo. I find that journey hard to imagine. We haven't seen any motor-canoes since joining the Sepik. The villagers would have to paddle against the

Plank seats for our customized raft.

current to Green River and then find a vehicle robust enough to transport their produce along the cratered road to the coast.

"And you hunt animals too?" I ask, noticing some of the boys have bows and arrows.

"Yes, for wild pigs, bandicoot, and cuscus. Sometimes birds."

The rain eases, and I ask if we can try firing an arrow or two. When a lad passes me his bow, there is widespread panic and a frantic dash for cover. I manage to hit someone's house fifty metres away and lose sight of my second arrow altogether. Nadya shoots her arrow into the top of a tree like she had a cuscus in her sights. The bows are remarkably powerful, the strings the same fibres that bind together our dugouts.

The boys return and pass the coconuts to their bigger brothers, who hack away the husks with their bush knives and lop off the tops of the nuts. We drink too greedily, and some of the juice dribbles down our chins. I offer Joseph ten kina, but he tells me we needn't pay. When we return to the water, he looks at our raft and shakes his head.

"All of you travel in that? Where do you sit?"

He yells something to the crowd of onlookers, and the boys shoot off again. They return a few minutes later with two planks, and Joseph chops them to size. Now we have seats. I wonder again if I should offer to pay.

|| "Tonight, we stay in Waku," Fice announces, taking up Oscar's paddle. "There is good guest house next to river."

He holds the paddle, I notice, further up the shaft than I do. At the end of each stroke, it almost swings itself back for the next, like a pendulum. His movements are slow and effortless, and he hardly bends. No digging, no yanking, no wild panting, yet I can feel the forward thrust. I look over my shoulder to see whether Alex is assisting at the stern. No. Just sitting steering, using a short paddle as a rudder.

The air is still, the water surface glassy, the sky patchy. But for the splash of paddles, all is quiet. I scan the banks for wildlife but see very little now that it's midday. Just the occasional blue-green-orange blur of a rainbow bee-eater, scooping the air for flies. Tom points to the far bank. A crocodile. Two metres long, perfectly motionless, and, apparently, unaware of our presence. Its spiked tail curls into the tall grasses. I ask the students if villagers get eaten from time to time. Children sometimes do, Alex tells me, especially when they venture out at night. I ask why it is we are not seeing more crocodiles. I was expecting to see them sliding down mud ramps at every bend.

"Hunter kill them," Alex replies.

"And they hide in swamp when rainy season come," Tom adds.

I take the tall paddle once again and try and mimic Fice's pendulum swing. The heat, reflecting off the water, is intense now, and sweat trickles down my spine and darkens my shorts. Every half hour, I stop paddling and take slugs of water from my canteen and munch

Em Nau crackers. None of the students have water bottles, I see. When they are thirsty, they simply scoop water up from the river with their hands. As the temperature climbs, they strip off their shirts—something I would love to do. Instead, I pull the brim of my hat over my eyes and button my shirt sleeves. I even have Dollarama gloves to protect my hands (last used to fend off frostbite). As we will be on the river all day, every day, we will keep our limited supply of sunscreen, Nadya and I have decided, for our noses.

An old man hails us from the riverbank. For some coconuts, can we take three more passengers on board? It's the Green River Christian Secondary students who took the motor-canoe on the Dio yesterday. They have been stranded all day in Bemath and need a ride to the next village. Is taking them wise? I ask Fice. Won't we sink with three extra? He says it's only for an hour or two, so I nod. We draw close to the riverbank, and the students clamber in, big smiles on their faces.

"*Masta em gutpela*!" the old man exclaims, clapping me on the back, and I remember a man outside a grocery store in Vanimo addressing me the same way. I am a visitor, I feel like saying, not your master. For older Papuans, I guess I am associated with a long history of colonial rule and an unbalanced relationship.

With the extra weight, our progress is slow, so sluggish at times that we barely seem to be moving. Nadya and I paddle cautiously, trying not to make any jerky movements lest water, which is now an inch off the gunwales, slops in. It's like ploughing through butter. When we lose the current, the raft is slow to respond to steering. Our passengers hop off late afternoon. It feels good to have helped them out.

It is dusk when we park for the night beside three dugouts. Kingston and Alex use the paddles as stakes to secure our raft, driving them down into the mud between the two hulls. We hump our gear onto the bank and set it down in front of a large house. I expect people to pour from it at any moment, like at Mockwai and Biwei, until I notice the padlock on the door. This is the guest house Fice spoke of. The village of Waku is further back from the river, and Tom heads into the trees to find the owner of the guest house while we do battle with the legion of *natnats* that has come to welcome us. The forty minutes it takes for him to return without the owner or the key are miserable ones. We must go to the village, he says, and bring all our stuff with us.

"Well, let's get on with it!" I say testily, grabbing the bin of food.

Tom, Fice, and Alex look at me, puzzled. They have been the ones carting it about, and I already have a pack on my back.

The path to Waku is porridge after the rain. We make squelching sounds as we walk, at times sinking to the ankle. Mud gets inside my flip-flops, and my feet keep sliding out of them. I tear them off in frustration and tuck them under my arm, but the soles of my feet are too soft to handle the rough ground. I stagger along, cursing. After ten minutes, unable to defend myself against the mozzies circling my head, I give up the bin. After a further ten, the path vanishes into a reed-choked swamp eight metres wide. I stand at the edge, blinking. Now what? The swamp is too deep to wade through. I put on my headlamp. The only way across appears to be via a partly submerged tree trunk, snapped in the middle and slimy with mud. Tom leads the way, performing a delicate balancing act, his widely spaced Papuan toes spreading around this bridge and giving him grip. As he nears the middle, though, his weight causes the trunk to sink. I expect him to back up. Instead, he leaps, landing smartly onto the other half, which shudders and also starts to sink. I sigh. Must the villagers do this daily to reach their canoes? I look at this bridge and the Tok Pisin word "*bagarap*" comes to mind. Buggered-up. Tom scuttles to the far side, hops off the log, and looks back at us, and I'm reminded of a kids' game at the county fair: walk along the greasy log without falling off and you can win a balloon.

"You should let one of the boys take your pack, Tony," Nadya says gently.

She is right. Since breaking my ankles in my twenties, I am hopeless at balancing. Can't even stand on one leg for long without keeling over. Yet I am reluctant to give up my backpack. No one should have to carry my belongings. As foolish as it sounds, I find accepting too much help—especially from high school kids—humiliating. Gives me the feeling that the trip has been taken out of our hands. Then I remember explorers like Hides and Champion with strings of porters carrying their supplies, tents, sacks of rice, bags of salt, and cooking pots. Jeffrey's high school students are not our hired hands, yet it is already clear they are way more capable in this environment than us, which is hardly surprising.

I yield my backpack reluctantly to Alex, feeling helpless. "Travellers are often in the position of children," I recall an American travel commentator once saying, "like students learning a new language." Taking Fice's hand, I step barefoot onto the log and try and grip its knobbly surface with my toes. Tom walks back along the log on the other side towards me and stretches out his hand. *Cross the snapped tree trunk, and we are done for the day. The village of Waku is on the other side, and the residents are expecting us.* Letting go of Fice's hand, I run and jump the moment I feel water washing over my feet. I try to land straight, bending my knees and snatching for Tom's hand. My other arm shoots out, and I wave it up and down like a bird's wing to steady myself. I feel water swilling around my ankles once again and so rapidly make my bid for dry land. I turn, relieved not to be neck-deep in the swamp, and shine my headlamp on the tree trunk. Nadya's turn. She manages her leap of faith with a great deal more grace and seems even to enjoy herself. For Alex, carrying my sack, and Fice, with the bin of food on his shoulder, the feat of acrobatics isn't one.

I shine my headlamp this way and that. Loads of mosquitoes on this side too, but no sign of a house. Then I remember how long it took Tom to go to the village and return to the river. The village is not located like the previous ones. We must climb a hill to get to it. I retrieve my pack from Alex. The path is steep and twisting, a mucky nightmare after the rains. I claw my way up it barefoot, mostly on my hands and knees, and slide back down repeatedly. At one point, I lose my footing entirely and fall flat on my face. I hear Nadya cry out a couple of times behind me. By the time we arrive at the first house, chests heaving, our shirts are sopping. I stop and wring out the front of mine. Sweat splatters over my knees. Whose idea was it to paddle down a tropical river in the rainy season? I take some deep breaths. My head is thumping and my mouth dry. Feels like I just did a hundred barbell squats in a steam room.

I become conscious that a crowd is watching us from above. I look up and suddenly behold forty or fifty people. My headlamp settles on the face of a bald man wearing a collared shirt and shorts, standing in front. He is staring at us with obvious concern, even embarrassment. Maybe the key for the guest house by the river should have been left with him, or is he embarrassed for us, arriving in such a dishevelled state and clearly in need of hospitality? He steps forward and offers his hand.

"My name is Rayut," he says softly. "Please, you follow me."

We climb further up the hill, past chattering houses, the occupants disembodied heads poking through windows. Another ten minutes and we are outside a tall house supported on three-metre piles. Every rung of the ladder leading to the raised floor supports a child. Rayut yells at them to make way and smacks the heads of those who are slow to comply. As I ascend, I try to wipe the worst of the mud off the soles of my feet. This seems rude, but ruder would probably be to pad mud into the room where we are likely to stay.

Like the floor of the guest house at Mockwai, this is made of a kind of bark that buckles when you put weight on it. I tread warily. Rayut ushers us into a room without furnishings, and I am relieved to shed my sack. I immediately dig out soap, towel, fresh underwear, and a fresh shirt and stick them in a plastic bag.

"*Mi go was-was*," I announce, squeezing past the people who have trailed us up the ladder. I should probably ask where the villagers go but feel too irritated. Must be a bathing hole somewhere near. Blissfully, now that it is pitch dark, the mosquitoes have gone to bed.

"I will bring coconut," Rayut responds, perplexed that I wish to leave having only just arrived.

There is a shriek from the corner of the room. Rayut gasps, and I hear shocked cries from the ground below. I swing my headlamp around. My wife is not as tall as I remember.

4 VILLAGE BIG MEN

It is essential for the well-being of the group that at least one of their number is a "big-man." A "big-man" has special powers and specialised knowledge which enables him to function as a mediator between the people and the ancestors or deities and to direct the various ritualistic activities of the group. The salvation of the entire group ultimately depends on the ability of the "big-man" to operate skilfully and successfully as a mediator of right relationships and of good order in society.

—KAY LIDDLE, *Into the Heart of Papua*

I awake at dawn to the sound of rain hammering the thatch over our heads. It feels like the roof is going to give way at any moment, and we will be buried under a pile of soggy palm leaves. Untucking the mosquito net, I roll out of bed and continue rolling in the direction of our packs near the door. Must spread my weight on this surface. Don't want to end up in an undignified heap on the ground below. This could have been Nadya's fate last night when her legs went through the floor.

I get to my feet cautiously and lean on the wall while putting on my shorts. My shoulder goes straight through it, and slats come clattering down. I stand like an idiot for a moment staring at the window I have created, then poke my head through and look left and right. Surely someone would come rushing. How should I explain? My Tok Pisin isn't up to the job although I do know the word for "fall down." Our phrasebook says that "*ren i pundaun*" means "it will rain," or, literally, "the rain it fall down." "*Haus i pundaun*" might work. For sure, I must say, "*Sori. Sori tru.*" I put the slats back carefully one by one, but there is nothing to hold them in place: no groove in the wood, no nails or pegs, no loops of cane fibre. I insert six and try and ease in a seventh, but the third pops out and then the fifth, smacking me on the temple. I grab them before they hit the floor but, in so doing, dislodge the others.

"Tony, what are you doing?" Roused from her slumbers, head propped on one elbow, Nadya is watching me with interest.

Fice's head appears at the window. Do we want to make breakfast? Nadya executes her own roll out of bed in the direction of the food bin and pulls out tinned fish, rice, and tea. She follows Fice down the ladder to the kitchen. A crowd has gathered, and I smell burning wood. Peering through a rent in the floor, I see one mop of straight, chestnut brown hair in a sea of frizzy, black ones.

Before going down, I look in the next room where our boatmates slept and see Alex, still sprawled out. With smoke creeping up through the hundred punctures in the floor around him, it looks like the room has been strafed from below with machinegun fire and Alex is a casualty. Father Liddle called the bark floors of Sepik homes "uneven and draughty," and I think back to the Belgian anthropologist we met in West Papua, who had put her tent up inside village guest houses. Alex tells me that the bark comes from the limbom palm. And the walls and roof? Leaves from *saksak*, the sago palm. The slats are the shaved spines of the fronds.

"How long does a house usually last?"

"Maybe ten years, but villager have to make new roof every five years."

I am amazed how well palm leaves shed water; there are barely any leaks in the roof. The villagers must be talented weavers.

By the time we are done with breakfast, the rain has stopped and once again we test our balance on the snapped tree trunk bridging the swamp. Alex has thoughtfully cut me a walking cane, but the swamp is too deep for me to use it as a third leg. I shake my head and practise gripping with my toes before stepping tentatively onto the log. It is especially treacherous after the rain. If the villagers can build shelters on a steep, wet hillside, how come they can't erect a serviceable bridge? Surely it would make their lives easier.

"How long has it been like this?" I ask Rayut when I reach the other side.

"Two years," he replies. "No, three years."

"Any plans to replace it?"

"The men will repair by end of year. Maybe."

Nadya thinks perhaps the owner of the swampland hasn't given permission for trees to be felled. She has learned from the people here that every square inch of land belongs to someone, even the jungle surrounding a village. A tribe is made up of family clans, each with a prescribed hunting ground and a garden. No fences or signs mark these, but everyone knows who owns this pandanus and its fruit or that tall hardwood suitable for making a canoe. Any evidence of violation is considered an act of war. "Pay-back" is necessary to make amends for venturing onto another tribe's land and taking resources, and this could be in the form of kina, betel nut, or crocodile skins. The exception to this rule is the river. No village or clan may claim a stretch of the Sepik as its territory. What this means for us is that, while we can paddle downstream unchallenged, we cannot pull in at a picturesque bend in the river at the end of the day and camp—unless we hack through the bush to the nearest village and ask permission from the Chief. It means that we should always travel with local people who can entreat on our behalf when we make landfall. These are sobering thoughts. I was under the impression that buying our own canoe would grant Nadya and I greater autonomy—as it had done in Indonesia in 1997. It appears we will be paddling with Papuans and staying in their villages all the way to the sea.

Folded fifty-kina note in my palm, I shake Rayut's hand and thank him for arranging our stay, Tom having suggested how much to give.

Yanking our paddles out of the ooze and saying *lukim yu* to the residents of Waku, we hit the water, and I am relieved to be free of the land. Feeling crap after a fitful night of sleep marred by dreams of falling down a bottomless well, I wish to work the tension out of my muscles and rid my back of its knots. I position myself amidships and begin digging purposefully with the tall paddle. Our raft saunters out over a glazed surface. The river is wider now, a good sixty metres. The two-metre-high cane on the far bank looks like a bad haircut after the rain. The only sounds are odd shrieks from the trees and, from time to time, the sloshing of the river over partly submerged branches, which are too heavy to float downstream. Some rounded, nodding stumps remind me of harbour seals in Maritime Canada, poking their heads out of the water and ducking down again.

Heat builds as the clouds disperse. I turn up my collar, roll down my sleeves, paste my nose with sunblock, and put on my gloves. Our destination today is Tipas, the end of the road for our students. If they are at all excited at the prospect of arriving home, they don't show it. They sit and snooze or smoke, and occasionally paddle. It is hard to say how fast we are travelling. Midstream, it seems at times that we are hardly moving; close to shore, we are racing. The murky water makes it tough to tell what is going on. You can't see the riverbed or any boulders passing under the hull. It's tricky, too, to tell how far we have come. Green River and Tipas are marked on our map, but none of the villages in between. And the Upper Sepik is so twisted it resembles an uncoiling snake. That said, about a hundred kilometres separate today's destination from our starting point on the Dio River.

At midday, roasting and light-headed, I lay down my paddle, rip off my sweat-drenched shirt, douse it in the river, and put it back on sopping. I fill my hat to the brim with brown water and return it to my head. Bliss. A daily ritual in the making perhaps. The river suddenly splits to pass around an island, reknits on the far side, then divides once again to circumnavigate another larger one. The second island supports an abandoned shack with broken stilt legs and a collapsed roof draped with vines, and I wonder, given that the river is ceaselessly gnawing at its banks, whether these islands were once part of the land.

In the afternoon, we make the first stop on our voyage that isn't at a village. We have yet to crack the coconuts the old man gave us

Tall paddles and muddy water.

Birdwatching.

at Bemath yesterday. There is an alluvial sandspit or rather mud-spit we might ride up on. Making it to terra firma proves, however, to be a challenge. We step off the raft and sink to our shins in hot mud. Five minutes it takes us to walk twenty squelching steps carrying a coconut under each arm. I imagine an opportunistic croc, seeing easy prey, sliding over effortlessly. Once we are all on firmer ground, Alex displays his dexterity with a bush knife. Holding a coconut in the palm of his hand and spinning it, he hacks away the thick husk. No chopping board required. Once he has exposed the kernel, he deftly nicks the top to make a hole, which he manages without losing a drop of milk. He passes the knife to Tom who demonstrates he is equally adept. They crack open coconuts for themselves. Once Nadya and I have drained our fruit, Tom takes them back and chops the kernels in half. He cuts spoons from the kernels so we might scoop out the innards.

While we drink and eat, we become aware of a riot going on in the treetops nearby. I fetch the binoculars: a dozen female eclectus parrots, with their unmistakeable red heads and purple wings, our frequent companions when we were trekking in the forests of West Papua. Eclectus parrots are characteristically voluble, but the women's guild here seems particularly so. Then I spot the sulphur-crested cockatoo to one side. Either the ladies are welcoming a newcomer in a hearty fashion or telling it to bugger off. The larger bird flares its flaming crest excitedly and answers the parrots with wild, stridulous squawks. I pass the binoculars to Nadya who chuckles as she watches. She invites the students to take a look. Fice tries first, but then looks at me questioningly. What possible use can the white guy have for this thing?

"Other way round," I say, gesturing.

They take turns with the binoculars and clearly enjoy getting close-ups of birds they must know so well. Watching the trio, I feel a surge of affection. It is a shame we have to part company. Lads almost a third my age have taken us under their wing, initiated us into river travel, and taught us some valuable lessons. I doubted how much help they would be when we met, a bunch of high school kids with little to say for themselves, but I will remember Tom's ingenuity on the first day, Alex's helping hand at the swamp in Waku, Fice's expertise with the tall paddle and his poise throughout the journey. Without Jeffrey Waino's high school kids, we could not have launched this expedition.

|| We leave the Sepik late in the afternoon. Tipas used to be on its banks until the river rerouted itself. The village is now at the end of an oxbow lake. Paddling across, we realize how much the current has been our ally these past days. The raft now seems weighed down with rocks; we must earn every metre. There are no longer any knots in my back.

Expecting to be the focus of attention on arrival, we pause before the final push to thank our crew. "What should we give them for helping us?" Nadya had asked Jeffrey Waino at Green River. "Just a drink," he said. Even if Tipas had a store, getting them sodas would be an insult after all they have done. Fifty kina each, Nadya and I decide. They are jubilant. They clearly weren't expecting anything. I ask if they can hook us up with John Youpa before heading off. John Mariati's uncle is our sole contact in Tipas.

I can see as we approach that the village is bigger than any we have visited so far: fifty or sixty houses. We aim for the largest one in the middle, and I brace myself for a commotion. But only six old men, sitting ruminatively on their haunches, watch us slide in. John Youpa's house? Easy. Right in front of you. John Youpa? Not as easy. He is away on business. Not expected back until tomorrow. The man who welcomes us is a cheery primary school teacher fluent in English who introduces himself as Jobby Molnobi. Perhaps we would care to see Tipas crocodile farm?

Packs on our backs, bin of food at our feet, we are caught off balance. Where might we put our belongings? John Youpa's house. One of the old men is John's father, and he gives us permission to stay there. The house is twice the size of any we have seen before and appears old. We climb a flight of plank stairs to a verandah more riddled with holes than last night's quarters in Waku. Must remember not to get up in the middle of the night for a leak. There we meet two sisters, Betty and Margaret, who are also John's wives. Polygamy, we learned in West Papua, is not uncommon in Melanesian tribes. They show us to our room, and I am relieved to find no daylight visible through the floor. There is even a table. We drop our stuff.

The crocodile farm is an artificial pond coated in thick, green scum enclosed by a rusty, corrugated tin fence. It contains seven-metre-long adolescent crocodiles that sit lifelessly with their mouths agape, staring at us with apparent loathing. I ask our guide if they were difficult to catch. Full-size ones are, he says, but these were raised in captivity.

"How do the villagers go about catching an adult?"

The hunters go to the swamps at night when the crocodiles are active, Jobby tells us, and shine their lights around the submerged tree trunks. "When they see eyes of crocodile, they paddle over. The light makes crocodile come to the canoe."

"That sounds dangerous," Nadya says.

"Yes. It takes three men to catch a big crocodile, one to paddle the canoe, one to shine the light, and the third to throw the spear. See that one at the back?" He points to a lighter-skinned reptile resting on a splintery plank in the corner of the pen. "That one is a real devil. That is salt-water crocodile. Very aggressive." It surprises me that a salt-water croc can be found this far up the Sepik. Evidently, they thrive in fresh water too. "Fresh water crocodiles don't usually attack people."

Once they reach full size—as long as 3.5 metres, Jobby claims—these crocodiles will be slaughtered. A hide can fetch K500 at the market.

I stare at the captives and remember what John Mariati said in Vanimo. If we are lucky, villagers might give us a baby *pukpuk* with the mouth sewn up as a pet.

"You can play with it in your canoe, even take it back to Canada with you."

"I am not sure customs would approve," Nadya had replied.

Back at Youpa's place, Betty is busy making pancakes. She is an attractive woman in her late twenties wearing a black dress decorated with purple flowers. We find her sitting cross-legged on a wooden pallet next to a fire, wooden tongs in her hand, infant daughter asleep in her lap. These are sago pancakes, and, rolled up, they resemble sea cucumbers. Would we like to try one? Nadya and I are ready for a change of diet, and maybe Betty is too, so we exchange sago for rice. The pancakes are bland and filling, crusty on the outside and gelatinous within. We have seen them before. Alex, Fice, and Tom got these from their *tambu* at Bemath together with pig knuckles wrapped in banana leaves (we have yet to see any pigs though). We dip our pancakes in tinned tuna to give them flavour. The fire, I see, is not making the house smoky as it is near the open end of the roof, neither will it burn a hole in the floor because it sits on a metal tray. Meat hooks hang from a grill positioned half a metre above.

Our night goes undisturbed until 2:15 a.m. A man is yelling outside. He must have a stick with him because we hear thrashing sounds. His shouts and smacks recede as he wanders off, but then amplify when he returns. The uproar lasts a good twenty minutes. Nadya and I listen intently without moving a muscle. At times, it seems like he is directly below us. It would be nice to have one or two holes in the floor to spy through. I expect someone to go out and tell him to shut up, but no one stirs. Could his sudden appearance have anything to do with our being here? Have we brought bad luck to Tipas?

|| The following morning, we have visitors. Not the head of the household, but a party of Elders from the village, including John's father. I find them sitting on the verandah smoking when I get up. Several were at the waterside when we arrived yesterday. I look around for Betty, thinking they wish to speak to her. No, says the youngest of the group, a crane of a man with protruding cheekbones and a walking cane. He wags the cane and then points it emphatically at me. I take a seat. In Tok Pisin, the Elders take turns conveying their message. We are in danger. I hear the words "*trabel*" (trouble), and "*peles nogut*" (dangerous place), something about *raskols* and "*katim i pundaun*" (cut him down). I want to ask where this dangerous place is and what exactly happened, but don't know how. It would be handy if Jobby were here to translate. A man with milky eyes and deeply fissured fingernails seems to guess what I want to know. "Ambunti *long* Pagwi." Oh. I immediately feel easier. Nothing to do with last night's caller. Ambunti is several days' paddle downstream, Pagwi further. The conversation continues, the man with the cane offering to take us as far as Pagwi in his motor-canoe. I decline.

"*Mi tok wantaim* John Youpa," I say. Hopefully, John will be able to shed some light on this.

They nod gravely and rise to their feet but seem reluctant to leave. I shake each of their hands, say "*Tenkyu tru*," and excuse myself to go to the bathroom. When I return, Nadya is up and doing her stretches on the grass. I tell her about our visitors. They are still there, chatting and shifting around on the verandah. Then, they are not. They are in a pile on the ground below. The entire verandah has collapsed. I drop my toothbrush, and we dash over. The Elders are muttering crossly and disentangling themselves from one another. I expect to

Betty and Margaret sieve sago.

see blood, gashes on heads, a broken bone, but, miraculously, they all seem largely unscathed. Just cuts and grazes. They get up and dust each other down. Snapped piles, shattered sago slats, and limbom bark litter the ground. Betty looks down, daughter on her hip, peering unfazed through the chasm that now separates her kitchen from the staircase.

Climbing the back stairs, Nadya and I join Betty and Margaret in the kitchen. They have a fire going again and are making more pancakes. They take cakes of sago, resembling tofu, out of plastic storage bags and grind them through a net sieve that they hold between them. The resulting flour they put into a handle-less pan, pressing it down firmly with their thumbs. On the fire goes the pan, and the flour gels to form a pancake. To keep it from burning, Betty sprinkles it every so often with water. After five minutes, Margaret seizes the pan with wooden tongs and flips the pancake. The topside is now light brown and crusty. More sprinkling of water and some shaking of the pan. Finally, the pancake goes on a plate and, once cooled, is rolled into a sausage.

The pair is making their third pancake when the shouting begins. The two women freeze. The enraged man is back. A rock hits the side of the house, making us all jump. Margaret removes the pan from the fire. More fierce yelling. Another rock. We duck our heads involuntarily, wondering whether the next will punch through the wall. Another voice. Someone trying to explain.

"His sister took his canoe while he was away," Betty whispers to us, "without asking permission. He is very angry."

"Who is?"

"John."

Oh, so not last night's caller. I ask if we should pack our things and leave, but neither sister replies. So we sit in silence, waiting for our host to mount the stairs and behold the remains of his verandah. I wonder if someone has told him that he has guests. The bright side is the verandah isn't quite the mess it was an hour and a half ago. Neighbours came with new piles and slats and started rebuilding. The speed of their response may say something about John's status in the village.

Hearing footsteps on the stairs, Nadya and I get to our feet. But Margaret and Betty are on theirs before us and quickly go to greet their husband. I take a good look at the man stepping gingerly across the verandah. Not at all what I was expecting. The image in my head was of a bear-like older version of his nephew. What I see matches my idea of a *raskol*: scrawny, shaved head, blackened skin around an empty eye socket, scar stretching from the socket down his cheek, curly moustache, chiselled beard, shirt as ventilated as his verandah. Not old. John Youpa, I would say, is in his mid-forties. He speaks to the women gruffly, but it is clear the storm has passed. Waving them aside, he approaches us.

"I heard from my men you were here." A gentle voice.

I offer my hand. "Sorry, your father said we could stay. If this is a bad time for you, we can leave."

He shakes his head, and I see a flap of skin in the socket twitch each time he blinks with his good eye.

"No, no. You are welcome. My sister cause me some problem while I was away."

Nadya and I nod. He tells us he is a payroll officer for a Malaysian timber company called Global, but he hates the job. The company only pays workers minimum wage: K35 for every 1 m³ of wood cut. The villagers come to him to complain. The correct rate is K100. Global is also destroying the forest around Tipas. All the wild animals have disappeared.

Nadya and I nod seriously.

"John Mariati sends his regards," Nadya offers after a short silence. She explains how we met in Vanimo. "We wanted him to come with us in our boat, but he had work to do in Green River."

"Yes, he said he would protect us from hungry *pukpuk*," I add.

Our host doesn't smile. "John is good man. I hear you want to go to Ambunti."

"That's right, but we understand a section of the river may not be safe."

"Some pirates attack boat near Ambunti. They point gun at passengers and make them take off clothes. Then they steal everything—money, cell phone, luggage, shoes, everything—and push people in water. One man say no, and they cut him bad when he don't give to them. They kill the owner of boat. When police find out, they go to village where *raskols* live and burn five houses, making *raskols* very angry. They lost all their things in fire."

"When did this happen?"

"Last year." He gets up. "Now I must find my boat. I will come back in the evening. Maybe I can find some men to go with you."

"*Tenkyu tru*," Nadya and I reply in unison.

In the afternoon, I lace up my running shoes and head out along a logging road behind the village. The heat is full blast, but I need to steady my nerves and be alone for a while. I run hard, dodging smashed logs and skipping over severed branches, and the sweat flows. Three hornbills pass low over my head, their characteristic downturned beaks with wrinkled casques arrowing forward. The odd whooshing sound of their wings makes them seem prehistoric. Then there are no sounds until there is only one: an obnoxious rumble I have not heard since leaving Canada, growing gradually louder. I slow down, dreading going around the next bend. There is freshly churned muck under my feet now, the dirt bearing the indentations of caterpillar tracks. The blunt rear end of a bulldozer, once yellow, now brown under its coat of mud, blocks the road ahead. Black smoke blurts from its exhaust, and I glimpse an Asian head in the cab and a nodding cigarette. I turn around, not wishing to see the destruction beyond.

When I arrive back, I cool down by walking around the village. It seems a little more well-to-do than others we've encountered. Tidy, knee-high hedges separate the dwellings from a swept bankside path. Grass, chopped low, surrounds John's house. Maybe Tipas, now distant from the mighty Sepik, isn't as vulnerable to floods. There are not many people about. I ask Jobby about this when I spot him sitting on the stump of a palm tree, chewing betel nut.

"Tipas was happy village in past," he tells me, even when the river left it. There were fish in the lake and animals to hunt. Then Global came. "Malaysia man trick Elder to sign paper and give away land! They promise people jobs and money if they cut down trees. Now there are no animals to hunt and no fish in the lake. Where have fish gone? No one knows. Maybe bad spirits come. Some people, they left Tipas and go to Wewak. They never come back. Their houses are empty."

I think of John Dademo Waiko's history of the nation and his reflections on the legacy of colonialism. In a country where environmental protections are inadequate or nonexistent, Japanese, Australian, Canadian, and Malaysian companies have found they can persuade local landowners to give over their land for resource extraction by promising to generate jobs and improve living standards. Most of the jobs on offer require little skill and are poorly paid: picking coffee beans, digging for gold, operating chainsaws, loading ships. Once the work is done, the resource extracted, the company moves on. I think, too, about our own presence here. Nadya and I are touring for personal gratification. Tomorrow, we will leave this backwater village and rejoin the Sepik. Not out of desperation because we can no longer make a living here, but because, as travellers, we have the privilege of arriving and departing when we please.

I ask Jobby to accompany us to Pagwi, promising to pay him a decent wage and feed him, but he declines. He only has a week off school: not enough time to paddle there and motor back.

|| John Mariati called Papua the "Land of the Unexpected." His uncle told us last night that we must rise at the crack of dawn so we have daylight enough to reach the village of Imombi, an eleven-hour paddle away. Two brothers, Bilicus and Estley, John's *tambu*, would accompany us. There, a motor-canoe coming down the May River and up the Sepik bound for Tipas could give the pair a ride home. A perfect plan. How he knew about this fortunate timing, given there is no cell phone coverage here, we could not fathom.

It is 7:30 a.m. at present, two hours since we got up, and I am watching a motor-canoe drilling across the lake in front of John's house. Is John also taking a trip? Is this the boat his sister borrowed now being returned? Neither. This is the boat that will return Bilicus and Estley to Tipas from Imombi, and we must pay for the fuel for it to do so (K256, about a hundred bucks Canadian), as well as hire them (K50 each). John thinks it would be swifter if we separate our canoes, and Bilicus has hacked away the bindings without asking us. He will join me in one dugout, towing the motor-canoe, and Estley will paddle with Nadya in the other. Neither Nadya nor I are happy with this, but we both sense it would be wise not to linger longer in Tipas. Having paid for our stay and given John a packet of cigarettes as a gift, we push off.

"Ask for Councillor Tobius when you get to Imombi," Jobby calls out. "He is big man there. He is our *wantok*."

Allegiances, we have come to understand, are critical in tribal Papua. First there is duty to one's immediate family: brothers hunting together, sisters helping each other to raise children. Then there are bonds to *tambu* (relations), to aunts and uncles or cousins, some of whom may live in a neighbouring village. Last, there is loyalty to *wantok*, to "one talk" or clan, which includes branches of the family established through marriage or friends who, again, may live far away. The *wantok* system cultivates a strong sense of intervillage kinship that is important in a setting where there are no social safety nets. It also fosters a network of obligation. Jobby was telling me yesterday about a marital custom in the Sepik. When a boy marries a girl from another village, and she moves to his village, his sister must leave and join the bride's family to fill the gap. Nadya and I are benefitting from *wantok* by association. John Youpa probably felt duty-bound to help us because we were his nephew's friends. If we had arrived yesterday without that connection, we might not have been made so welcome. Back in Vanimo, Jeffrey Waino may have felt obliged to assist us as Dorothy, the manager of CBC Guesthouse, who took us under her wing from our arrival, belonged to his *wantok*. Nadya has also discovered that John Mariati is Dorothy's brother-in-law. Our journey so far has been made possible through a network of connections. I am starting to realize how dependent we are on kinship relations and how indebted we are.

It takes me less than half an hour to detest the new boating arrangement. Bilicus is standing at the stern paddling in the customary fashion; I am sitting up front with a short paddle, lurching from side to side and trying to harmonize with his strokes. My back is starting to play up. I briefly consider kneeling, but, with my *bagarap* ankles, this has never really been an option. We have lost the glorious stability of our double-hulled raft. Worse, each time we thrust forward, the "anchor" out back with its weighty outboard engine acts as a brake. Nadya and Estley shoot ahead in their canoe, and I privately curse dead-eye John for forcing this situation upon us.

"Bilicus, *dispela nogut*!" I say before we rejoin the river. A strapping fellow probably in his late twenties, my new shipmate doesn't appear to speak any English.

Noticing that the motor-canoe has a painter, I gesture with my hands that we should bring the two boats side by side and hook the rope over my bow. Bilicus nods. I still have one of the plank seats we were using before. The two canoes aren't precisely the same height off the water, but close enough. I can use the plank to bridge them and sit more comfortably to paddle. We start to make better progress, particularly when the current seizes us, and catch up to the other canoe. I don't like Nadya being in a separate canoe and suggest she remain within earshot.

Mid-morning, I hear what sounds like the buzz of a hornet. The buzz deepens in pitch and becomes a chainsaw. Then it is a biplane before it turns into a motor-canoe, gunning around a bend in the river ahead of us and creating a wide bow wave. I stop paddling and brace myself for waves, but, fifty metres from us, the boat throttles down and draws to a halt. It is two-and-a-half times the length of our canoe and twice the girth; it has a 150 hp Yamaha engine on the back and "Labour Boy 1" painted on the side. Ten passengers have their arms around gunny sacks of cocoa or copra. The bare-chested captain chats with Estley and Bilicus in Tok Pisin, then in English warns us about pirates.

"Sorry, but that is Papua New Guinea!" he says, shrugging helplessly before refiring the engine and shooting off.

Five hours of steady paddling brings us to a fishing camp occupied by Bilicus and Estley's sister, her husband, and an older man with grizzled hair and badly abraded feet and ankles, the dark skin worn white. And what kind of fish do these muddy waters conceal? What do the eagles swoop down to catch from their roosts? Piranha. Evaline has a hundred fish blackening on a rack above a fire, and she gives us one each to try. They are almond-shaped with gawping eyes and mouthfuls of spiked teeth. Some are the size of dinner plates, their teeth like a baby shark's. And to think, earlier in the day, fed up with the heat, I had stripped down to my briefs and dived overboard. Yet Nadya and I have heard no talk of these fish biting lumps out of people. None of the villagers we have seen bear such wounds. These can't be the piranha fish of the movies. I think of Blofeld's pets in *You Only Live Twice*. We sit cross-legged under an awning, scratching off the crispy, scorched skins and gnawing the flesh while Evaline catches up on the news from her brothers. Maybe it's the smoking process, but piranha is chewy and hasn't a distinctive flavour.

The day is well advanced when Imombi materializes. Our approach does not go unnoticed. People are calling each other out of their homes and pointing. We quickly dig out some kina to pay our escorts. Once we hit land, Bilicus and Estley waste no time unloading our bags and are soon roaring away in their motor-canoe. We are left alone in a crowd of about a hundred and fifty people. Most are clearly astonished. When I move too fast, the children scream in terror and scatter. Nadya and I smile broadly and shake as many adult hands as possible. *Councillor Tobius, where are you?* I practise saying the name in my head: *To-bee-us* (not *To-bye-us*). We have no idea what he looks like. Someone who exudes an air of authority, I suppose. A high school student introduces himself as Justin and asks where we are heading. Ambunti. His school is there, he says, and he must return soon. A classmate also needs to go. Maybe they could join us. Sounds promising. Nadya and I could avoid the wallet-thinning gasoline costs associated with getting a paddler back to his home village. All we need now are the blessings of the village big man.

5 “CANADA TENT *NOGUT!*”

While we were making camp that night, more natives arrived with food for sale; and I parted with the last of my trade goods (and some of my personal cutlery too)...At one time, I counted sixty-seven men in the camp: all clamoured for tomahawks and I had to explain to them—a very difficult task—that...I still had a long way to go, and that the remainder of the axes, &c., would be required for the use of the party. They listened rather sullenly to this; and I could see they were disappointed, but I couldn't help it. However, soon afterwards, two men came into the camp bearing a large pig, and persuaded me to part with my last tomahawk.

—JACK HIDES, *Through Wildest Papua*

“Welcome my village!”

A stocky man of about fifty, dressed in blue shorts and a yellow T-shirt printed with the words “Bilas Peles,” descends the ladder from his hut and comes to shake our hands. We need not ask who this is. Clean-shaven, silver watch hanging loosely from his wrist, safari hat with a floppy brim on his head, Councillor Tobius stands out from the crowd. Once again, we have arrived by chance in front of the village big man's house—unless, that is, all visitors are obliged to pull in at this spot. Our dugouts are tucked behind a floating log moored to the bank, chopped flat on the unsubmerged side so it can serve as a catwalk. I am relieved to see our contact. The crowd seemed alarmed at our sudden appearance.

"The children are frightened of us," I say to him, swinging around and watching them flee shrieking once again.

"They never see *waitman* or *waitmeri* before," replies Tobius, chuckling. "But I remember *waitman* come here one time. Old man from Australia."

"How long ago?"

"Long time before. Maybe fifteen year."

Fifteen years ago? I wasn't expecting there to be such villages in twenty-first century Papua New Guinea. I had assumed you would need to delve deep into the hinterland to encounter Papuans who hadn't seen white people since the wide-roving Australian district patrol officers (*kiaps*) of the colonial period marched through. Surely Aussies have been paddling or motoring along the Sepik over recent years, photographing crocodile hunters, collecting tribal artefacts, or tracking down birds of paradise. And yet we haven't seen a single white person, Australian or otherwise, since crossing the border from West Papua. Looking around at the bemused faces, I am reminded of the tribesmen in the famous photographs Michael Leahy took in the 1930s. Only Papuans living on the coast had encountered whites until the Leahy brothers from Australia ventured into the Highlands hunting for gold.

"I was terrified," Kirupano Eza'e from Seigu village in the Eastern Highlands said when interviewed by Australian documentary filmmakers Bob Connolly and Robin Anderson decades later. "I couldn't think properly, and I cried uncontrollably. My father pulled me along by the hand and we hid behind some tall kunai grass."

Whites may rarely visit Imombi, but manufactured clothes are plain to see, kids in soccer jerseys, women in dresses printed with elaborate designs. Some of the villagers must make the long trek to town from time to time, whether to Vanimo via Green River or to Maprik via Pagwi, or else merchants in their motor-canoes supply them. Judging from how torn, bleached, and saggy-necked the shirts are on the kids, if the second be true, I would say it has either been some time since the last shipment or the villagers can't afford the prices.

Tobius has his men heave our belongings up the ladder to his house. His wife Jenny brings hot water for tea, and we sit cross-legged in a circle on the floor around the big man. He removes his hat, revealing a bald head, and I note, regarding his equally hairless arms and legs, what a contrast he is next to his compatriots. Hair, its curliness, its abundance, was the feature of the Papuans that most struck the Portuguese when they first touched on New Guinea's shores in the sixteenth century. "Ilhas dos Papuas," they named the archipelago (Islands of the Frizzy Hairs), Papua deriving from the Malay word *papuwah*, meaning curly hair. Spanish explorer Yñigo Ortiz de Retez, arriving shortly after, came up with the name New Guinea as the Papuans reminded him of Guineans in Africa. I find it remarkable how similar in appearance the Papuans are to sub-Saharan Africans and wonder about their heredity.

I break out a packet of pineapple creams to have with the tea, and Nadya and I tell Tobius our plans. What fortunate timing that Justin and his classmate must return to their school in Ambunti. We travelled with high school kids from Green River and found them very capable. He smiles and tucks into the cookies, telling us that we must travel safely on the river. Nadya and I nod seriously. I expect our host to pass the cookies around, but the tray remains in his lap, lightening by the minute. They are clearly a treat for the big man.

Nadya and I wondered in Vanimo whether to bring gifts or items for trade to the Sepik. Ivan Champion had taken mirrors, steel adzes, and tomahawks with him when he crossed the country in the 1930s and bartered for food. Eric Hansen had carried salt, flashlight batteries, and shotgun shells into the Bornean interior in the 1980s for the same purpose. Jeffrey Waino advised us to buy small bags of sugar or salt, and we have been exchanging these for sago. To foster good relations, I have also been handing out Gudang Garam cigarettes I bought in Jayapura, and these seem popular among the men. What is appreciated or regarded as valuable here no doubt changes over time. I thought the villagers would be envious of our clothes, medical supplies, bedrolls, and water purifier, and petition us for them, but so far this has not happened.

As light is fading fast and there is obviously no electricity, I excuse myself to go for a *was-was*. I stink after the long day's paddle. Is there a place where Imombians bathe? The river, of course, says our host. Noticing there is still a crowd on the riverbank, Nadya decides to pass. Today, I must not—*must not*—drop the soap as I did in Mockwai. Anything that goes into this cloudy river does not come out. We have only one bar remaining, and there are no stores. This reminds me as I step tentatively onto the floating log beside our canoes that I must get Justin to find some cane string to bind our dugouts together so we can have a stable raft once again. I place the soap carefully in a shallow indentation in the log and slide my body into the water. The current immediately sweeps my legs downstream, and I have to hug the log to stay put. Invisible objects bump into my body. I duck my head under and then climb back onto the log to soap down. Back into the river again to rinse. Throwing my arm over the log and groping blindly for a handhold to heave myself out, my hand smacks the soap. Away it flies, and I hear a fateful plop. I expect to hear roars of laughter from the bank, but, when I return to my perch and look around, I find myself practically alone. Guess it must be dinnertime.

In my absence, Nadya has managed to buy a fish, and Jenny has cooked it over the house fire and made sago pancakes. After dinner, Councillor Tobius introduces us to three men sitting patiently on his verandah, waiting for us to finish eating.

"They want 300 to take you to Iniock."

It takes a moment for this statement to sink in. I look over at Nadya.

"Um, please thank them for their offer," I reply, "but actually we already have an arrangement."

"Justin is worry about *raskol*. He will not go with you."

Another silence.

"That is unfortunate," Nadya says, the first to recover. "He has a classmate who also wants to go to Ambunti."

Tobius doesn't respond, and we can't very well ask to speak to Justin. We are in no position to offer him protection. I would like to dig out our map and find Iniock, but it is too dark. Can't get an impression of the three men either, and it wouldn't do to shine my headlamp in their faces.

Light from the embers of the fire plays over the empty plastic cookie tray, making the corners glint. Guess we won't be tossing pineapple creams to a hungry *pukpuk* to persuade it "not to eat tasty Canadian" as John Mariati suggested.

"*Ol gat seken prais?*" Nadya asks after a while. Are the men willing to go for less? This is the first time either of us has tried to bargain.

Tobius puts it to them. No. They will not budge. They want a hundred each.

"*Mipela tok gen tumaro,*" I say wearily. Let's talk about it again tomorrow. At least they are not asking us to tow a motor-canoe and pay for gas.

|| Ill-rested after a sweaty night spent too close to the dying fire, I ease my stiff body down the ladder and splash some river water on my face. Standing by our canoes is one of the three men who visited us last night—at least, the silhouette I saw seems to match. He introduces himself as Jimmy, and, judging by his easy smile and wiry physique, he looks like he might make a good boatmate. *Tiktik* is Tok Pisin for the cane string Papuans use for bindings, and I ask him to unite our canoes using the two sticks we have on board. I stress with suitable tugging gestures the importance of pulling the string taut to make the sticks hold fast. Nodding cheerfully, he heads off, and I feel encouraged. But where the hell is Iniock?

Back at the house, I see that Nadya has found it on our map. However, as neither Tipas nor Imombi are marked, it is hard to say how far away it is. About half yesterday's distance, we reckon, and for this we are going to pay three times the hire price? Jenny serves breakfast: leftover sago from last night and fire-blackened bananas, which I find tough to swallow, as they are mealy and juiceless. Thanking her, I pay for our stay and go and check on progress at the waterside. I expect to see Jimmy and a river-worthy raft. I find neither. What I see are two lengths of fraying *tiktik* wound loosely around the bridging sticks and tied in attractive bows. Neither string, I notice, goes under the hulls. I look up and down the riverbank.

"The men don't want to go," Tobius says when I return and mention Jimmy.

Life on the Sepik.

"Oh dear." I do not ask for the reason.

"But my son Benjamin will go...and another man with a motor."

Nadya and I frown at each other. We don't want a rerun of yesterday if we can help it.

"Actually, Councillor, we came to paddle down the Sepik," Nadya says phlegmatically. "A motor disturbs the birds."

I expect Tobius to reject this. Do we expect his son to paddle back from Iniock against the current? Instead, he goes in search of Benjamin.

An hour passes. Tobius returns to report that his son has no wish to go. It seems we are stuck, and we find a spot beside the river to sit. It is an overcast, windless day, and the air seems soupy and stale. There is little movement on the river. A solitary canoe containing two women and three children edges upstream, all five pumping hard, the kids with mini-paddles mimicking the adults.

Nadya tells me she also had a restless night, jolted awake repeatedly when the hut creaked on its piles or she heard voices outside.

"I am starting to wonder if this is worth it, Tony."

I look at her for a while, not sure how to respond. There's no turning back now.

"Well, we have to give it a chance. This is only our fourth day on the river."

"I know, I know, but the villagers clearly don't want to paddle with us unless they feel duty-bound, and who can blame them? We're asking them to drop what they are doing and waste a day escorting the *waitpela* downstream. Then they have to paddle home upstream in the dark on a river in flood."

She is right. We have assumed the villagers are willing to help us because they need the money. But they have shown themselves to be largely self-sufficient: hunting in the forest, fishing in the river, and growing fruit and vegetables in their gardens. They are generally in fine shape. Many of the men look like trained athletes. The fact that the villagers live in basic shelters and their kids dress in ragged clothes does not make them needy, yet I realize I have assumed this. They probably have most of what they require to survive in this setting.

"And they may not wish to go with us," Nadya adds, "because they, too, are afraid of pirates. Travelling with us makes getting robbed more likely, doesn't it?"

"Probably. I didn't think it would be like this. I thought we'd be canoeing on our own for most of the time."

"And, frankly, it is scary. The warning you got from the old men in Tipas about *raskols*, same again from the motorboat captain yesterday. And that man screaming and beating the ground under John's house, what was that about?"

"You know, I found John scarier," I reply. "I couldn't understand why he was chucking stones at his own house."

"There are no police around if we get into trouble. Remember when we canoed in Indonesia? Stopping at little fishing ports along the Javan coast. The fishermen were friendly, and there were no pirates. The only threat was the sea. Here things seem so unpredictable, like anything could happen."

Tobius returns, a man at his side in his forties, smoking a cigarette. He bears something of a resemblance to the councillor but has short, curly hair and a sullen look. Trailing behind them is a teenage boy.

"My brother Jeffrey has canoe. He will take you to Iniock, and this boy will go too."

"For how much?" Nadya asks, folding her arms.

"Same price. Hundred kina for Jeffrey, hundred for Melwin."

"Seventy each."

Tobius mumbles to Jeffrey. Jeffrey shakes his head firmly.

"Hundred kina each man." He sees that we are about to protest again. "Life is most important! You pay money, you have good safety!" He does not shout, but it is clear that negotiations are over.

We gather our bags while Melwin chops down and peels fresh cane. I join him on the catwalk but need say nothing. In twenty minutes, we have a sturdy raft once again.

The big man of Imombi in his "Bilas Peles" T-shirt and floppy hat stands on the log catwalk and smiles as we shove off. The villagers line the riverbank and wave; the children hoot and jog along the bank, keeping pace with us. *Bilas* means "gem" in Tok Pisin, *peles* "place."

For part of the day, Melwin paddles alone in Jeffrey's canoe, and, for part, he draws alongside, and we are a tri-hulled vessel. This leg of our voyage is a quiet one. I try to engage Tobius's brother in conversation, Tok Pisin and English, but he just grunts. He spends the entire day seated, paddling without effort or just steering and smoking. This Jeffrey is hardly the inspiring Jeffrey who launched us on our expedition at Green River. Melwin, by contrast, is cheery and does his fair share. Better if he were on the raft rather than his senior, but we are not in a position to propose this. Then I realize that, without Tobius's brother, we would still be in Imombi; Jeffrey is enabling this leg of our journey.

I paddle slowly and deliberately, happy we have a stable platform once again. As the muddy river reveals little, my eyes rove over the dense, green mass that it bisects. In places, the forest erupts over the river, trying, it would seem, to colonize it. Thirty-metre vines, some adorned with vermillion flowers like candle flames, plunge from the canopy and sway as they rake the surface of the river; sturdier branches with waxy, tongue-like leaves fan over it. Some of the branches have monstrous swellings in their forks. Hornets' nests? But I see no hornets arriving and departing. Brown ribbons spiral down the trunks from these goitres. When we draw near, I scratch at one and uncover the ant highway beneath. The dirt tunnels must protect the ants from predators.

Perched on a tall branch, a bird the size of a Canadian blue jay but with the bluey-green sheen of a rusty blackbird monitors us. I try in vain to train our binoculars on him, but he keeps shooting off. I get flashes of an orange beak fat as a finch's and a head too big for its body. I recall seeing this fellow in the bird book I ordered in Canada but cannot recall the name. A roller perhaps? When the bird takes off for the eighth or ninth time, I spot the circular white splashes on the underside of its wings that resemble coins. This is the dollar bird.

I think of my late father and his love of birds. He liked to stand at the kitchen window watching blue tits, great tits, greenfinches, and chaffinches visit our bird table, on which he religiously poured birdseed every morning. I remember him tossing grubs he had unearthed while digging in the garden to a robin perched on his wheelbarrow. I can see him in his tweed jacket, flat cap, and gumboots, setting off on one of his rambles in the English countryside, binoculars around his neck, bird book in his pocket. He favoured walks around reservoirs so he could see ducks, geese, and grebes on the water, as well as linnets, yellowhammers, and dunnocks in the surrounding hedgerows. He also knew which birds were about without seeing them. "There's a green woodpecker in that wood. Can you hear it?" "Listen to the rooks in those elms!" "Clicking pebbles. Hear that? Call of a stonechat."

We invariably spent our Easter holidays in the Lake District, a national park a three-hour drive north of Coventry, where I was born. The place was a rambler's and birdwatcher's haven as it was studded with lakes and sparsely forested at altitude. This meant spectacular views and sightings of eagles. "Prize for the first one to spot a golden eagle!" Dad would say on the drive up. My brother and I peeled our eyes at the first signs we had arrived in Cumbria:

sheep, stone walls, and scree-sided fells. The emperor of eagles was difficult to spot as it typically soared alone over high valleys or crags. A solitary buzzard or even a crow, flying at height, could easily be a golden eagle until binoculars disclosed the imposter. Invariably, my eagle-eyed mother, binocular-less and flicking through a gardening magazine in the passenger seat, would be the one to get the jackpot.

Dad had a way of passing on his passion to his sons. "See that field? Look out for fieldfares. Saw them there this time last year. A fieldfare is a like a thrush, only bigger and dressier." At a reservoir: "Now, if we are lucky, there might be a red-breasted merganser or two and maybe some shelduck." At the Lake District: "Keep an eye on the streams," he would say. "You might see a dipper or perhaps, higher up, a ring ouzel. Ring ouzels look like blackbirds but have white collars."

Interestingly, I know he wouldn't have wanted to see the birds of Papua, however "dressy." He preferred to remain on home territory with the birds he grew up with and loved, watching them arrive and depart with the seasons.

We have been on the Sepik a week now, and the sun has left its mark. I have pink ankles and itchy blisters on my wrists. I must wear socks on my feet and make sure my shirt sleeves extend over my gloves. I am glad these canoes aren't made of fibreglass or plastic, or else I would probably be sliding about in my socks, struggling to keep balance. My stocking feet can grip the rough wood well enough, but the downside is that my socks pick up the slop that inevitably collects in the bottom of the boat. My gloveless, unsocked wife does not seem to have these problems. For her, inhaling the thick sauna air is the challenge. In the afternoon hours, she must take breaks from paddling, sit down, and breathe deeply through her mouth. I thought two months in West Papua would have been enough to harden our skins to tropical heat, but then, I realize, we spent all our time on the coast or in the highlands where it was often breezy in the afternoons and cool at night. Here, the setting sun brings little relief.

The day's paddle ends when we run up on a mud bar in front of two huts leaning out over the water. Both are in miserable condition, slats missing from the walls, stilt legs at odd angles, palm-leaf roofs patchy and sagging. They look more like hunting shelters than homes. I imagine a tropical storm reducing them to piles of sticks or lifting them clean off their skinny legs and tossing them in the river. Melwin jumps overboard and squelches through mud toward the huts.

"*Dispela* Iniock, Jeffrey?" I ask, squinting and trying to make out the outline of a village through the trees.

"Melwin have *tambu* here," our captain mumbles. It is his third sentence of the day. "You pay now" is his fourth.

"*Mi wetim* Melwin *kumbek*," I say, turning away. Not until Melwin returns.

Looking at the great brown river swirl by, I find my mind floating back to a brief voyage I made by dugout canoe along the Ubangi in the Central African Republic in 1993. In my late twenties then and single, I was travelling with a feisty Frenchman a few years my junior called Olivier Chotard. Through an agent, we had hired two village men to take us from Mobaye to Limassa, a four-day paddle upstream. It was also post-monsoon season and the going was tough, the pair at times having to hug the riverbank and shunt the canoe forward gondolier-fashion using long poles, dodging fallen trees and avoiding the current. The trip lasted only a day and a half. At noon on the second day, our paddlers beached the canoe and demanded their pay: 4,500 francs a piece (about Can$25 at the time). But we were not at Limassa, Olivier yelled. They wouldn't get a centime out of us until we had arrived at Limassa, the arrangement agreed in writing with the agent in Mobaye. He would have come to blows with the older of the two paddlers had a policeman not appeared on the riverbank. We had arrived at the village of Satéma, and he marched us off to his station and had us sit on a bench to explain ourselves. Olivier got to his feet several times, shaking a signed contract at the officer indignantly and yelling about being cheated. He was told firmly to sit down and not speak again unless invited. Having listened to what everyone had to say, the policeman adjudicated: much to Olivier's disgust, he and I would pay our paddlers 3,000 francs each despite the fact that Satéma was clearly not two-thirds of the way to Limassa from Mobaye. I remember how angry the paddlers were as they returned to their canoe. Despite them dishonouring the contract, it seemed unwise to part company in their world on such bad terms.

Melwin returns with a man of about forty-five in a red ball cap, blue T-shirt, and jeans rolled to the knees who introduces himself as David. His bare feet are shod in mud slippers.

"Apinun," Nadya says, shaking his hand. *"Wanem nem bilong hia?"*

"Iniock," he replies and points downriver.

I see smoke above the trees. We must be at the outskirts. I dig four fifty-kina notes out my wallet and hand two to Jeffrey and two to Melwin. Jeffrey says nothing and avoids my eyes. David gives us a hand carting our gear over to the huts, and a man called Anton comes over to carry our paddles. Hearing their outboard start up, I turn and watch Jeffrey and Melwin depart. Their canoe slices across the river diagonally to where the water is smoothest on the far side and then drills upstream. Melwin looks back and waves.

David has an amiable, welcoming face with rounded features and a broad grin, and I sense immediately that he is a decent man. He shows no surprise at our appearance and even seems to have been expecting us—although I know that is not likely. There has been no cell phone service since we left Green River. We are to lodge in the first hut, he says, which we discover to be a kitchen. There's a fire in one corner, a heap of yams resembling stone boulders in another, a cobweb-coated battery rigged to a solitary lightbulb at one side, bags of peanuts and cooking pots hanging from the soot-blackened roof, and a black-and-white cat with lumps of fur missing stretched out on a heap of fishing net. First cat we've seen since arriving in the country.

It is hard to get our gear up the tree-trunk ladder, jamming the edges of our feet in the divots macheted in the side. It is also hard to step off the ladder into the kitchen as a very old lady is clinging to the top of the ladder, her legs fleshless and twisted beneath her. She stares at us, baffled, as we step carefully over her, apologizing for the intrusion. Perhaps this is the safest spot in the house as the limbom flooring is in terrible shape. Again, I fear that, at any moment, we will fall through. Maybe we should have brought snowshoes with us.

It is a tricky evening. David and Anton, the only English speakers, vanish into the woods on a hunting expedition, and Nadya and I struggle to converse with a band of elderly men who come to visit. When we return to the kitchen, it is like a tramp steamer's engine room. A teenage girl has stoked the fire. We open our food bin and hand her rice and a tin of pork luncheon meat, which Nadya detests and I haven't eaten since I was a boy scout. We are not quite sure who the pint-sized kids are helping with the cooking—David's children, presumably—but they are obviously quite used to the fire. I last ten minutes. Sweat trickling down my forehead and spine, eyes smarting from the smoke, I grab a nylon bag from my pack and a headlamp and make a dash for the ladder, almost dislodging grannie in my haste. Now I understand why she is stationed where she is; hers is the coolest, least smoky spot in the room.

I have an idea, one that has been on my mind since our stay in the sago sieve in *natnat*-infested Waku. Old men and small children gather around in a circle as I unroll the tent and peg out the groundsheet. Like a magician, I snap together the elasticated aluminium poles and produce three gleaming antennae. The children help me thread these through the colour-coded canvas loops of the inner shell. To the wonderment of all, our Terra Nova Voyager tent, with its space-age geodesic curves, its mosquito-proof mesh inner, its taut rainproof fly, and its Waterbloc groundsheet, rises from the jungle floor. Dusting off my palms, I retreat for dinner, assured of a dry, cool, *natnat*-free, restful night with my wife. A cuddle for the first time since we left Vanimo might even be on the cards. I will not be tormented by dreams of falling headfirst down a well. I give the thumbs-up to the watching men, now seated on a log, and get nods of approval.

When we are done eating, I gather up our bags. Nadya is reluctant to follow but humours me. David's invalid mother must be wondering what's going on as I make for the ladder. Leaving already, are you? Thought you were spending the night with us. Unable to see where to plant my feet, I half slide down the ladder and bark my shins.

Our tent has a roomy porch at the entrance: plenty of space there for our packs, and we can zip the fly over them. The old men watch us wriggle in. We last two minutes. If the kitchen was hot, the inside of the tent is a furnace.

"I...can't...breathe," Nadya says, her chest heaving.

"Better get the flysheet off. It's trapping the heat."

Out I slide and quickly peel it off. But this means our bags are now exposed. Someone could wander off with them in the night. They will have to sleep with us. I open the mesh door and shove them in. By the time I am back in and the mesh door zipped shut, there is no room to move. My wife and I are scrunched up in one corner, knees tucked into our chests. Nadya is desperate. She has enough trouble breathing outdoors.

"Tony, I...CAN'T...BREATHE!" she rasps.

Uncoiling herself, she rips open the door and shoves her head out, gasping. Out she dives. There will be no romantic cuddles tonight. Our camping experiment is over.

"Canada tent *nogut*!" I yell at the men while ripping out the pegs and collapsing the poles. The men shake their heads and mutter *nogut, nogut*.

"Em tumas hat!"

The men nod. Yes, yes, too hot. David, I see, has joined them.

"You want to come back inside house?" he asks gently. He sounds more concerned than amused.

"Sorry. Yes, David. Do you mind?" It kills me to say it.

The geodesic marvel becomes a black slug once again, and I coax it back into its nylon sock. I have been carrying around 2.2 kilograms of weight for nothing.

What is the old lady going to think when I heave our bags up the ladder once again? But no one is in the kitchen when we return. The only signs of life are the winking coals in the grate. Nadya yanks our mosquito net out of her pack, unravels the string that suspends it, and stands on her toes to tie it to a rafter. I am glad to see that her breathing is back under control.

"Can I help with that?" I am a little taller than she is.

Nadya chucks the string four times before it goes over the rafter. She grabs the end, pulls hard, and ties a knot.

"You know, you didn't have to join me in the tent."

No response.

"You could have stayed..."

"No, Tony. No, I couldn't. You don't understand. It is too dangerous for a woman to sleep alone in a place like this. And it would have sent the wrong message about our relationship, wouldn't it?"

She turns, pulls out her bed mat, and unrolls it. I follow suit, and we spread the mozi net over them, tucking the edges under the corners of the mats.

"True. I hadn't thought of that. Sorry."

While Nadya crawls under the net and changes her clothes, I sit leaning against my pack and dim my headlamp. Wind off the river gusts through rents in the walls and carries off the heat of the embers. I take a deep breath and listen to the river. Sounds like it is right below us, tugging at the legs of the hut. Last thing I see before switching off my headlamp and ducking under the net is the cat washing itself in the corner.

6 YANAK THE SORCERER

A number of half-starved village dogs, as they are accustomed to do, were standing around watching the men eat, hoping that they would be thrown a few scraps. But after picking the bones clean, the men carefully placed them in the fire, and burnt them...I asked them why they didn't throw the bones to the dogs. One of them gravely explained that Kwoma never did that, since the dogs are in the habit of dropping small particles of the food when they eat, and if these were found by sorcerers, they could be used against the people whose leavings they were.

—ROSS BOWDEN,
Sorcery, Illness and Social Control in Kwoma Society

I wake up with a rotten stomach. I must make a dash for the forest. Wrestling on my pants, I sprint bare-chested for the ladder, apologizing, as I tumble down it, to grandma who is back at her post and cowering. In the suburbs of Iniock, there is no shed for ablutions, only a hole in the ground, hidden under a banana leaf. I peel it back, disturbing a battalion of flies. Not a moment too soon. A jet of relief. I breathe out, closing my eyes.

What was the villain? The fire-blackened bananas we carried from Imombi and ate for lunch yesterday? There couldn't be anything blander. Last night's dinner? Perhaps New Guinean pork luncheon meat contains more than the obvious. But tinned meat should be safe. Nadya would have noticed if the tin had been punctured or rusty. My lack of hygiene since donating our last bar of soap to the

Sepik? I am surprised I haven't had more gastronomical rebellions since arriving in Papua. The irony is I have more trouble in Canada—especially during winter for some reason. My stomach no longer copes easily with the constant onslaught of every kind of food imaginable. The simple village food we have been eating here has, until now, done me no harm. Sago and fish, fish and sago. Straight from the fire.

Then I remember. We spotted a creek early afternoon yesterday, a rare sight on the flooded river. Our bottles were dry. Topping them up on river soup again was not attractive. It is not so much the knowledge that anything and everything goes into the Sepik, but the foul taste of the chemicals we must add to make it drinkable. Our SteriPEN, running on local batteries, has been unreliable. Over to the creek we paddled, euphoric. The water, cascading over a log step, was clear and cool. I thrust my head under the falling water. My mistake, having refilled and chlorinated our bottles, was not giving the Aquatabs time enough to do their work. Busy birdwatching again as we headed off, I waited only fifteen minutes instead of the necessary thirty before slaking my thirst.

It doesn't help, as we load the boat this morning, that David shows us the spoils of his evening hunt: a flying fox. He stretches out the wings so Nadya can take a picture. Looking at the head tilted to one side, eyes glazed, the wings held open like this, I am reminded of Christ on the cross. I think back to the very alive ones we saw in Vanimo, clamouring for roosting space on their favourite tree, their eyes bright, their orange coats radiant in the sun. I see that the arrow struck near the head of David's prize. One wing has ripped away from the shoulder; a mushroom of pink tissue sprouts from the neck. Is this to be breakfast for the family? The way he is displaying the creature, it seems like an invitation to us. I imagine sitting across from him, each of us chewing on a leathery wing. My stomach turns.

"*Lukim yu*, David. *Tenkyu tru.*"

If he had a hand free, I would shake it. He has taken our unannounced appearance in his stride and made our stay as comfortable as possible. We didn't even have to ask if he knew of paddlers we might hire. Last night, Anton and Nicodemus simply presented themselves, prompted, we assume, by the big man. This pair would accompany us five hours downstream to Oum Number 1, a village that must be of some size as it is marked on our map. For this, we should pay them fifty kina each. Nadya and I nod without hesitation. The two men are burly and mature, Anton probably in his early forties, Nicodemus his thirties. Anton speaks English, Nicodemus not (I scribble a reminder in my journal to stop referring to Papuan men as "burly").

We shove off. The Iniockians stand shoulder to shoulder, watching. Nadya takes a picture of them, and a burly young man in an Adidas shirt takes one of us with his cell phone. I look at the villagers. They seem very serious, and I wonder what is going through their minds. Were they pleased to have visitors for a night or were we intruding? Did they rest easy? Through their legs, I spot grandma, faded blue-and-yellow dress with pleated collar hanging off her sagging shoulders, looking equally as grave. Someone has carried her down to witness our departure. Or is she there to make flying fox stew?

I start spooning the water with the crocodile paddle, but rhythm does not come easily this morning. I keep dusting the surface and sending spray back at Nicodemus who is steering our tri-hull, Anton's dugout being tethered temporarily to our raft.

"We can paddle," says our captain after a while. "You don't need to do."

I open my mouth to say what I have said before: Nadya and I came to the Sepik to paddle the Sepik. But I know I am tired. Our night in the kitchen was far from peaceful. In the early hours of the morning, a tropical storm marched through Iniock and rain spanked the palm roof of the kitchen. Suddenly, we were getting drenched. Our mats were too close to the window and directly under a hole in the ceiling. We shifted to another spot, but by then the storm had moved on. We enjoyed silence for about ten minutes. Then scurrying feet and a vicious scuffle between two animals. The cat was in mortal combat with something that had come in to take shelter. We groped about again for our flashlights. Suddenly, a tortured squeal. The cat bolted by our mosquito net and shot down the ladder, chasing something of similar size. A bandicoot? Round two of the duel happened beneath the house and went on for several minutes. We shone our lights through the gaps in the floor but could only see shadows. More stricken yowls and thrashing about. I tucked in the mosquito net. Would the cat return, bloodied but victorious, midnight snack swinging from its jaws? Or the mysterious intruder, perhaps, licking its chops?

I sit and then lie down. Anton's steady sweeps propel us forward smoothly. I make sure my legs are covered by my rain jacket and pull my hat down over my face.

When I wake, Anton is sitting, looking closely at a tri-pronged bamboo spear, one of two he has brought along.

"Is that for your *tambu* in Oum?"

"No, I will use when we come back. It is for piranha."

I pluck a salty Em Nau out of my pocket and take a bite. My gut is playing up again.

"And the other?" The other is thicker and has a single barbed iron spike with a string attached that coils down the shaft. A harpoon.

"I think you can guess."

"You are *sutman pukpuk.*"

He grins. "When we get close to home, it will be dark. Best time for hunting *pukpuk.*"

"Where do you aim? At the head? The stomach?"

"Here!" He taps his temple. "Behind eye."

How he manages that in the dark I will ask later. Right now, I insist that we head immediately for shore. I have a pressing need. But shore after the rain looks like a greasy nightmare. So I strip down to my undies and, as Nicodemus approaches the bank, dive overboard. Our *sutman* can keep an eye out for crocs. I hang on to the side of the boat and screw up my face. Nadya takes another photograph. Anton peers down at me with amusement.

"Let it go down the river, Tony. Let it all go." He makes a sweeping gesture with his hand as though waving traffic through an intersection. Anything and everything goes in the Sepik.

|| "I think best you pay us now," Anton says, pausing between strokes.

Oum Number 1 is on the horizon, a cluster of huts on a mud flat. Two ribbons of smoke unravel into the still air. A hundred children have emerged from the huts and are jumping up and down, pointing at us and screaming. Either they have eagle eyes, or they already know about the two *waitpela* paddling a local boat down their river. Feeling giddy after a day on salty crackers, I am relieved to see, as we draw closer, two men in their midst, standing with their arms folded. The moment we hit land, we head straight for them. Hopefully, one is the village big man and can offer us lodging.

"Put your bag there," says the stockier of the two, pointing at an isolated stick shelter a little back from the water.

By the time we have piled our gear under it and said farewell to Anton and Nicodemus, the two men are gone. So we sit leaning against our things proprietorially as a wall of bodies, five-deep, presses in. I do not prosper in such situations maybe because Nadya and I don't have kids of our own. Before leaving Canada, I should have learned how to juggle or perform magic tricks, reach behind a little boy's ear for a coin or ask another to choose a card from a deck but not show it to me. The Papuan kids we have met ask no questions. They stand and stare. If you move too suddenly, they run away. Blissfully, I am travelling with a social marvel. Listening to my wife, you'd think she just got out of bed after a night of undisturbed slumber.

"And what's *your* name?" "Do you have any brothers or sisters?" "Do you go to school?" "Where is your school?" "What grade are you?" "How about you?" "Is he your brother?" "Are you in the same class?" "Where do you live?" "Which one is *your* house?" Many of the Tok Pisin words are close to the English: *nem* (name); *skul* (school); *brata* (brother); *haus* (house). She hardly needs to translate. That said, many of the questions are answered only with embarrassed giggles. But that does not seem to matter.

After an hour and a half of this, I begin to see double. There are two hundred children now. They are cloning themselves. Now four hundred. I rub my eyes and take a swig from my water bottle, but it doesn't do any good. Maybe this is a test. The Elders of Oum are observing us from a distance, checking to see if we mean well. Finally, I hear a shout that definitely belongs to a man. Heads turn.

Another, more impatient bark, and a corridor opens in the crowd. A compact man with a broad nose and furry chin, dressed in sawn-off jeans and a Jim Beam T-shirt turned inside out, steps forward and thrusts out his hand. Behind him, a taller man in a flat cap and Puma shirt, carrying a *bilum*, does the same.

"I am Walter," says the first. "His name is Clifford. Welcome to our village."

These are not the men we met when we arrived, and neither is old enough to be the village big man. Late twenties, early thirties perhaps? Walter would seem, however, to belong to an important clan, for he leads us to a house the size of John Youpa's but in finer shape (sturdy plank stairs, limbom flooring without holes, furniture, an electric light powered by a solar panel). I collapse on a bench by a window, head thumping, enormously relieved to be off the baking mud. A breeze wafts in, and I close my eyes and breathe deeply. Another sound reason in tropical swampland to build houses on piles. I ask Walter if the village has a rainwater tank, remembering that Tipas did. Yes. He sends two boys off with our empty water bottles, and Nadya digs out rehydration salts.

When the heat of the day subsides, and I have pulled myself together, Walter and Clifford show us around Oum Number 1. Woniam and Pauwon tribes cohabit here peaceably. The main avenue is tidy, and the houses to either side large and in good shape, the sago slats of their walls slotted together without gaps, the palm fronds of their thatched roofs tightly woven and neatly trimmed. Fruit trees grow between the houses. I see clusters of yellow-husked miniature coconuts; goitrous *pawpaw*; ribbed, yellow or brown cocoa pods bursting from trunks; and sprays of giant green bananas like plantain that Clifford calls "*mau*" and says must be cooked before eating. He picks two shiny red pears from a tree loaded with them. Their watery, white flesh dissolves in our mouths, the taste nothing like a pear. "*Lau lau.* Water apple." On the ground near one house are edible berries called *tulip*, meaning "two leaves" in Tok Pisin, which are also edible.

Each house has a vegetable plot, a raised square of dirt shored up at the base with coconut husks. Walter points out mustard, chilli peppers, pumpkins, and taro plants.

"And do you know this one?" he asks, fingering the waxy, stretched-heart leaves of a vine. Nadya and I shake our heads.

"Vanilla. This we sell at market."

Ah, yes. We did notice the wrinkled, desiccated pods tied in little bundles on tables at Vanimo market. The hooked, dark brown pods resemble the mummified claws of some prehistoric creature.

"How much do you get for vanilla?" Nadya asks.

"1,100 kina for kilogram." Can$440. An extraordinary sum, although it would take a lot of dried pods to make a kilogram.

We walk on. Many people have decorated their houses with ornamental arches: palm branches bent over and festooned with hanging grasses and cut flowers. The village is preparing for a belated Easter convention, Clifford tells us, Pastor Ivan Lesley of the Assembly of God presiding, Pastor Godfried Wippon of the Revival Church in attendance. I ask him which church he follows.

"AOG. I want to be Revival man, but I like *buai* too much. Look at my mouth! I cannot belong. You must have white teeth to belong to Revival Church! You cannot chew *buai* or drink beer or smoke cigarette. If I want to join, I must repent my sin."

I ask him what the villagers of Oum believed before the arrival of the Christian churches. He points solemnly at a more dilapidated house that has no decorations.

"That was the house of a great sorcerer called Yanak. Everybody afraid of him because he had big power, like a god. Yanak was killing man, woman, even children when he had problem with them."

"How did he kill them?"

"He takes little bit food from enemy's plate and put it under fire where it heats up, and, when this happens, the enemy gets sick with fever and die. Or another way is when Yanak sees his enemy leave village, he sends his men and they knock him down unconscious. Then they take water from stomach of dead dog and pour it in enemy's mouth. Then they take needles from hands of flying fox and push into his arms. When enemy wakes up, he feels sick, his blood is contaminated, his stomach is rotten. And doctor comes, and he say, 'Do you know me?' and if the man say nothing, he will soon die."

I had read of such gruesome goings-on in Papuan villages, of sorcerers collecting the leavings (the leftover food, cigarette stubs, betel nut discharge, feces, or semen) of their victims and casting spells that caused illness and death. British anthropologist Anthony Forge, studying the Abelam tribe of the East Sepik in the early 1960s, told of Kwis'ndu, a sorcerer who gathered his victim's leavings and cooked them, apparently causing that person to have an epileptic fit, suffer a debilitating illness, or go mad. Apprehensive tribesmen took pains to leave no traces of their passing, especially when visiting a neighbouring village. If they needed to go to the toilet, they did so in streams. Bruce Knauft, an American professor of anthropology, noted something similar while with the Gebusi tribe of the central-western jungles in the 1980s. Sorcerers practised "parcel sorcery," meaning they stole their victim's leavings, especially their food scraps or excreta, and tied them up in a *bogay* or bundle. With their leavings bound up in this way, the victims could no longer digest their food or defecate and would quickly lose their appetites and waste away.

Papuans feared sorcerers, but they also feared being accused of sorcery. Knauft reported how the Gebusi held divinations and spirit seances to bring to light the malefactor responsible for a villager's sudden sickness and death. In this case, anyone in the community might be accused of witchcraft. One grisly trial by divination after a mysterious death required that the accused shake the decomposing corpse. If juices gushed out or the eyes bulged or burst from their sockets, the suspect was deemed guilty of sorcery and could be struck down there and then with an axe. Once despatched, the "sorcerer" was typically cooked and eaten—fitting retribution, supposedly, for having spiritually consumed the sick person. Knauft noted that, between 1940 and the end of his fieldwork in 1982, one in three adult Gebusi had died by homicide, 87 per cent of those through being identified as sorcerers or sorcerers' assistants.

"So what happened to Yanak?" I ask Clifford.

"He passed three year ago. He was old man."

"And the Woniam and Pauwon feel better now he's gone?"

"Yes, yes. We are no longer frighten. We are free people!"

"What about sorcery? Do people still believe in sorcery?"

Returning to the Papuan rainforest sixteen years after his first visit, Knauft discovered that sorcery was miraculously a thing of the past for the Gebusi. By 1998, the tribe had, apparently, "internalized Christian beliefs concerning morality, sin, and the need to leave judgments about death in the hands of God."

"No. Yes. Sometimes. When friend is sick when yesterday he was laughing, we get...suspicious."

We arrive at Clifford's house and meet his wife outside. She is beaded with sweat, her arms and legs coated in white slime and wood splinters. Skinny chickens squawk and chase about her legs. She laughs, embarrassed.

"Today, she beat *saksak*," her husband explains, grinning.

Beat *saksak*? She beckons and we follow her down a path behind their house. It terminates at a fallen tree, the trunk equal in girth to a canoe. Half of this has been sliced open and the bark removed, revealing the soft fibre within. A teenage girl sits beside the trunk and beats the white pith with a bamboo adze. This is the sago palm, and its innards will eventually become the pancakes we have been eating on our journey. Although there must be an intermediate stage in the process as the coarse, woody fibres we see here look nothing like the cheese-like cakes of sago Betty Youpa kneaded into pancakes and fried in Tipas.

Nadya asks Clifford about the division of labour in the village. Men, he tells us, make canoes, hunt animals, build houses, clear forest for gardens, and cut down sago. Women fish in the river, cook dinner, raise the children, make *bilums*, and prepare sago.

"And look after the chickens," I add.

"No. No one look after chicken."

"Do you eat them?"

"No."

"Their eggs?"

Clifford shakes his head. "Chicken eat insect. Then insect do not eat our food!"

We head slowly back to where we started, shaking people's hands on the way and saying, "*Yu orait*?" and "*Wanem nem bilong yu*?" At one point, we walk past three men squeezed onto a stick bench. They also welcome us to their village, but, as we move off, one seizes my elbow. I don't get what he says but can tell he's in deadly earnest. I turn to Clifford.

"He says you must only go to Kubkain. No further."

He means Ambunti. Only as far as Ambunti. Our map says Kubkain is the next village down the river.

|| Evening is *was-was* time. I go first with the men. Nadya will go with the women after dark.

This is the first time I have had bath buddies, and I am not sure about protocol. Guests first or guests last? Jump in and make a happy splash or slide in regally? Undies on or undies off? Wallow and chat or do your business and be on your way? We march along the riverside—there are twenty-four of us—Walter leading the way. I am the only one carrying a towel and bottle of lady's shampoo (the only lather we have left since the Sepik ate our last bar of soap).

Something tells me when we arrive at the bathing hole, a reedy inlet with eddying water and frogs, that the white guy should not be bashful. Walter is regarding me inquiringly. So I strip down with purpose and dive in naked. Well, almost. At the last moment, I decide to preserve my modesty. My warrior bath buddies grin at one another, tear off their clothes, and wade in, cupping their genitals in their hands. I go to work with the shampoo: head, armpits, some down the front of my briefs, and then submerge to rinse off. I offer the bottle around, but there are no takers.

On our way back, we pass an open-sided pavilion inhabited exclusively by men. About fifty of them, mainly young, sitting cross-legged in tight groups, an older man presiding over each.

"*Haus boi*," Walter says. "Place where young man sleep before married."

"What are they talking about?"

"Bride price. To get a wife, the boy must pay money to bride's family."

The Dani tribe Nadya and I visited last month in the highlands of Indonesian New Guinea practised the same custom. A young man's family had to compensate the bride's parents for the loss of a daughter from their household—only there, the bride price was not paid in money. Ten pigs was the going rate for a wife.

"How much does a man pay for a bride here?"

"Five thousand."

"Five thousand kina?" Can$2,000. "How can he possibly raise that much money?"

"His father and brother and uncle help. They hunt crocodile and sell skin, or they sell vanilla, or they go to mountain and look for gold."

"Maybe two of them would like to earn some kina paddling with the *waitman* and *waitmeri* down the river."

"You can ask."

|| 6:15 a.m. Sun slices through the clouds and settles on a small boy squatting alone in the mud beneath our hut. Deep puddles and snapped palm fronds surround him. A dog with furless ears wanders over, and he strikes it smartly on the nose and laughs as it jumps back. All the dogs here have ripped ears. I asked Walter about this last night, expecting him to say that they fought over food scraps. "*Natnat*" was his reply. Mosquitoes? I understood what he meant at dusk. The dogs tear their own ears to shreds.

I lean further out the window and look about. The river is shrouded in mist, and the forest on the far bank, leached of colour, seems to brood. No birds are singing this morning, and I don't hear the customary drone of insects. All is quiet in the village too. Woodsmoke creeps up through the blackened, dripping thatches of a few huts. The ditches people have dug around them are brimming with water. At the riverside, our dugouts have become bathtubs. Just as well we didn't camp out last night. The torrential rain would have washed Terra Nova downstream.

Nadya and I have a decision to make. Jamesy and Lee Matthew, our hired hands for the day, refuse to go further than Kubkain, a four- or five-hour paddle from Oum Number 1. The length of the "no-go zone" has stretched. It was Ambunti to Pagwi, a day's paddle. Now it is Kubkain to Pagwi, a three- or four-day paddle. John Youpa, the big man of Tipas, told us the ambush story, of travellers stripped and robbed and slashed with bush knives, and we keep hearing versions of it and warnings. But that attack happened last year and between Ambunti and Pagwi. How are things *this* year? Have there been other incidents of piracy? More raids on those foolish enough to voyage without an outboard engine? We keep getting warned that pirates are still operative, but no one has recent news. Makes me wonder just how often villagers stray from their villages.

"*Raskol* need money for drug and beer. They looking for money, killings, trouble," confirms Jamesy, a cheery father of three, once we have gotten underway. "If use motor from Kubkain, you be okay."

I paddle with purpose, feeling well rested despite last night's explosive thunder and hard rain. Nadya and I lay awake on our mats during the offensive, waiting for drops to smack our foreheads, but this time none did. Oum Number 1 recedes in the mist, and we pass a smaller village, specializing, it would seem, in building canoes. Oum Number 2. Six men work on three tree trunks resting on cradles. *Chok-chok* go their axes, the sound echoing across the water.

"What wood do they use?" Nadya asks.

"Kwila is best. Wood is hard and last very long time. But it is difficult to find now because logging company cut this tree. We also use catma or ewa."

As the sun burns off the last of the cloud and the mist evaporates, the forest regains its lustre and magnificence. Again, I marvel at its intricacy, its knottiness. As Nadya remarked the other day, you can walk through the woods in Canada and into the company of individual species of trees. White pine here, maple over there, birch to the left, poplar to the right. Not so here. The Papuan equivalent is arboreous anarchy. Trees growing through trees, vines coiling up trees and between trees, lianas cascading from the tops of trees and snaking around lower-storey growth, epiphytes erupting from branches, long-fingered palm fronds reaching out for their share of the sun. There is something unnerving about this riot of growth, like it is capable of plucking the unwary out of his tree-trunk canoe and swallowing him whole.

We glide past tribal gardens, the leaves of the banana palms looking like slashed tents, the phallic peduncles supporting tiers of skinny green fingers; past fields of storm-routed sugar cane; past vines ignited with flaming orange flowers, newly open. The current is brisk after the rain and the river lumpy with debris. No other canoes are out. Storks are our company—as they have been from the start. We stop paddling here and there to watch them fish. The intensity of their concentration and their lightning stabs remind us of herons back home.

"This bird we call White Saun," Jamesy says.

"Saun?"

"Saun is name of great ancestor."

At times, amusingly, White Saun overtakes us, standing on a floating log, the slender captain of his own canoe. Maybe this is the spirit of the ancestor remembering his days as a villager.

"We must not kill this bird," adds Lee Matthew.

|| Kubkain must be buried in the bushes as the only bankside presence is three huts, one of which stilts venturesomely into the river, and some dugouts parked behind a floating log. One of these canoes is almost twice the length of ours and has an outboard engine weighing down the stern.

We give our hires fifty kina each for escorting us from Oum, and Jamesy introduces us to Gerry and Israel, a pair in their twenties who shuttle passengers up and down the Sepik in the motor-canoe for a living. It is only midday, so we immediately enter into discussions. They usher us into the hut over the water, and we sit together cross-legged on the floor.

No, they can't paddle with us to Ambunti. Too dangerous. Not even if we tether our raft to their motor-canoe and pay for their fuel to get back. No, they don't know anyone who might be willing to do so. What are they willing to do? Take us in their motor-canoe to Ambunti for K900. If we leave right away, we can be there by nightfall.

"Nine hundred kina?" I splutter. "You have got to be kidding."

Eight gallons of fuel to get to Ambunti, fifteen for them to get back, Gerry explains patiently. A gallon of gas costs K28 in Kubkain, but K25 in Ambunti, where they can buy what they need to return home. Then there's the hire fee for the boat: K150. And hire fee for the crew: the same.

Nadya and I scramble to do the math and ask to be left alone for a while. I turn to my wife.

"What do you think?"

"Seems like a rip-off, doesn't it? But it's hard to say."

Does it take eight gallons of gas to reach Ambunti? Is K28 a gallon the going price here? Seems right: it was K30 in Oum. Do they need fifteen gallons to return? About double to motor upstream? Is K300 the going rate to hire a motor-canoe and crew? It occurs to me that we could offset the last fee by persuading Gerry and Israel to buy our dugouts.

"Let's see how much money we have left."

We dig in our wallets and check our hidden stash. About K1,200.

"So that's another problem if, somehow, we paddle from here," Nadya says. "We need to get to Pagwi and the road. That's another day from Ambunti. So four more pairs of paddlers to hire and four more nights in villages to pay for."

We do more calculations. If it is K100 for crew, that's K400 for four days. Lodging is usually K100 a night, so there's another K400. This seems fine if all goes according to plan. But, as we found in Imombi, the hire charge can be as much as K100 a man, and, on a stretch of the river known for banditry, we could get hit with jacked-up prices. We might have to pay gas for those who refuse to go unless they can buzz home. Or we could get stuck in a village because no one wants to go with us.

"Food? How about that?"

"Food is no problem," Nadya replies. "I checked last night. There's still quite a bit in the bin."

We sit in silence for a while.

"Shame we can't just head off alone, hey?" I say, gazing through a gap in the bark floor at our little vessel, tucked behind the floating log and looking capable of travelling all the way to the sea.

"That's one thing we can't do. There have been too many warnings."

"I don't like having to motor a part of the river."

"Nor do I. It's not what we came to do."

"And I still wonder how real the threat is."

She goes to a window and looks down at the river. "Who knows in this place? If we are attacked, there's no one around to help us. Can't expect our hired men to defend us. We'd also be putting them at risk."

I remember the Australian ornithologist we met in West Papua, determined to see all of New Guinea's birds of paradise. He had been to PNG five times and had one word to describe the country: lawless. The tribes of the Upper Sepik make their own laws. We have enough food; we may have just about enough money; we have a river-worthy raft. But we can do nothing to protect ourselves or our hires from pirates.

When Gerry and Israel return, they are with Valentine, an older man with a long, unruly beard and owner of the motor-canoe. He has inspected our dugouts. The going rate for one of this size is K50, he assures us. He will take them and knock K100 off the hire charge. Take it or leave it. He is cheery and relaxed and knows we are short of options. His son brings sugar cane, and we sit ruminatively nibbling the ends and sucking out the sugar.

|| The motor-canoe drills along, engine at full throttle, Israel at the helm. He sweeps around the bends without easing up, causing White Saun to panic and spread their broad, snowy wings. They cry out in displeasure, spanking the *tiktik* canes in their desperation to escape. I sigh and watch them circle above us, snaky necks retracted, and flap to the other side of the river. A steady wind beats our faces. For the first time, my wife and I are not sweating.

Late afternoon, we pass the turn for Wagu Lagoon. We had hoped to make a stop here. According to our guidebook, there is a lodge run by a man who knows a display tree for birds of paradise. The entry doesn't say which bird of paradise, but "display tree" suggests one of the ethereal plumed performers that dance in the tall branches: the greater bird of paradise, perhaps, or even the

Raggiana bird of paradise, the national bird. We have seen neither before. Staying at bird lodges in West Papua, we beheld dancers of the forest floor: Wilson's bird of paradise, western parotia, and magnificent bird of paradise, brightly coloured, enigmatic creatures, the males endowed with flicking antennae or tail-springs. But for a glimpse of the red bird of paradise in Raja Ampat in West Papua, we have yet to see any of the canopy performers.

At times, our helmsman takes shortcuts through the swamps, and we catch whole flocks of storks by surprise. Nadya tries to capture their alarm on video. I sit and sulk. Just when we were getting into a rhythm on this river, goddammit, a third of our way from Green River to the sea, we have to quit. It takes many bends of the river for me to let go of a personal mission. Paddling the length of the Sepik is an objective, merely a theme, I remind myself. It need not be pure or without breaks.

We arrive in Ambunti after dark and put up for a night with Israel's *tambu*. The following day, we're in Pagwi. From there, a truck and then a PMV minibus take us north along the road that connects the Sepik to the coastal town of Wewak.

7 RETREAT FROM THE RIVER

Raskolism, as criminal activity designated by this term, is a relatively recent phenomenon in the Sepik. In the early 1980s, it was still thought of as something that happened elsewhere in PNG but—apart from some petty harassment of residents in the provincial capital of Wewak—not in the Sepik. Within a few years, however, gang activities had become a matter of some concern in Wewak, and by 1987 they were beginning to spread into the hinterlands...By 1990, highway robbery had expanded dramatically to include every sort of vehicle travelling the highway, including police trucks and ambulances... People walking along intervillage tracks were frequently waylaid and robbed, vandalism against mission and station property was almost commonplace, and occasional raskol-instigated rapes and murders had occurred.

—PAUL ROSCOE, *"The Return of the Ambush:* 'Raskolism' *in Rural Yangoru, East Sepik Province"*

After a breakfast of rice, *tinpis*, and black tea—the remains of our boat rations—we get ready to hit the streets of Wewak. No money belts, no camera, no cell phone, no wristwatches. All valuables must stay locked up in our room at the CBC Guesthouse. Empty daypacks go on our backs. The cash we need goes in the button-down breast pockets of our shirts so it is right under our noses.

"Take Manox with you," Joseph, the manager, advises, referring to the gateman. "There was a murder downtown last night."

The gateman is short and far from young, but he has the stony face of a fellow who doesn't put up with any nonsense. He shoves a 45-cm bush knife down the back of his pants as we depart.

"Should we pay him?" Nadya asks Joseph.

"Just buy him a Coke."

Wewak, like Vanimo, is situated on a polyp of land bulging into the Bismarck Sea and has an idyllic sheltered beach running down one side of the isthmus. It is difficult for us, looking down on the peninsula from the hillside guest house, to imagine it being the scene of heavy bombing in the Second World War. The occupying Japanese had their largest airbase here until the Americans, in a concerted series of raids lasting five days, all but obliterated it in August 1943. The Imperial Japanese Army Air Force lost about 174 planes, seven-eighths of its fleet in New Guinea. The Japanese surrendered to the Allies two years later at Cape Wom, just west of Wewak.

Most of the stores in town are on a single street, and on a Monday morning the place is buzzing. Women with *bilums* stuffed with fruit and vegetables weave through parked Land Cruisers and trundling Toyota and Isuzu PMVs trolling for passengers. One has "Angoram" painted on the front, a second "Aitape." In a glossy red-and-black national flag T-shirt with a yellow bird of paradise on the chest, the conductor of a third hangs out the door, calling "Maprik! Maprik!" Men huddle in groups of three or four in front of the stores, leaning on each other and sharing betel nuts, and teenage girls with canvas shopping bags at their feet chat under parasols. I look left and right. Ours are the only white faces. And I notice we are the only ones wearing boots; everyone else is in flip-flops.

Our destination is Papindo supermarket, which was founded, Joseph told me at breakfast, by a naturalized Indonesian called Sir Soekandar, who made his fortune selling vanilla and was knighted by Her Majesty the Queen. Villagers in Papua grow the vanilla and sell it on the streets of Maprik, and we saw many of the buyers there on our way up from the Sepik. The buyers then sell to Papindo Trading, which, in turn, sells to foreign merchants. This year is apparently a good one for exporting vanilla since last year a cyclone devastated crops in Madagascar, the world's principal supplier.

I feel tense approaching the entrance to the supermarket even though Manox is with us. Twenty-five or thirty young men line the spiked metal fence, and their eyes are on us. "It's like being in a Western!" Nadya says. Men with whiskery chins standing outside the general store, eyeballing the strangers in town. No six-shooters here though, thankfully, and no visible bush knives.

"Gude. Tude hotpela!" I say to the three men closest to the door. The nearest has a conker of a face bordered by tight frizzles, a string of beads around his neck, a *bilum* under his armpit, and jeans rolled to the knee. I shake his hand firmly, then the hands of his two pals. "I need skin like yours that doesn't burn!" They look at me, puzzled, but nod and smile.

The store is much like those in Vanimo. Guards wield batons at the entrance and exit, and Chinese men perch like hawks on tall stools at the end of each aisle, quietly watching the activity. We fill a basket with Em Nau crackers, instant noodles, Teistim peanut butter, Bea Fruity toilet soap, pasta tubes, and a frozen chicken. We order beef pies from the *kai bar*, the Papuan equivalent of an English chippy, likely introduced by the Australians. The stainless-steel bins behind the counter contain fish in batter, finger-thick fries, breadfruit slices in batter, dough balls in batter, fried chicken legs, and garishly red jumbo sausages.

"Those men you shook hands with outside," Nadya whispers, adding a refrigerated bottle of Coca-Cola to our basket. "Manox just told me they are thieves."

Nadya pays for our groceries. We squeeze everything into my daypack and head out, careful to avoid making eye contact with anyone.

After a diet of predominantly rice and tinned food on the Sepik, we also want fresh fruit and vegetables. Some of those leafy greens we see ladies carrying about in their *bilums*. The open-air market has tables for vendors sheltered by a tin roof and a forecourt under the sun, where women spread out their mats beneath parasols. A market-phile under normal circumstances, Nadya does not linger or attempt to barter this morning. Bananas. Mangoes. A pineapple. *Kango*, those leafy greens. A yellowing papaya. Peanuts. Quick stops, trial squeezes of fruit. *"Hamas long dispela?"* (How much?) *"Faivpela ten toea."* (Fifty toea.) *"Wan kina."* (One kina.) *"Bai mi kisim."* (I'll take it.) I pay and stuff the items in her pack. Manox watches our backs.

In the evening, Nadya makes a chicken casserole and invites four school administrators staying at CBC to join us for dinner. They came to Wewak last week from the remote highland villages of Telefomin and Oksapmin for a district meeting and now find themselves stuck, their return flight repeatedly postponed by poor weather or because of "technical difficulties." Den, the principal of a boarding school in Telefomin, tells us how hard it is to feed the four hundred students in a place where food is limited and there is no road to town. The school must charter an aircraft to bring bags of rice and cans of meat and fish every two weeks at a cost of K6,000 a flight (Can$2,400).

"That's K15,000 a time, including the food! When we can't pay for the flight or the plane doesn't come, I have to send the children home."

"Can't local farmers grow sweet potatoes and sell them to you?" Nadya asks, remembering the highlanders' staple in West Papua.

"They do, but it is not enough. And many of the farmers do not live near the school. They must carry their potatoes for a day or two days, and potatoes are heavy."

"Couldn't you grow them at the school?"

"We have only small land," Tommy, the school accountant, says. "When we try to take more, the villagers tell us we are on their land."

I shake my head. Surely, Telefomin Secondary is educating the sons and daughters of the farmers. Yet Nadya and I know from our time on the Sepik that land ownership in PNG is critical, a matter of life and death.

"How do you raise the money?" Nadya asks. "Does the government help?"

"The government give some fund," Den replies, "but it is not enough. We must charge each student a fee of 1,500 kina for a year."

"Can the parents afford to pay that?"

"Many have trouble, but they understand how important school is, and they understand we have few resources."

Despite these challenges, the administrators tell us they have high hopes of increasing student numbers next year. Nadya asks if there are any food co-ops in the Highlands, in areas where agriculture is thriving. If so, these could be useful models for their region. She asks if the United Nations Food and Agriculture Organization is active in PNG. What role does it play?

I listen for a while, then retreat to our room. Now that we have Wi-Fi, I can post an entry on our travel blog. I look up the tall stork we saw daily on the Sepik, the "White Saun" of the river, on the internet and discover it to be the eastern great egret. The eagle with the shaggy pants is the white-bellied sea eagle and its fawn branchmate a whistling kite. It takes a while, but I also find the name of the vine with flaming orange flowers: d'Albertis creeper, named after naturalist Luigi Maria d'Albertis who travelled by steamer up the Fly River toward the end of the nineteenth century, the first Italian to do so. Apart from collecting specimens of plants, insects, and birds en route, d'Albertis got into regular skirmishes with the river dwellers, ransacked villages and stole local artefacts, practised dynamite fishing, and, on his third and most eventful voyage in 1877, shot and killed several Papuans. Even more repulsively, he put the head of one he decapitated in a pickling jar and took it home to add to his private collection. It shocks me that a gorgeous flower, as well as a New Guinea beetle and python, bears his name.

|| "You will feel relax and free on my island! In town, there are many people around, always looking what you doing. On my island, you not worry about a thing! You leave your bag, you go anywhere you want. You feel relax at Naigboi Guesthouse!"

Nadya and I have arranged to spend a week on a tiny island in the Bismarck Sea about an hour by motorboat from Wewak. A jolly man in his late fifties with a bald head and white beard has come to pick us up. Yuo is a kilometre square, and Robert has spent his entire life there. Lithe and energetic, his skin dark brown and lustrous, he looks the picture of health. As the boat roars away from the quay and the air freshens, our host rolls a wooden spool toward me.

"Tony, you will catch dinner for us!"

King and Mark, Robert's sons, equally as sun-scorched and radiant, regard me hopefully. I look down at the lure, a pink rubber squid with gawky eyes and an ear-sized hook tucked beneath its skirt of tentacles. Can't see how this little guy, swimming at a speed of thirty knots, will fool a tuna. Nevertheless, I let out the line and jam the spool under my foot. The foam erupting in our wake swallows the bait. The hour passes. No tuna. But Robert has a trick up his sleeve. King takes the line while his father draws big circles with the boat in front of their island. The squid, now out of the boat's wake, skips about, breaking the surface. Then it no longer does, and the line is taut. King reels the thrashing fish in, and Robert strikes it smartly on the head with the handle of his knife. It is silver and black and has a triangular, pointed head. Not a tuna. Spanish mackerel.

Our skipper eases back on the throttle, and suddenly we are in shallow water and approaching the island. The colour switch is dramatic: from ultramarine to turquoise. Coral heads like cauliflowers bubble up from below, and schools of iridescent blue minnows dart around them. The boat weaves through the coral and makes for a white sand beach and a cluster of thatched huts similar to those we encountered on the Sepik but with shorter, thicker piles. A stout Papuan woman in a dress decorated with hibiscus flowers stands in front of one, holding a little boy in her arms. We ride up on the beach under a sprawling tree with broad, spatulate leaves and two hammocks suspended from its lower branches. A lean white man in a blue wetsuit, reading a book, occupies one. I rub my eyes to check I am not hallucinating.

The woman is Catherine, Robert's wife, and she shows us to our bungalow. The skinny man in the hammock is Paul, who is on holiday with his wife Clare. When we've settled in, he invites us over to their bungalow for a cuppa. The pair are expatriate British Christians who have spent the last fourteen years in PNG and have a house in Wewak. Paul flies Cessnas for Mission Aviation Fellowship (MAF), an outfit that brings aid and the gospel to remote regions of the country.

"I adore my work," he tells us as Clare pours the tea. "No two flights are the same. Sometimes I carry boxes of medicine to clinics deep in the jungle or food packages to Highlands communities when their harvest fails. Other times there might be a medical emergency, and I have to get to some place fast. A villager gets a cut that turns septic or someone has a bad case of malaria. Usually, they're in a bad way by the time I reach them. I medevac them out. Then there are government officials who need ferrying about, or politicians canvassing for votes, or church leaders going to seminars. Sometimes I restock community development projects, or I'm taking bibles to sell. It used to be that MAF took missionaries from the West to remote villages to spread the word, but that no longer happens."

"Seems like a tough country to fly in," Nadya remarks.

"Yup, but the scenery is magnificent, especially in the Highlands."

"Must be a risky business in a Cessna though," I say.

"Landings at small places can be, places where there's no paved runway, just grass. And some airstrips can be really short and, in the mountains, on a slope. Factor in a side wind, and things can get pretty hairy. But weather is the biggest threat. Can be a perfect day when you fly out of Wewak, nice again when you arrive at a village in the Highlands. Then, while you're unloading or getting a patient ready to fly, in come the clouds and rain. Sometimes I have to stay the night in a village. You have to put your trust in God."

"Do you worry about him, Clare?" Nadya asks.

"You kind of get used to it," she replies. "One problem is there aren't enough pilots. Paul has to fly extra missions or make stops on his way back from somewhere." It helps, she tells us, that she gets involved. "I prepare the medevac packs for new mothers, putting in blankets, bandages, antiseptic, emergency food, and baby items. I also visit the patients after they have been admitted to hospital."

I can imagine Clare as a no-nonsense chief ward sister in a London hospital.

"You know, we worry more about other things," Paul says, draining his tea and getting up. "I won't walk anywhere alone in

Wewak. Too dangerous. One time, we had to stay inside a whole week because of riots."

Clare nods, and I picture the couple drinking Tetley's behind a fence topped with razor wire, a guard like those at Papindo supermarket minding the gate of their home. Paul picks up his snorkel and flippers.

"Well, time for one last swim, then it's back to Wewak. I have a mission to fly first thing in the morning!"

"Where are you going?"

"Oksapmin." Taking the stranded school administrators back home perhaps.

> *April 18, 2018: Yuo Island*
> *Life simplified. Bamboo hut, flask of hot water for tea, hammock, old books, coral gardens, charming family, no natnats. I jog around the island. Hermit crabs shrink into their shells. I carry two stones to throw at dogs. Yellow hibiscus flowers. Breadfruit tree with sawtooth leaves. Croton hedges with striped leaves. Screw pines. Betel nut palms with skinny trunks. Plumeria. Green butterfly the size of a saucer. And the sea, scrubbing the skin, massaging away the aches. Worry dissolves.*

Nadya and I spend our days snorkelling, eating, and reading books bush pilots or other expats have left behind. Now that Paul and Clare have gone, we are the only guests, and Catherine treats us. Boiled eggs for breakfasts, donuts in the afternoons, fresh fish for dinner.

It is hard to believe we arrived in PNG just sixteen days ago. So much has happened. I am sure Nadya feels as I do: stunned and a little overwhelmed, like we've been carried along on a breaking wave that kept threatening to topple on our heads. But this surely is one of the magical effects and validations of travel. There's a kind of assault going on, a bombardment on the senses, and the traveller reels and tries to understand, adjust, and cope, aware she is living life intensely. I find it ironic that we have achieved this intensity by deliberately slowing down, by travelling at a jogger's speed, our pace determined by the flow of a river and by the routines of the people who live on its banks.

We are taught in industrialized society that we should never be idle. If we aren't occupied every waking moment, then we are wasting time, not living life to the full. It is small wonder that smart phones are so popular: they fit perfectly with this erroneous belief. Those minutes when we could be looking around, thinking carefully, reviewing our actions, making considered decisions, or just wondering about stuff, we have replaced with texting, watching videos, or playing games. We can go for a walk in the park, listen to the birds, and talk directly to one another. Or we can go for a walk in the park, stare into a little box, and block our ears with headsets. It is true that Nadya and I have found our cell phone handy for booking places to stay and sending messages home, but I am glad that on the Upper Sepik there was no electricity and no cellular signal. Consulting the phone would have taken from the intensity of the experience, the sense of being immersed in a world alien and fascinating to us.

Twice a day, Nadya and I swim out to the coral wall (where the sea water turns ultramarine) and bask with our arms outstretched, marvelling at another alien world. Beaked, purple parrotfish peck at the undersides of ochre fans, yellow-and-blue-striped surgeonfish weave through spiky branch corals resembling deer antlers, and orange-and-white clownfish dart in and out of sea anemone clusters. When the urge seizes us, we take deep breaths, dive down, and swim along the streets of their city, pretending we belong. On the sand are pink sea cucumbers with black thorns rising from their backs, and in crevices lurk feather-finned lionfish or moray eels. I think back to our snorkelling forays two months ago on the reef at Raja Ampat, a group of islands at the westernmost extreme of New Guinea. For ten days, we kept company with lump-headed napoleonfish, spotty-skinned map pufferfish, maze rabbitfish, hawksbill sea turtles, whitetip reef sharks, and, most memorably on the final day, giant manta rays, gliding effortlessly and gracefully through the water, the wingspans of some reaching five metres.

Sometimes Catherine drifts over to our bungalow for a chat, her smallest kids in tow. She has eight children in all, ranging in ages from three to nineteen. What an idyllic place to raise them, I remark one afternoon. She agrees but worries about the five attending school on the mainland.

"Worried that your boat might capsize in bad weather?"

"No. Sanguma might put a spell on them while they are away."

She tells us a story about a woman who lost her baby while crossing a river in flood last month. The woman stumbled and fell, and the baby was snatched from her arms and whisked away by the current. She dived into the water after it. Both mother and baby vanished without trace. The two bodies were discovered on a little beach downriver a few days later. Of the baby, only the heart, liver, and throat remained, all "in perfect condition." This was the work of Sanguma, who people pay to perform evil deeds.

"Sometimes Sanguma suck the blood or pick the liver. The cursed ones must drink urine to be cured."

Nadya and I look at Catherine, unsure how to respond. I think of American anthropologist Bruce Knauft's talk of Sanguma (Ogowili to the Gebusi): the spirit of a crocodile or the reincarnation of a nasty old man who tears out and eats the innards of his victims. Sewing them up afterwards, he magically makes them forget the assault happened. Back to their villages they stagger, become violently sick, and die in great pain a few days after, striking fear into their fellow tribesmen and women. This Knauft called "assault sorcery."

"Why does sorcery continue to exist, Catherine?" Nadya asks.

"Because many people are short of land, so they pay Sanguma to put curse on neighbour. They hope they can gain land after owner is dead."

This is the second sorcery story we have heard since coming off the Sepik. Den, the school principal from Telefomin, told us one the other night at CBC about a sorcerer who was abusing young girls.

"One day, he went to a house and took a young girl. The father went after him and speared him through the face, but, next day, the sorcerer was completely healed. So the father called the police, and they arrested him and put him in jail. However, when they returned to the cell the following day, the sorcerer had escaped, and there was a big hole in the wall. The police recaptured him and put a ball and chain on his foot, but he escaped again and told them to stop chasing him or he would kill them."

Again, Nadya and I weren't quite sure what to make of this. Den had been talking before about the logistical challenges of increasing enrollment at his school in the new year. Such tales seem to go with the one Clifford told us in Oum Number 1 on the Sepik about sorcerer Yanak's misdeeds. It would be good to find out more about local beliefs and the extent to which the introduced religion, Christianity, has displaced them.

On our sixth day in paradise, we go on a road trip of sorts: northeast to Kairiru, a larger island a twenty-minute boat ride away. Nineteen-year-old Tony, Robert and Catherine's eldest, is our skipper, and three of his little brothers our crew. On the way, he tells us news from Wewak. A PMV got ambushed yesterday on its way to Maprik. *Raskols* killed the driver and robbed the passengers. The police have closed the road. The attack happened at a partly collapsed bridge I remember crossing when we travelled up from the Sepik. Our PMV had had to slow down to a walking pace to cross it. So now we know: *raskols* are real, and they are active. I feel a twang of apprehension and look at Nadya, trying to gauge her reaction, but her eyes are fixed on the band of palm trees ahead.

Kairiru is volcanic and has vents along the shore belching scalding water. We stop at the house of an elderly Kiwi pastor and buy eggs, go to a cove, wrap the eggs in the leaves of a brass palm (which are pliant), and shove them in the vents. While we are waiting for the eggs to cook, an old man from Karesau, an island west of Yuo, joins us. We are on contested land, he informs us. Long ago, his ancestors sailed here, defeated the Kairiru, and took possession of part of the island—the part where we are now. Here it is again. My land, your land. So aren't we welcome? Do we need his permission to be here? It is okay that we are here, he says, because he is "little daddy" to Tony and his brothers—Robert on Yuo is his nephew. So why mention the territorial dispute? Because he must keep an eye on all comings and goings on Kairiru, and Nadya and I are unknown to him. We share our eggs with him when they are done, and I think of the words of Papuan historian John Dademo Waiko: "Land is our life. Land is our physical life, food and sustenance. Land is our social life; it is marriage; it is status; it is security; it is politics, in fact it is our only world." Disputes over land are common, we have been told, as some tribes don't have enough land, or they don't have enough good land.

The island setting belies any tribal tensions. The clear water around the hot springs is an enticing mix of heated turquoise water and colder blue from the sea. We wallow, warming up, cooling down, and warming up again, and the kids play, little King launching himself off his older brothers' shoulders. Black sunbirds chase about the trees leaning over the water, squeaking as our warblers do back home. They are about the same size too, but have decurved beaks, handy no doubt for extracting nectar from flowers.

On our way back to the boat, we pass through a Kairiru encampment. The people there have coconut kernels laid out to dry under the sun on canvas sheets. This, I understand from our companion from Karesau, is not the ideal way of producing copra. Coconut kernels must be thoroughly dried. The Tolai of East New Britain, responding to the arrival of European traders, were the first Papuans to get into the business late in the nineteenth century. To get good-quality copra, they placed the kernels on racks in a drying shed, the hot air passing along a flue from a slow-burning fire of coconut husks. By 1880, the tribe was producing almost a thousand tonnes of copra a year. By 1965, Papua New Guinea had 262,000 acres of land given over to coconut plantations and produced 77,100 tonnes of copra that year.

Slurping coconuts on our seventh day in paradise, we discuss options. We can spend the rest of our lives fraternizing with coral fish and lazing in hammocks "with half-dropt eyelid," like Tennyson's lotus-eaters, or we can push off and "smite the sounding furrows." It is cooler today, and we have our long-sleeved Sepik shirts back on.

"So should we go back to the sauna?"

Nadya has continued to struggle with heat despite being back on the coast where the wind picks up in the evenings.

"We could," she replies after some thought, "when the road reopens. We have yet to see the art."

Our guidebook calls the Sepik the nation's "'treasure trove,' overflowing with masks, shields, figures, canoe prows, and story boards." The key villages to visit, apparently, are Palambei, Kanganaman, Kaminabit, and Timbunke, all on the Middle Sepik downriver from Pagwi. The only piece of tribal art we have seen so far is here on Yuo, resting on the sand near our bungalow: a section of tree trunk with a slot in the top. Through this, I can see that the trunk is hollow. Fixed to one end is the head of a crocodile, fixed to the other its tail. The body is notched with scales. If Catherine hadn't identified this object as a drum, I wouldn't have guessed. It's called a *garamut*.

"Trouble is," Nadya continues, "we saw no dugouts like ours at Pagwi."

"True. We'd need to ask around."

"We'd need to ask about *raskols* too. Your Black brother said the Lower Sepik wasn't safe." The bear-like electrician at Green River Christian Secondary had indeed said as much. "But you know what Tommy told me?"

"Telefomin Tommy?"

"Yes. He said the tribes in the Upper Sepik were the dangerous ones."

"I'm getting the feeling that PNG is dangerous. There's a reason we haven't bumped into any tourists."

Yet we have not been attacked, or robbed, or sent packing. The villagers we met on the Upper Sepik were suspicious of us, and some of the men appeared fierce, but, once we had shaken hands and asked for their help, we got along fine—despite our rudimentary Tok Pisin. Affiliation has been critical to our progress. Papuans paddled with us from the start, and our escorts served as envoys. We were passed between *tambu* and found ourselves sheltered by village big men. I think of the gentle Rayut, the irascible John Youpa, the avuncular Councillor Tobius. Our passage has not been cheap, and at times we likely paid *waitman* prices, but this is to be expected. We can't expect to know the going rates after such a short time in the country.

"And we need to get to know people better," Nadya adds. "Hire paddlers for longer periods, a few days, say, rather than for a few hours. And spend more time in the villages. I'd like to talk more to the women as we'll likely be with men again during the day. Like at Green River."

I nod, remembering how she went to the creek each day for a *was-was* with the girls after they were done class. Back she came with wet hair and a new revelation. "Girls must always use the same bathing hole, and theirs has to be downstream of the boys' one." "Girls must never wash alone lest a witch carry them off into the forest or cast a spell on them." "Some girls think teachers tell them never to wash alone not because of witches but so boys won't bother them!" On the third day, two girls asked if they could touch her hair, saying they didn't believe it was real.

And I think back to our week-long trek last month in the highlands of West Papua. We hired a Yali tribesman called Kanak to guide us and a Dani called John to help carry our food. We learned little about either man or his tribe on the first day of our trek, but, by the end of the week, we had discovered that the Yali prefer to roof their homes with wood rather than grass, unlike the Dani; that Yali women like to wear their skirts higher up the thigh than their Dani counterparts; and that the Yali bride price is a lot lower than the Dani one: three pigs rather than ten. By watching the pair, Nadya and I came to understand the importance of stopping on the trail whenever you meet someone, regardless of tribe, and shaking hands, squatting to share a cigarette even. We realized only by the fourth day that Kanak, exercising a duty to his tribe, was sharing his share of the food we cooked for dinner with the family hosting us in a village. "Only when you spend time with local people," I recall Nadya reminding me, "do they show you who they are."

Catherine hugs Nadya the following morning and ties a bead necklace she made around her neck, saying it is the sort worn by women in her clan. It has a gleaming white cowrie shell the size of a thumbnail at the bottom. Robert, who has been away all week on business, takes us back to Wewak. Brown noddies, tell-tale white paint splashes on their heads, streak across our bow, flying low over the waves and scanning for fish.

|| "The *raskol* come out of the bush, pointing guns at the bus...and, and the driver try to reverse back, but they come and bash him in the head and hit him with knives...and they come onto bus and say to passengers, 'Give us your money!' and they slice one on the knee... and punch another on the head...and PMV come from other direction and another one from same direction, but they, they don't stop... then some men from different tribe chase off *raskols*...eventually, police came and try to calm situation. I hate to live in a place where such things happen."

Sarah is from the village of Sibilanga, near Nuku, west of Maprik, and a stranded guest at CBC in Wewak. Her distress is palpable, and we feel our own stress levels rise. The road to Maprik is still closed, confirms warden Joseph. We have no choice but to wait in Wewak. There is no alternative route to Pagwi. Perhaps we should have dawdled longer on Yuo. Staying at CBC is expensive: K200 a night for a room (Can$80); we were paying K75 for our bungalow on the little island.

Thinking of Paul and Clare, I see what I can find out about Mission Aviation now that we are connected once again to Wi-Fi. Apparently, the Lutheran Church was the first to use an aeroplane in Papua New Guinea to spread the gospel. Wishing to Christianize the Highlands more efficiently, the church bought a Junkers F13 passenger aircraft in 1935. It arrived from Germany with First World War flying ace Captain Fritz Loose, who flew missions out of Lae for the following three years. This he did without an aerial map, traffic control, or even a radio, and at times to destinations as far away as 600 kilometres. I picture him flying through cloud and rain, searching desperately for a grass airstrip in the middle of the jungle. How astonished villagers must have been to see for the first time a metal bird drop out of the sky and spill bibles from its belly. After the Second World War, Christian pilots in the US and UK created Mission Aviation Fellowship to serve missions worldwide. Service in PNG resumed in 1951 out of Madang by means of a four-seater aircraft called an Auster Autocar, but that didn't last long. The pilot, Harry Hartwig, formerly of the Australian forces, crashed and died in the Highlands. MAF bought a Cessna 170 to replace the Autocar. Today, MAF has a fleet

Mission Aviation Fellowship Cessna aircraft.

of Cessna Caravans, flying from nine bases to 213 airstrips around the country, doing God's work. The effect of this on the health of Papuans, their understanding of the world, and on their beliefs has no doubt been profound.

But Christianity had gained a foothold in Papua New Guinea long before the arrival of the first aircraft. How on earth did it manage to do so? Missionaries started showing up on Papuan shores in the mid-nineteenth century. French Marists tried to establish a station on Woodlark Island in 1847, and Italian missionaries attempted the same on Umboi Island five years later. Neither lasted long. The London Mission Society, using evangelists from Polynesia (Rarotongans, Samoans, Loyalty Islanders, Fijians), met with greater success and built stations in Port Moresby in 1874, the Gulf region in the south and the Fly River in 1878, and at Milne Bay in 1891. In the northern half of the country, occupied then by Germany, the early missionaries were Lutherans, making landfall at Finschhafen in 1886, some 550 kilometres south of the Sepik estuary.

The challenge for any pioneering missionaries was how to get the villagers interested in the gospel. Johann Flierl and Karl Tremel, the first at Finschhafen, discovered that delivering sermons—the customary mode of transmission—was a waste of time. "We are tired of your words," the villagers complained. "Our ears hurt. Your axes are good, but your talk you can keep for yourselves!" They wanted the glass beads, iron tools, and tobacco the missionaries had brought. Flierl and Tremel responded by making half of the mission house they had built into a school. By teaching their young, they would gain the trust of the adults, they reasoned. This also failed. The children saw no reason to sit in a classroom and so ran away. Then the Lutherans' luck changed. A Chief and fourteen young men from a neighbouring village appeared one day at the station, saying they were willing to devote five months to working with and learning from the missionaries. So began *kostschule* (boarding school) in which Papuans, immersed in a Christian community life, learned how to read and write, say prayers, sing Christian songs, and use iron tools.

In his history of the Anglican Church's involvement in PNG between 1891 and 1942, David Wetherall notes a similar strategy adopted by missionaries: "Nothing in the missionary duty was thought more important than the duty of educating the young...teaching in the school and introducing the gospel were the same process, the schoolboys hearing with delight the bible stories and being led unconsciously into Christian doctrine." Papuans were, to some extent, brainwashed into following Jesus.

The first baptisms at Finschhafen happened in 1899, thirteen years after Flierl and Tremel had arrived. A man called Kaboing was given the baptismal name Tobias and another called Kamunsanga became Silas. Thirty-six more followed over the next five years. Baptisms meant Christian converts who might themselves spread the word, and the Lutheran Church spread its tentacles inland. With Catholics, Methodists, and Anglicans equally determined to bring the good news to the "heathen," the twentieth century saw Christianity establish a solid footing on the Melanesian island. By the 1970s, there were over thirty church denominations operating in the country. Today, approximately 96 per cent of Papuans are Christian.

What of traditional beliefs? In the villages of the Upper Sepik, Nadya and I saw no signs of these: no carved deities, no "pagan" rituals, no lucky charms around necks, no sacred sites or holy structures, no dances to honour the gods of the river. But for a brief mention of a deceased sorcerer, we could have assumed, if we hadn't known better, that Christianity was the Indigenous religion. A truer picture—one that an anthropologist would probably get—might come through living for months in a village and witnessing the habits of the tribe season by season. From our transient contact, it appears that Christian churches have suppressed or swept aside local beliefs. When we return to the Sepik, we must find out whether this is true.

Online, I discover an article written by Robert W. Robin, the Visiting Lecturer in Psychology at the University of Papua New Guinea in the 1970s, referring to the wealth of mission literature testifying to the glory of God and "the good works" of his servants in the country. According to him, a primary focus of missionary efforts was directed toward "deterring Melanesians from observing and participating in traditional customs and events, while at the same time striving to replace these indigenous practices with forms of Western Christian culture and ritual." Some missionaries even "encouraged their followers to physically destroy spirit houses, sacred tree groves, and artefacts" to demonstrably affirm their rejection of "heathen practices."

For a moment, I don't feel so far from home. I think of Catholic and Protestant churches reprogramming First Nations kids at residential schools, of the Indian Act and its outlawing of Indigenous religious ceremonies and cultural activities, of the desecration by white settlers of sites deemed sacred by Indigenous Peoples in Canada.

|| "You will be alright until Angoram. After that, there is nothing—all the way to the sea. I don't know that part of Sepik, but people say it is dangerous."

Leo Singut is the owner of Sangra Guesthouse in Pagwi. He is a brawny man about my age with a barrel chest, a crewcut, a bulldog jaw, and a roaring laugh. He drives a black Toyota Jeep with "Such Is Life" painted on the hood. When I called him to make a reservation at Sangra this evening, I didn't expect to see him on CBC's doorstep twenty minutes later. He comes to Wewak frequently to see his wife and three kids and do business. His daughter is studying in Mysore, India, he tells us, and his eldest became a "crocodile man" last year. He has another wife and two kids in Pagwi, where he owns a store as well as the guest house. He offers to help us look for a canoe when we arrive there.

Rumour has it the road to Maprik will be open tomorrow. Nadya and I restocked our boat bin (including several bars of soap) this afternoon and hit the BSP teller machines. And hit them again. And then again. Until they grew tired of swallowing our cards and coughed up enough kina for us to continue our voyage. Manox was too busy at the guest house to accompany us, bush knife in his undies, so we had to pretend we were no-nonsense bad asses.

"I would drive you to Pagwi," Leo says, "but I have to stay here longer. When the road opens, many PMVS will go. I will see you there. I think you will have no trouble to find my guest house."

Nadya and I feel encouraged and remember that it was a man called Leo (an Australian expat) who helped us buy and customize *Monique*, the fishing canoe we bought for our travels through Indonesia two decades ago. How far Pagwi is from the Bismarck Sea is hard to say, so like a broken guitar string is the Sepik, but a good three hundred kilometres. Will there be bandits hiding in the bends? Maybe I should buy a bush knife and stick it in my undies.

8 CROCODILE MEN

Before earth there was nothing but endless water in which there lived a crocodile. Layers of his excreta built up land areas and so the earth was created. The crocodile gave birth to man who was completely dependent to the point of being carried about by him on his back and at times in his mouth. After some time, man determined to end his complete dependence upon the crocodile and seek a life for himself. He selected a large stone and while the crocodile was sleeping killed his parent with a mighty blow. Gazing remorsefully at the dead crocodile he burst into uncontrollable tears. For days, weeks, months, he cried. His nose became elongated and his tears flowed steadily. This torrent of tears penetrated the earth's surface and flowed towards the sea. Thus man's lament for the beginning of his separate existence on earth formed the mighty Sepik.

—FRANK HODGKINSON, *Sepik Diary*

Sangra Guesthouse is by far the most striking building in Pagwi. About three times the size of the average Sepik stilt hut, its thatched roof and gables rearing extravagantly into spires, it could be the home of a tribal Chief. From the tip of one spire, a carved eagle launches heavenward on outstretched wings, and fixed to the gable at the front is a wooden head with cowrie shell eyes, a nose with spreading nostrils, and a red tongue. Plank siding instead of sago slats, painted white and decorated with murals. A woman waves bird of paradise plumes while dancing on the back of a crocodile; a man holding a spear stands in the bow of a canoe. Iron grills cover the windows, and rattan chairs are on the porch. Out front, a sago-leaf parasol shades a bench.

While we wait, I walk around the guest house on the trimmed lawn and examine the legs of the structure. Each is carved with figures and patterns: a warrior's head like the one under the gable...a crocodile with bug eyes and a fish in its jaws...the head and torso of a man with jug ears and a toothy smile...another with a star on his belly and triangular cuts going from his chest up over his shoulders. A wavy motif banding all the pillars resembles an opening flower, the petals breaking away from the bud. The cuts on the man's chest are the same: made to stand out, like the flesh is peeling off.

Peter, the manager of the guest house, approaches from the river. He is a stocky, earnest fellow who already knows from his boss what we want to do.

"My job is give visitor way to go," he told us when we arrived two hours ago. "Otherwise, those guys charge you very big money. You want to go slow. That is good. You want to see how people of PNG live. That is very good. If not I do job here, I go with you!"

Exactly who "those guys" were, we weren't certain, but once he'd checked us into the guest house, off he went to search for a canoe.

"Any luck, Peter?"

"We will go together, and you decide."

The sun is low in the sky. Another day on the Sepik is winding down. I expected to spend a day or two discovering Pagwi, but I am not sure there is much really to discover. Long canoes unload passengers and sacks of produce onto the riverbank, and those passengers and sacks go into waiting PMVs, destined for Maprik and Wewak. The faster PMVs are minibuses, the slower ones pickup trucks with benches in the back sheltered by canvas tarpaulins. A crew heaves sacks ashore, and I ask one of them what they contain. Cocoa. A sack of sixty kilos goes for K450 (Can$180) in Wewak.

After a fifteen-minute walk upriver, Nadya, Peter, and I arrive at a meagre hut, its stilt legs partly submerged in water. A thin, bare-chested, long-bearded man, the image of an Indian sadhu, is standing outside and introduces himself as Moses. Nadya and I shake his hand. He looks neither of us in the eye. The dugout canoe he has for sale is of a similar size to the ones we had before but sits lower in the water. It is obviously old. There is a wide crack in the bow and several holes in the hull that have been plugged with clay. I step in tentatively and note as I transfer my weight that the clay plugs are weeping.

"How much does he want for it?" Nadya asks.

"Sixty kina."

I look up and down the river: no small dugouts about, not one.

"Is this the only canoe Moses has?"

"He does have another one, but he says it won't suit your needs."

"Can we see it?"

Moses drags it out from under his house. A baby canoe. About two metres long and thirty centimetres wide in the middle, it has curvy gunwales and a crocodile head prow. Perfect for a six-year-old.

"Does anyone else around here have a canoe for sale?" I whisper to Peter.

"I don't know any others."

Perhaps we should wait for Leo to return from Wewak. I look at Nadya, who is running her hand along the hull of the baby canoe.

"It could work, I guess, if somehow we attach the little canoe to the big one. The little one can be like an outrigger."

She is remembering *Monique*, bamboo outriggers on either side making the canoe stable and practically unsinkable.

"How much is this one, Peter?" I ask.

"Same. Sixty kina."

"Tell him we will buy his canoes if he can join them together and plug the leaks in the big canoe properly."

Exactly how I expect him to join them, I can't say. Obviously, the previous arrangement we had isn't going to work. Can't simply lay sticks between the two bows and the two sterns and bind them. The big canoe sits low in the water, but the little one even lower. I expect Moses to frown, shake his head, and refuse to indulge the whims of the *waitpela*. Instead, he looks at me for the first time and nods. Come back tomorrow. Do we need a paddle? His neighbour has a short one for ten kina. Peter says he can find us a tall paddle for twenty kina.

|| Nadya buys donuts for breakfast from a stall selling them to passengers transiting between road and river, and we eat them on the guest house porch while waiting once again for Peter to return. Crammed into a plastic bag, pink icing gluing them together, the donuts look far from appetizing, but they turn out to be like traditional homemade ones, far more satisfying than their glistening equivalents at Tim Hortons back home. Pied herons and masked plovers pad across the lawn, seeking their own breakfast: grasshoppers and frogs to supplement their fish diets. With their bright yellow cheek wattles resembling lavish sideburns, the masked plovers look comically erudite and donnish.

Leo returned briefly last night and told us that a friend of his called Kami would accompany us to the village of Kaminabit, a three- or four-day paddle from Pagwi, but Peter said this morning when he brought our paddles that Kami wasn't interested and had gone to Maprik anyway. He would find someone else. Now he joins us on the porch with a man in khaki shorts and a baseball cap.

"This is Fresher," Peter announces. "He is river taximan. He say he can go with you to Kaminabit for K200."

The short man standing before us looks like a war veteran or a retired henchman. He has grizzled stubble speckling his chin, a chipped eyebrow, and a crewcut. Probably in his late forties. His lower lip is crusty with chewed betel nut. He doesn't smile when we greet him.

"He can carry your bags and food in his canoe."

Fresher's ten-metre motor-canoe rocks in the shallows over where the cocoa haulers were unloading yesterday, a 40 hp Yamaha outboard engine weighing down the stern. Nadya and I know we cannot entirely dismiss an escort such as this unless Moses has worked a miracle and turned a leaky old canoe and a baby "outrigger" into a robust raft capable of carrying us, our belongings, and a hired paddler or two.

"Um, we don't actually have a canoe yet," Nadya replies evasively. "Can he come back in an hour or two?"

Peter explains in Tok Pisin. Fresher looks at us expressionlessly and nods. We grab our paddles and head off down the riverbank.

"What do you think?" Nadya asks when we are out of earshot.

"Doesn't seem like an ideal travel buddy, does he? You?"

"Difficult to say."

Ahead of us, moored to the leg of a stilt hut, is a curious vessel: a miniature catamaran of sorts. A big canoe and a little one joined at the hip by means of a bamboo and bark platform. I wade over and plant my foot on the platform. Sturdy. How has our skinny boatbuilder managed this? We crouch down to appreciate the twin sticks supporting the platform, strapped tight to the hulls with cane twine. Moses has made the platform flat by having the supporting sticks rest on the gunwales of the small canoe but slot into semicircular grooves gouged out of the port gunwale of the big canoe. Smart. The gap between the canoes is about a metre. He has plugged the leaks in the big canoe with fresh clay, and I see a banana leaf scoop to bail water comes with the sale.

Moses emerges from his hut, and we settle up, tipping him for the labour. He seems content, and, as we shove off, Nadya and I are too. We have found a way to continue our canoe trip down the Sepik. We must tip Peter for making this possible. The problem is, however—and this becomes glaringly obvious in the ten minutes it takes us to paddle back to Sangra—that our catamaran will only bear the weight of us, not our luggage. The waterline is too low. To improve *Monique*'s buoyancy, we strapped empty jerry cans to her sides. None are available here; Pagwi doesn't have any stores selling that kind of stuff.

"We have a decision to make," Nadya says as we ride up on the mud in front of Sangra. Peter and Fresher are still on the porch. We stop at the bench in front of the guest house and ask Peter to join us.

"Who is Fresher?" I whisper to him.

"He is river taximan. He take passenger and cargo to Ambunti or Kaminabit, sometimes Chambri Lake."

"Yes, but *who* is he?" Nadya presses. "How do you know him? Is he your *tambu*?"

"No, not my *tambu*. Leo's. His younger brother."

"Is it just him?" Nadya asks after a short silence. "He is willing to follow us for three days on his own?"

"No, no. He will bring Tolly, his brother's son."

"Leo's son?"

"No," Peter says. "Tolly is Leo...*pikinini man bilong brata*."

"His nephew?"

Peter nods. Leo has clearly been in touch with his kin. We join the river cabbie on the porch. His name is not Fresher, we learn. It is Fraser but pronounced *Frezzer*.

"You know we will go slowly," Nadya says to him, making paddling gestures. "Is that okay?"

Fraser nods.

"So please stay close to our canoe," I add, wondering whether this new boating arrangement is going to be our undoing.

Fraser nods again, and Nadya and I shake his hand. We agree to settle up when we reach Kaminabit.

It takes four hours for Fraser to return to his home village, pick up his boatmate, and get fuel. Nadya and I chat to the only other guest at Sangra. Albert Mossie works for Global as a security officer, travelling up and down the Middle and Lower Sepik on a timber barge, protecting Malaysian employees from pirates. He seems to know everyone living along the banks of the river. We should look up Sam the policeman in Kanganaman, he says, Ronnie in Kaminabit, a school inspector called Francis Masam in Angoram, and Father Patrick in Marienberg near the estuary. I jot the names down and thank him. The feeling of being connected once again is reassuring.

|| Much to the amusement of the local cocoa haulers, a *waitman* and *waitmeri* on a customized catamaran plunge their paddles into the Sepik early afternoon on April 26th. Waiting fifty metres away is a motor-canoe containing a stony-faced Papuan, his young companion, a plastic bin of food, a fancy, high-tech tent (practically unused), and two backpacks. Destination for the day is Korogo, first village of any

Seaworthy vessel, I don't think.

size east of Pagwi on the Middle Sepik. I look back at the guest house. The wooden head grins down from the eaves, red tongue lolling out.

A hundred metres wide at Pagwi, the river churns and boils restively. The current takes hold of our little boat and carries it seaward with the flotsam. The buzz of arriving and departing motor-canoes fades behind, and we find ourselves back in the company of White Saun, whistling kites, and the dollar bird, the last a blue-white missile streaking across the water. Then, just as we're finding our rhythm, all hell breaks loose.

Six dugouts, the size of our larger one but with outboards on the back, come jetting up behind us. Nadya and I freeze and stare as they rocket by, incongruous with their bows rearing up out of the water. One cuts devilishly between Fraser and Tolly's canoe and ours, and waves slop into our small canoe. Nadya drops her paddle and starts bailing. The egrets flee, protesting. I wave over our comrades.

"Who the hell are these guys, do you know?"

One dugout draws a circle around us, and we hear the youngsters on board scream with laughter.

"They are practising for motorboat festival in Pagwi next month," Tolly yells. "They put big engine on little boat and race for prize!"

"Stay right behind so they can't come between us, okay?"

We sit tight and watch the racers cross and recross the river ahead, doing tight turns and almost losing control. I keep expecting one to slam into another. After ten minutes, they turn upstream and scream past us again. Waves bash at our canoes. Land of the Unexpected. I chuckle, get to my feet, and take up the tall paddle. Nadya empties the bailer for the last time and retrieves her paddle. Our catamaran has survived its first test—although I notice the clay plugs have begun to weep again. With the cost of gas, it surprises me that Papuans would have money to burn in this way. The winnings at the festival must be worth it.

Nadya and I recover our tempo, paddling close to the riverbank now—until Tolly shouts, "Follow the logs! Follow the logs!" Yes, of course. We must make use of the current. Jeffrey Waino's students taught us that.

After four hours of paddling, we are at Korogo with Keith, the village big man, in front of a thatched hut resembling Leo's guest house, although this one does not have such soaring spires. It is a *haus tambaran* or spirit house. Beneath the leering head pinned to the gable is the word "Sumboruman," which Keith tells us means "Eagle." Unlike Sangra, the stilt legs of the hut are hidden behind a skirt of hanging grasses, suggesting that what goes on inside this house is not for all to behold. Keith must be used to receiving visitors for he immediately assumes we are here to see inside. He sweeps aside the grass curtain at the entrance. Women are forbidden to enter, he says, but a *waitmeri* is an exception. This is the first time we have entered a village house in PNG without having to climb a ladder or stairs.

We are standing on packed dirt, and the air is cool. It takes a while for our eyes to adjust to the gloom, but the first thing we see

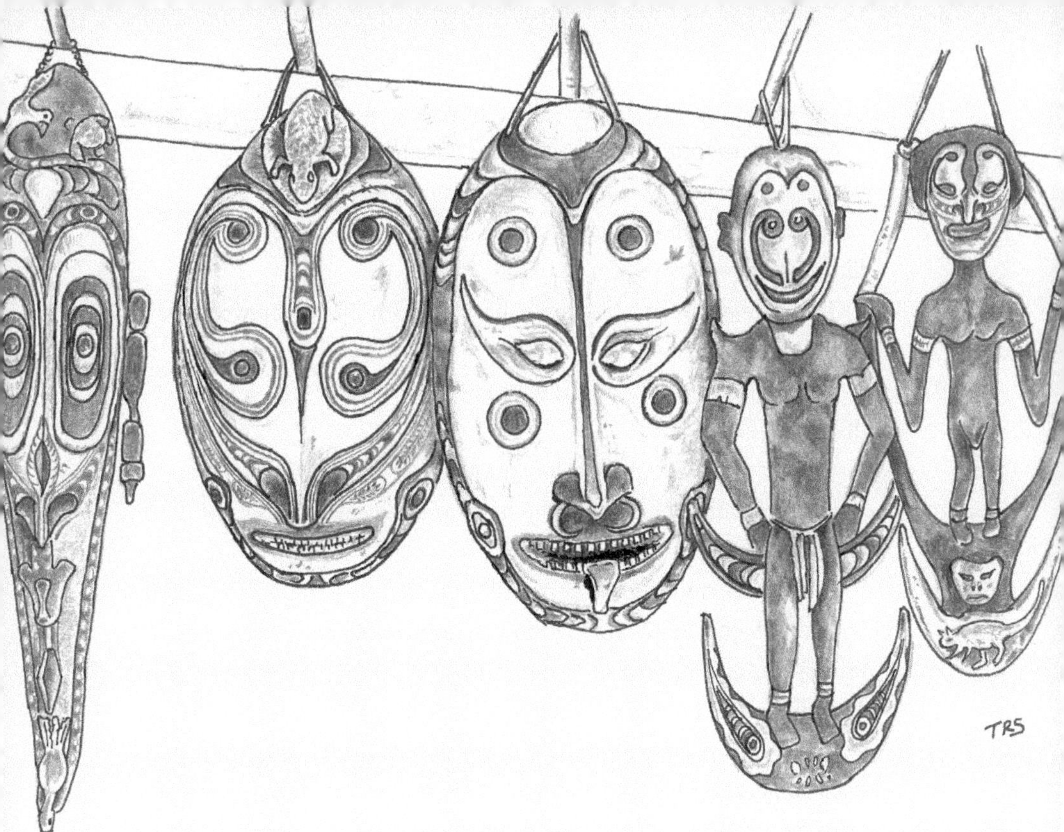

Tribal masks, Korogo.

are disembodied heads hanging from the rafters. Their faces are white, their eyes wide, and their cheeks tattooed with patterns.

"Who are they, Keith?" I ask.

"*Tumbuna*, our ancestors. They watch and listen what we say."

The wood heads stare down at waist-high berths made of bamboo slats and limbom bark, same materials as the platform on our catamaran.

"This is where clan members sit," Keith says, patting one with his hand. "Each clan has different place in the *haus*." He points to one corner. "That is for Pig Clan," then to the one opposite, "that for Eagle Clan," then to the other two corners, "that for Crocodile, and last one for Dog."

I notice that the pillars supporting the spirit house are carved with these creatures.

"What do the men discuss when they meet in here?" Nadya asks.

"Important thing for village. About land or marriage or which boy who will become man, or good hunting place in forest. Our ancestor guide us to make good decision. When we want to call clan for meeting, we beat drum."

Two *garamut* drums the size of bathtubs rest on logs between the Eagle and Pig berths.

"And those?" Nadya points at long bamboo flutes tucked into the rafters.

"We blow in skin-cutting ceremony or to send crying baby to sleep."

"But the father must bring the baby into the spirit house, not the mother, right?" Nadya guesses.

"Yes, yes. Only man can come in."

We each give Keith K10 for showing us around, the amount Leo told us was customary.

Dehydrated, unused once again to paddling under a tropical sun, we ask to buy some coconuts. Keith has two girls shin up a palm and fetch some, and they hack them open for us. He then takes us to the official guest house. The owner there wants K50 per person for a night's stay, and he considers Nadya and I with our hires a party of four. On the Upper Sepik, we never once had to pay lodging for our hired paddlers; they were invariably treated as *tambu*. We ask Keith if there's an alternative.

We walk along a well-maintained avenue further into the village, home, Keith tells us, to a thousand people belonging to the Iatmul (*Aye-yat-mul*) tribe. He steers us toward what appears to be the most battered hut of all, one as patchy and worn as some we stayed in upriver. A short, stout woman stands in front with her arms folded. She is wearing a red dress and has dyed brown hair rising vertically from her scalp. This is Mathilda, and I can tell before she says anything that she is a woman of strong character. The hut turns out to be her kitchen. Guests stay next door. We carry our bags into a house twice the size with a corrugated tin roof and plank siding. Inside are rooms with padlocks, beds with mosquito nets, and an electric light—the first we've seen in a Sepik village. Mathilda says a friend of hers can put up Tolly and Fraser, and we thank her for offering this.

Mathilda's husband, Collis, arrives while we are eating a dinner of smoked piranha, sago pancakes, rice, and tulip leaves. He has been out fishing and says he had a bad day. He only caught thirty fish.

"And how many do you catch on a good day?" Nadya asks.

"Three hundred," Collis replies.

They must be fed up of swimming around in muddy water. What does he use for bait? Seeds, he says.

Our hosts show not the least surprise that we have turned up out of the blue to stay. Collis is a tour guide, and the couple are used to looking after tourists. From time to time, groups of fifteen or twenty come to Korogo for two or three days to witness a skin-cutting ceremony.

"How much do they pay for that?" I ask.

"Usually K20,000." Gulp. Can$8,000. "The group share the cost. The clans divide the money between them."

"How long does the cutting last?"

"About two hours."

"What do they cut with?"

"Before, Elders were using sharp bamboo, but now they use razor blade. The boy lies in uncle's lap on a canoe. They cut first his chest and shoulder, then his back and buttock. After finish, Elders put mud and tree oil in cuts, and the boy must not wash for a week. The oil smells bad and keep flies away. The boy must not stretch or stand up straight to stop blood from coming out cuts. If he does, the Elder will beat him or charge a fee, like a chicken or betel nut. He walks around bent over with stick. After a week, he washes in river, and this is very painful. Over next two weeks, he adds more mud and oil in cuts so they get scar and his skin is like crocodile. The boy stays with others in *haus tambaran* for this time, and his sisters and mother bring him sago and fish to eat. Elder teach him many things about becoming a man. After, the boy may enter *haus tambaran,* and he has confidence to act like man. He can say things, and others will listen. And the Elder says, 'You are a man now. Anything that comes, you can take it!'"

"Did you become a man this way?" my wife asks Collis.

He nods and grins. "Yes. I am a crocodile man."

Benedict Allen, a British adventurer, endured such an initiation while living with the Niowra in the Sepik village of Kandengai in the 1980s and wrote a memoir about his experience. An image comes to mind of him coated from head to foot in clay, cakes of it flaking off his face, after his skin-cutting, blood trickling down his back. He shuffled around Kandengai village with his hands on the shoulders of another hunched-over and bleeding *bandee*. The Elders he called *avookwaarks* or "embodiments of the crocodile spirit," the blood he shed his "female blood," a necessary purgation on his path to becoming a man. I remember how difficult he found it to relinquish his Western identity. "I was still a white man, still needed Hardy, Lawrence, Larkin, and all that; required annual stocks of Aunty Joan's and Uncle Geoffrey's tomato and apple chutney." Satisfied finally that Allen had let go, *avookwaark* Lamin said, "*Nau naim bilong yu 'Wumbunavan.'*" The Englishman now had a Niowran name: Wumbunavan.

Nadya asks Collis what the Elders taught him in the *haus tambaran* during his six-week initiation.

"How to beat drum and how to play flute," he replies with a smile. "And, of course, how to hunt crocodile."

|| "This morning, I will go to barter market," Mathilda announces as we are taking down our mosquito nets after breakfast the following day. "Do you want to come?" Nadya and I nod enthusiastically.

Canvas sack of fish under her arm, Mathilda leads the way to the swamps behind the guest house, and we board a motor-canoe. Five boats are waiting to go, crammed with women carrying sacks like Mathilda's. Somehow Fraser and Tolly manage to squeeze into another. It is slow-going cutting a path through the water hyacinths, but this gives two men in our boat the opportunity to use their slingshots. Eagles circling low over the canoes know what the women have in their sacks. I am happy to see none of the clay pellets they shoot hits its mark (although some come darn close) as I have become partial to kites and eagles and wouldn't fancy eating either for lunch. After twenty minutes, we arrive at a clearing in the forest.

The barter market goes something like this. The fish ladies of Korogo settle down on the grass but do not display their merchandise.

Barter market.

The sago ladies from the inland villages of Selai, Aurimbit, Kosingbi, and Yamok arrive, also find spots to sit, and lay out their fruits and vegetables. Some women have brought bushels of betel nuts for sale. Before the market starts, the fish ladies walk around to see what's available and make agreements with other sellers. For the first hour, people buy veggies, fruits, and betel for kina. These are mainly for local officials. Nadya buys bananas, tulip, papaya, peanuts, sago, oranges, and a cucumber.

"Give some cash to Fraser and Tolly so they can get betel nuts," Nadya says to me, dropping her bag of goodies at my feet and heading off again.

Another ten minutes of cash transactions to buy fish, now on display, and then, as if someone had rung a bell, the ladies tuck their money away. The inlanders extract sweating cakes of tofu-like sago starch from their bags and walk around presenting them for exchange: a smoked piranha for two fist-size boulders, three tilapia for two bricks, a catfish for a wedge like a loaf of bread. The exchanges are fast, the ladies neither arguing nor haggling, both groups seeming to know what the going rate is. After twenty minutes, the inlanders have all the fish and the river dwellers all the sago.

"Why can't the Iatmul grow their own vegetables and sago?" I ask Hendrick, a Korogonian who has also been watching the frenzy of activity.

"Because of floods. This year is good year, but some years, our village is under water for four months. We depend on the other tribe for *kaukau* and sago. They depend on our tribe for fish and crocodile. They know crocodile meat is best protein!"

"That worked amazingly well," I remark when Nadya returns.

"Their system ensures that no one goes home with what they brought, which is particularly good for the inland women. Mathilda says some have to walk a full day to get here, sago curd and vegetables on their backs."

Sago is on the menu for lunch when we get back to the village, although not the pancakes we know from the Upper Sepik. The quivering, glittering blob Mathilda cups in her hands resembles a jellyfish, and it is hard to believe it derives from the same starch as a pancake. Nadya asks her how to make it. Pour boiling water over fermented sago flour in a basin and stir vigorously. Add water until the white slurry turns to transparent glue. Get a pair of jumbo chopsticks, and, holding one in either hand, pick up the glue by winding it onto the chopsticks. Drop the gathered blob into a bowl and serve with fish boiled in coconut milk. I remember the dish from West Papua, where it is known as *papeda*. There, we ate the glue by stabbing it with a wooden fork made especially for the task. Stab, twist, and suck off the elongated tines. I grimaced eating it there, and I do so again here. Sucking blobs of glue into her mouth, Mathilda laughs. Jellyfish that go uneaten she wraps in banana leaves, where they cool and become floppy sausages that are easier to eat.

Impressed by Mathilda's industriousness, Nadya asks her about the division of labour in the village.

"Women do most of the work here," she says. "We fish, cook meals, look after children, go to market, look after house. Most men spend all day in *haus tambaran*, smoking, eating betel nut, and doing nothing. I say to wives, 'If your man spend all day in *haus* man, don't feed him when he come home!'"

Collis, fortunately, is not typical. He goes fishing daily, does housework, guides tourists when they come, and attends to the guest house. He is also involved in the larger Sepik community. With Mathilda, he is organizing a weekend of canoe races, soccer matches, and cultural activities in September called "Avisat Is Bleeding." *Avisat* means "river," and the event aims to raise awareness of the potential environmental threat of a proposed copper and gold mine on the Frieda River, a tributary of the Sepik. Given the infamous pollution of the Ok Tedi and Fly rivers by a copper and gold mine, the Sepik villagers downriver of the Frieda have every right to be alarmed: they drink from the river, eat fish and hunt crocodiles that live in the river, wash themselves and their clothes in the river, and travel on the river.

In 1984, the Ok Tedi Mine, located in the mountains of Western Province, began dumping some 73,000 tonnes of mining waste (crushed rock, sand, and metals) per day into the Ok Tedi River, a tributary of the Fly. This continued for almost two decades and fouled 1,300 square kilometres of land near the river. For the fifty thousand people living in the 120 villages downstream, the effect was devastating. Swathes of forest were poisoned, animals disappeared, fish numbers declined by 70–90 per cent, and contaminated mud carpeted the flood plain where the villagers cultivated sago, taro, and bananas, their staple foods. The tailings raised the level of the riverbed, disrupting boat traffic. It took eleven years for the villagers' complaints to be heard and for BHP Billiton, the Anglo-Australian company and majority owner of the mine, to acknowledge fault and pay compensation. The mine did not cease operations. As the single largest contributor to PNG's economy, accounting for 10 per cent of GDP and producing 18 per cent of its total exports by 2001, it continued to dump waste into the river. Unhappy with the media attention, BHP Billiton withdrew in 2002, handing over its shares in the mine to the PNG government in exchange for legal indemnity from all future claims for compensation. The Ok Tedi ranks as one of the world's most environmentally damaging mining disasters.

The story is similar for the Porgera Gold Mine in Enga Province in the Highlands, the largest gold mine in the country. Owned by Canadian mining giant Barrick Gold, this mine dumps 14,500 tonnes of waste rock and mining tailings into two major tributaries of the Porgera River every day. A "red river" of iron-ore-rich tailings descends from the site, and high concentrations of toxic heavy metals like nickel, arsenic, cadmium, mercury, lead, and zinc make water in the valley unsafe to drink. A French investigative documentary made in 2014 highlighted, too, the human rights abuses. In 1989, local residents signed over their lands to the mining company in an agreement, apparently unaware of what it contained. Barrick Gold promised to relocate them but then failed to do so, leaving the dispossessed Porgerians on a ripped-open, barren, and contaminated land, where they could only eke out a living as "illegal" gold miners. Company security guards beat or gang-raped any women they caught scavenging for gold on the waste dumps, a practice Barrick Gold initially denied was happening but later acknowledged.

Mathilda and Collis come down to the waterside to see us off, and Nadya and I wish them luck in their efforts to save the river. Multinational corporations from developed countries no doubt have an easier time going about their business in the backwaters of an undeveloped country, where environmental standards are lax, human rights violations tolerated, and protesters few. Mathilda hugs Nadya and gives her a catfish to cook for dinner.

"I will miss them," Nadya says as we paddle away.

|| On our way from Korogo to Yentchen, our next port of call, I see swirling water ahead. Keep away, Peter advised us at Sangra: "Bad spirit live in whirlpool!" I regard whirlpools more as a maritime phenomenon, created when two opposing currents meet. Nadya and I steered around a few when we crossed the Sape Strait between Sumbawa and Komodo islands in Indonesia in our outrigger canoe. A little extra throttle on our tuk-tuk propelled us out of harm's way. Maybe they are a feature of the Sepik because it twists so: plenty of opportunity for the water to curl back on itself.

"Let's try going right," I suggest. Wouldn't want to provoke a bad spirit.

To go right, Nadya must paddle like a madwoman as she is on the port side. This she tries but to little effect. I cannot help by paddling on the same side because the outrigger is in the way, so I try a J-stroke on the starboard side to assist the turn. Fruitless. Suddenly, the whirlpool is upon us. Thankfully, the hole at its centre is not of tree-trunk-gobbling proportions but the diameter of a soup bowl. We paddle hard, bumping right over it, and enter a patch of choppy water beyond.

"Well, that wasn't so bad," I say.

Nadya sets her paddle down and catches her breath. The truth is we have very little control over our new vessel. Standing with one foot on the bark platform and the other in the adult canoe, I am able to get much more thrust with the tall paddle than Nadya can with the short one while sitting. She perches on the edge of the platform, one leg tucked beneath her, the other stretched out in front of her in the baby canoe. Every two or three strokes I take, the catamaran spins to port. We have tried to compensate: two strokes from Nadya for every one of mine.

Tolly and Fraser look at us, amused. Why are the *waitpela* doing this? What do they hope to gain? Earlier, though, they seemed impressed by our efforts. "Tony is strong man!" Fraser shouted after watching me paddle for two hours without pause. Madman, he probably meant. I am hoping they don't get bored, trailing behind us, engine off or idling. I wonder if they are having second thoughts about taking a break from their work as river cabbies to accompany us. They could, if they wished, toss our bags overboard, I suppose, fire up their outboard, and head home. What could we do? Not give chase, that's for sure. They chew betel nuts from the barter market and flick the husks in the river. I wish we had thought of buying betel nut for our paddlers on the Upper Sepik. Betel is, we have come to realize, like a goodwill currency. Papuan men give each other nuts persistently. The exchange builds and maintains relationships.

Noticing the big canoe is becoming a bathtub again, I wave to our escort.

"Can you find some more clay, Tolly?"

This is the second time we have asked him to do this since departing Korogo. Fortunately, Tolly is like one of Jeffrey Waino's students: willing and capable. A somewhat bizarre-looking character probably in his mid-twenties, with stumpy dreadlocks and a beard that bursts out of his face in all directions, he is as vivacious as his senior is taciturn.

The motor-canoe buzzes away again. Not just any clay will plug the holes. Taken from the riverbank, it is too wet. Tolly must seek firmer material farther inland.

The heat of the day is now upon us. I look down at my wife, under her Tilley hat, one arm brown, the other pink. On our way back from the market, Mathilda daubed Nadya's arm with clay to protect her from the sun. The clay is now crusty and flaking off. She seemed pleased with this alternative to sunblock, and I imagine her coated head to foot in it like Benedict Allen after his initiation into the Crocodile Clan.

We learned last night that both Tolly and Fraser are crocodile men. I asked tentatively if we might see their scars, uncertain whether the request was impertinent. They did not hesitate. Off came their shirts, and I saw Fraser grin for the first time. A map of diamond-shaped welts covered their chests and shoulders and cascaded down their backs. Being cut around the nipples must have been especially excruciating. The scars there resembled curled-up earthworms. Tolly told us that Fraser was his *wau*, the mentor in whose lap the bandee lies while being sliced. Skin cutting is a rite of passage to manhood, and I wondered if Fraser might have known Benedict Allen. The Brit was in Kandengai, Fraser and Tolly's home village, about the time our senior boatman turned adult.

"Yes, I know him. We become crocodile man together."

"What was he like?"

Fraser said nothing for a while, and I thought I might be prying. The process of becoming a crocodile man happens largely behind closed doors.

"He can speak Yatma, and he dance like Papua man in *sing-sing*," he said finally. "He was kind man."

Our new boatmates, Tolly and Fraser.

The motor-canoe returns. Nadya bails the water out of the bathtub, and Tolly caulks the holes. The clay resembles fudge and is compact enough to resist the water pressure.

It takes us five long hours to paddle the twenty or so kilometres to Yentchen. Nadya gets backache in her awkward sitting position, and I can't propel us forward powerfully on a bark platform that buckles with each thrust. We are both ready for a relaxing dip when we pull in.

Unfortunately, we have arrived at *Natnat* Central. We are able to hump our gear to the guest house unmolested, but the sun is rapidly sinking in the sky. I am quicker off the mark with my soap and towel than my wife or Tolly. There is no question of sitting dreamily on the riverbank, kicking the water and admiring the tropical sunset. I hurry back after my *was-was* and quickly get dressed on the guest house verandah just as my compadres are heading riverward. The air fills with black dots.

I have never seen such accelerated ablutions. A chatty saunter toward the river becomes a speed walk with hunched shoulders and swearing. At the river, there is much wild and ineffectual flinging of water, and a lot of shrieking and slapping. The much-hoped-for relaxing dip becomes a brief sloshing of water over head and under armpits and little application of soap, if any. I see two desperate people dashing for sanctuary, hair dripping, arms windmilling frantically. Fraser pulls up a chair beside me and observes, stroking his chin and grinning.

The guest house is of the highly ventilated sort Nadya and I experienced in Waku on the Upper Sepik—although this one is endowed with intermittent electricity. A creaking fan lurches to life and blasts away the mozzies parked on its grill for a few minutes, then coughs, nods forward, and dies as if exhausted with the effort. A solitary lightbulb hanging over a dinner table flickers on and off. The only way to keep the *natnats* at bay is to cook on a smoky fire, and Tolly gets one going. Dinner is brief. Once the fire dies, the aerial assault begins again. Our buddies excuse themselves; a wall-less hut next door is theirs for the night. Nadya and I quickly string up our net beside the wilting fan, tucking the bottom edges under our sleeping mats lest the mosquitos rise up from below, passing through the rents in the floor. The problem with this is we must lie on our backs like cadavers, arms at our sides, and try not to move. Roll over and lean a body part against the net wall, and we will be needled and scratchy all night.

"So how did you feel bathing with a Papuan cabbie?" I ask.

"Comfortable," Nadya replies without hesitation. "He asked me if I wanted to go alone but said it would be safer at dusk if we went together."

"What a gent. Did he strip down?"

"Only to his shorts. And he went downriver just far enough for me to have privacy but still be able to hear his voice. It was funny. I didn't expect him to be as freaked by the *natnats* as I was."

"His uncle was certainly amused," I say, closing my eyes. "Guess Kandengai doesn't have as many."

"They seem close, these two men."

"*Wau* and *bandee*."

My last thought is that PNG needs geckos, like Indonesia. I haven't seen a single gecko since arriving here. They adore dining on mosquitoes.

9 SUNK

The spirits are as real as the phenomena of the material world; to enlist their aid to ensure a good piece of work is a matter of caution and common sense.

Such precautions will be especially necessary for the erection of large buildings which have special significance in the ritual by which the deities and spirits are propitiated. The particular purpose of such structures may vary a good deal from one place to another. The emphasis may be on their function as a club for the mature men, or there may be a heavier emphasis on the religious purposes. Generally both needs are met. Christianity, of course, has made a big difference in many places. But there are still many others, as in the Sepik District, where the great haus tamberan *remains.*

—CHARLES ROWLEY, *The New Guinea Villager*

"Put more in middle," Tolly urges, peering over Nadya's shoulder. "It is too thin there."

Nadya extracts another gluey brick of sago starch from the bag she bought at the barter market in Korogo, breaks off a chunk, and crumbles it into the frying pan. Sago, before it's fried, resembles feta cheese. Today is my birthday, and she is trying her hand at making pancakes.

"Now press down or pancake will be bumpy like Papua road!"

Nadya does so with the heel of her hand. She needs the mesh sieve John Youpa's wives used in Tipas to turn the starch into flour before putting it in the pan. Tolly watches her movements curiously, his fingers twitching. He wasn't expecting to give a cooking lesson this morning. He has the puzzled look of our hired guides on the Upper Sepik when we insisted on taking over the paddling or humping our gear ashore. Weren't we paying them to do that work? At the same time, Tolly is clearly happy to teach the *waitmeri* a trick or two.

"How much water should I add?" Nadya asks as the crumbs in the pan begin to stick together.

"Just *liklik*."

She sprinkles some over. Lifting one edge of the pancake with his hand, Tolly slips the other underneath and deftly flips the pancake. It lands without breaking.

"You want to try?" he says, smiling.

"Sure." Nadya laughs. "Take cover!"

Chuckling, Fraser goes out to lop off some banana leaves to serve as plates for our pancakes. The day is fine, the sun streaming in through the gaps in the sago wall. With my pancake comes a homemade birthday card, Nadya's drawing of a leering tribal mask on the front of the sort we saw in the *haus tambaran* at Korogo.

After breakfast, we cross the river to Yentchen village and meet the gods of the Sepik. Presiding over the affairs of men is Sukundimi, a deity whose oval head is the seat back of a wooden chair positioned at the centre of the *haus tambaran*. When an Elder wishes to speak, he sits on this chair so the god may inspire his words and endow them with wisdom. In a debate—there are four clans here: *Pukpuk* (Crocodile), *Tot* (Pig), *Wawe* (Eagle), and *Saksak* (Sago)—speakers approach the chair in turn from their berths, holding finger-length leaves. To deter garrulity, they must tuck these behind Sukundimi's necklace and utter brief, well-considered statements. The god has a rear-viewing face, too, keeping an eye on clan members sitting behind him. This one has gawping eyes with seashell irises and a stretched nose pierced through the septum with pig tusks.

Dennis, our guide, takes us around the *haus*, pointing out images carved into its pillars: an eel, a prawn, a frog, an egret. I ask him about the zigzag pattern circling most of the pillars. Crocodile scales? No, he replies, the waves of the river. This surprises me, as the Middle Sepik has, so far, not been choppy.

Haus tambaran *(spirit house), Middle Sepik.*

An athletic figure stands behind a pillar at the end of the *haus*. This is the warrior god Suabandi. He has a face like Sukundimi's backward-looking one and wears a grass tunic with a pouch.

"Before we go hunting, we come here and we say, 'Suabandi, why don't you come with us?' and we put some betel nut in his pocket so he will guide us to find cuscus or bandicoot or wild pig."

Our guide points at the cobwebby rafters over our heads. Two more gods are watching us: a spiky-toothed fish called Ramis and a giant snake called Kinjin, both crudely fashioned wooden effigies. Dennis, like most Papuans, is a Christian, so I ask him if his belief in the gods of the river conflicts with his commitment to Jesus. He laughs.

"I cannot work for two god! We respect our god, but they are god with small 'g.'"

I think again of Pastor Liddle at Green River, intent in his mission to turn Papuans away "from the power of Satan to God" and feel saddened that an intrusive religion has shoved aside local beliefs. Jesus, it would seem, has relegated Ramis and Kinjin to the rafters.

Two men enter the *haus* carrying what look like cudgels: short polished sticks, weighted at one end and tapering to a point at the other. Both sticks are carved with crocodile scales. The men mutter a few words to Fraser and Tolly who are standing at the door.

"They wish to welcome you to their village," Tolly announces.

The men go to a pair of coffin-sized *garamut* drums located near Suabandi. I expect them to start beating the sides vigorously, using the sticks like hammers. Instead, holding them by their fatter ends as one might a pencil, they begin rapping the tops of the drums near the slot openings. The beat is a fast rat-a-tat that gains resonance as it echoes in the drum. I imagine the sound travelling far on a still day.

"They use drum for calling clan member or telling people there will be *sing-sing*," Tolly informs us. "Or telling other tribe there has been a death in the village."

"Different beat for each occasion?"

"Yes. And they have special signal to call village big man. When he hears it, he will come. *Garamut* is their telephone!"

"How much time do you spend in the *haus tambaran*?" Nadya asks Dennis when the drummers are done, and we have shaken their hands and paid for our visit. She is probably recollecting Mathilda's complaint that men hang out in a spirit house to shirk their chores at home.

"We men are here more than we are in our homes!" he replies. "It is bad for a man to spend too much time in his family house. Too much time with wife and children make him weak. He lose his power. He lose his respect among other men."

Our two boatmen nod seriously. Fraser has seven children, I learned at breakfast this morning, and Tolly three. Neither appears inconvenienced at having to leave his family at short notice to escort the *waitpela* downriver for three days.

An hour's paddle and we are in Kanganaman, the location of the oldest spirit house on the Sepik. This wooden cathedral is three storeys high, the largest we have seen of its kind, and has towering spires. Unlike the previous *haus tambarans*, the sides are open: no grass curtain to keep men's business a secret. I imagine angry wives spotting their husbands, stretched out chewing betel nut on the berths in the *haus*, and yelling at them. But Vincent Yarme, the diminutive, bare-chested wood carver who shows us around, assures us that women are chased off or beaten if they come near the *haus*. Over the entrance, a naked woman spreads wide her muscular legs, exposing her enlarged vulva, reminding me of an Irish sheela-na-gig. A *haus tambaran* symbolizes the womb of the mother, Vincent explains. After initiation into crocodilehood, young men are reborn when they pass through her legs. They have purged themselves of all harmful "female" emotions and are ready to assume their masculine roles.

Inside the cathedral, we find the kind of richly patterned masks we saw in the Korogo spirit house—although these ancestors, bathed in sunlight, seem much less ghostly. To one side are two *tumbuan*: tall, cone-shaped wicker costumes used at *sing-sings*, one an embodiment of a male spirit called Kambaragu, the other of a female called Memburasi. They seem like cheery characters. Each is endowed with two grinning faces, a lower face that conceals the head of the wearer, and an upper one that gives the figure an imposing height. The costumes are ornamented with grass, which hangs from the shoulders to below the waist, hiding the dancer's body. It would be good to see them in action, but we are not visiting at the right time of year.

The most notable *sing-sings* take place in the Highlands, where tribesmen and women paint their faces, dress up in all their finery, sing traditional songs, and dance. The largest festival, held each September in Goroka, the capital of the Eastern Highlands, attracts warriors from over a hundred tribes. Red-and-white-faced Goroka warriors wearing shell necklaces and flamboyant bird of paradise feather headdresses rub shoulders with ghoulish Asaro "mudmen" daubed head to foot in clay, their faces hidden behind scowling clay masks, their fingernails extended into fearsome spikes. Early August is when the Sepik River Crocodile Festival happens. In Ambunti, dancers dress in tanket-leaf skirts, beat *kundu* drums, and cavort with trussed-up baby crocodiles slung around their necks. The World Wildlife Fund supports the festival to promote conservation and to raise awareness of the threats to the local reptile population posed by logging, mining, and other commercial operations.

Australian patrol officers came up with the idea of *sing-sings* in the 1950s, apparently, a patriarchal attempt to get warring tribes to interact peacefully, although I assume tribes were performing dances way before that. Our guidebook has nothing to say about the meaning of the dances or why tribes choose to look the way they do. Why red and white face paint for Goroka warriors? Why stretched fingernails on mudmen? I look again at the static double faces of Kambaragu and Memburasi and get the feeling Nadya and I can only really skim the surface as we float down this river. Why do these spirits have two faces? I ask Tolly, but he doesn't know. Perhaps all is made clear at the *sing-sings*. The costumes and dance routines probably reflect traditional beliefs or align with mythology.

We return to our canoes and cross the river again. Another *haus tambaran* is at Palambei, this one a dim repository for the most intricately carved and painted masks and figures we have yet seen: a face as large as my torso with lidless golf-ball eyes and zebra cheek markings, White Saun in flight with its wings outstretched, a life-size village woman in an eagle headdress with grass tassels dangling from her ears, miniature *garamut* drums with crocodile heads. The work belongs to master carvers and is remarkable to behold in this elemental world of hollowed-out tree-trunk pirogues and gap-floored huts with leaky palm leaf roofs. Once again, we listen to a drum recital, performed this time by three men on two *garamut*. We would learn later that they welcomed us this way because Fraser and Tolly had *tambu* in the village.

We emerge blinking into the light and immediately start sweating. The sun has vanished, and the air has turned soupy. The mosquitoes are biting. I am keen to return to the river and find some wind, but

Fraser has a proposition. One of his daughters lives in Maringei village, a short walk upriver from Palambei. Would we like to have lunch at her place?

"Why not?" Nadya says breezily.

The way is along a puddle-dented grass avenue toward a row of huts stilted high off the ground. The largest of these has been elevated a good six metres; Maringei must see severe flooding. Fraser's daughter Alison lives here with, it would seem, a hundred children. In fact, as Fraser tells us, only four of them belong to Alison. Neighbours' kids come here during the day to play. Fraser brings two chairs for us, and the children sit in a circle at our feet. We look at the staring eyes, wide smiles, and torn shirts. The average age would seem to be about four. It's like being put in charge of a kindergarten class. Nadya slides off her chair and switches on her question stream, prodding little stomachs and getting giggles. Alison brings us smoked fish and sago in enamel basins. I look over at Fraser, standing by the door. There is no mistaking the expression on his face: he is the proud grandfather.

By the time we get back to the boats, it is 4 p.m. Nadya and I plod through the puddles, swishing away mozzies with our hats. Grey clouds roll by overhead, and I hear rumbles in the distance. From Palambei, we have about fifteen kilometres to paddle to reach Kaminabit.

The voyage begins well. Ready for some exercise after our cultural tour and lunch, Nadya and I are quick to find our rhythm, her sitting and me standing to paddle and coordinating as best we can. Fraser and Tolly follow behind, sometimes close by, at other times farther off. When they lag too far, Fraser starts the motor. Annoyed by this strategy, I shout at them to switch it off and use their paddles. They are not the ones paying for the gas, and the noise disturbs the birds.

The wind picks up, an easterly blowing in our faces. I take some deep breaths and feel renewed. Maybe this lopsided vessel will carry us all the way to the Bismarck Sea after all. I dig an "Extra Cheesy" Em Nau cracker out of my shirt pocket and take bites between strokes, savouring the artificial flavour. A decent cheddar. Now there is something we have not had in quite a while. The wind is creating little waves. The boat bumps over them, and we must concentrate to keep it pointing downstream.

"Tony, I'm going to have to stop and bail," my wife says.

I look down at the baby canoe. Every third or fourth wave is slopping over the bow, and a pool is collecting in the stern. I look left and right. We are right in the middle of the river.

"Um, this is not an ideal place to stop. Why don't we head over to one side or the other so we're less exposed?"

I plunge my paddle into the water and try with some forceful pulls and a J-stroke to steer to the south bank, where there seems to be shelter. The catamaran responds lethargically but eventually turns.

"Tony, stop paddling! You're making it worse."

I stop and catch my breath. "How about we try paddling fast? Maybe we can skim over the waves."

"That, that's probably not going to...What if we get Fraser and Tolly to give us a tow?"

I bend my knees, grasp the paddle lower down the shaft, and start digging like there's no tomorrow.

"No, no. Stop! *STOP*! It's coming in over the side and the bow now."

Chest heaving, I look again at the baby canoe. Should've turned the other way. The chop is now hitting it broadside. Waves are washing over the curvy gunwales, and we are beginning to tip.

"Ah, shit. Fucking midget canoe! Knew in Pagwi the waterline was too low. Can't even carry our gear on this buggering thing!"

Nadya throws down her paddle and starts bailing furiously with the banana-leaf bailer, but it is too late. The wind is stiffening and the waves getting larger. So this is the wavy water carved into the pillars of *haus tambarans*—maybe the gods of the spirit house were trying to tell us something.

"It's no use. I'm coming to your side," she yells. "Take my bag."

She scrambles across, and the small canoe fills practically to the brim. I wave frantically to our escort fifty metres away. Tolly is sitting sideways in the canoe, legs dangling over the side, and tossing betel nut husks idly into the river. Fraser waves back and pulls the cord on the engine. Perhaps I shouldn't have yelled at them earlier.

"Oh, this is not good," Tolly says as the motor-canoe draws alongside. Fraser tells him to tie up to the now fully submerged baby canoe. He does so and starts bailing using their scoop.

As he works, we start levelling out, and I feel relieved. Then I look at the hull of the adult canoe and see that this, too, is swimming in water, perhaps the weight of two people putting the clay plugs under greater stress. The motor-canoe propels us to the riverbank, and we enter a shallow inlet.

"You want that we tow to Kaminabit?" Tolly asks.

"No," I say. "What we need is more clay to plug these bloody leaks."

He shrugs and wades ashore to find some while Nadya bails out the rest of the water. Fraser looks on impassively. I try and size up the river. No whirlpools. Bit of rough water. Perfectly paddle-able in a Canadian Prospector. What if we hug the bank? Use the bends of the river to our advantage. Where we are now, the water is relatively calm. We should paddle hard on the open stretches and duck into inlets for breaks. Can't be that far to Kaminabit.

Tolly returns with two cakes of clay and caulks the holes, and bails out the remaining water. Once we are seaworthy, our escort withdraws. As soon as we depart the inlet, the wind is once again in our teeth. Waves slap the hulls and smack the underside of the bark platform. However, if we paddle steadily and keep the catamaran pointing downriver, we can make headway without taking on too much water. I look ahead for dents in the riverbank where we can hide. What I see is a dark bank of cloud rolling toward us.

A few fat raindrops hit the boat, the splats audible. Nadya performs a sweep stroke that angles us to shore, and we draw to a halt. All is quiet for a moment. The wind dies. Then the storm is upon us, the kind of lashing rain that drenches in seconds. We exchange looks, shrug, and go back to work. Tropical storms never last. Waves bash the baby canoe and spill over the sides as we paddle; the clay plugs in the big canoe become pitted, then crumble and dissolve. After fifteen minutes, we realize there is no point in paddling anymore.

The Sepik has claimed our boat. We don't need to wave the motor-canoe over.

"Now you want a tow?" Tolly asks.

Defeated, Nadya and I climb aboard. Heck of a way to end a birthday. It takes a full hour to get to Kaminabit, dragging the waterlogged catamaran, rain pelting our heads the entire way.

|| I sit on the steps of the guest house and watch the great watery brown beast roll by, hauling its booty. We've heard that some trees the river claims are so massive they are worth salvaging and turning into canoes. After a storm, the men keep half an eye on the river. The sun is just up and the air uncannily still after yesterday's meteorological offensive. I hear a lonesome hoot from a stand of coconut palms. A friarbird.

I walk to the river's edge. Our catamaran sits swamped in the muddy shallows. With the buckled platform practically ripped off the bigger canoe, it is hardly a catamaran anymore. The tall paddle, driven through the snapped bamboo slats of the platform and into the mud, keeps the boat from joining the debris rushing downstream. Three days this rig lasted. Why did we waste fuel towing it here?

Getting a tow brings back memories of our efforts in '97 to extricate ourselves from Grajagan, a port on the south coast of Java. Small canoes like ours should not enter the port, we had been told. The entrance, rocky at one side, was too narrow and the waves too big. Only fishing trawlers with big engines could enter and exit safely. Outrigger canoes should land on a beach outside the port. Knowing that we needed supplies, I chose to ignore the advice. Throwing the throttle on our tuk-tuk to max, I risked our necks by charging in through the surf. We got lucky and took on little water, but, having loaded up on fuel and food, departing from Grajagan was another matter. The waves rolling into the port were far too tall for us to crest. We successfully mounted two, which were already spent, and then got summarily crushed by the third and fourth. Swamped and helpless, engine dead and hissing, supplies spread out over the water, we were at the mercy of the waves that followed. We were lucky not to get tossed onto the rocks.

Our Indonesian canoe was also a dugout: far too heavy to portage to a safer put-in. So back in the port we begged for a tow. Would one of the departing trawlers be willing? We paddled around, holding up a rope and a carton of Gudang Garam cigarettes. Finally, one agreed. It was a rollercoaster of a ride getting dragged at twice our normal speed through toppling waves, and we almost didn't make it when the rope snapped. Fortunately, we were far enough through the surf zone to finish the job with some manic paddling and help from a resurrected tuk-tuk.

"Now what?" Nadya says, joining me on the riverbank. We stare at the submerged wreck. Strips of bark peeling off the platform wag like tails in the current.

"Good question."

Laughter comes from the kitchen, an open-sided shelter with a firepit beside the guest house. Soaked and shivering, we took refuge from the storm here when we arrived yesterday. Cyril, the owner of the guest house, a lean, bald man in his early forties, showed no surprise at our sudden appearance. He promptly put the kettle on and asked his wife to prepare dinner. The shelter has berths like in a *haus tambaran*, and our crocodile men are lounging on them, eating fried bananas and yakking. I thought they would be itching to get paid and go home after yesterday's shenanigans.

"How about we go with them to Chambri Lakes?" Nadya says. Fraser mentioned the possibility in Pagwi, a two-day side trip from Kaminabit. "They are decent guys."

Tough, too, and patient. I admired their composure during the storm. No grumbling, no criticism. In their shoes, I might have questioned the clients' obstinance. Why do you insist on paddling in these weather conditions? And in that ridiculous boat? Can't you see it's *bagarap*? What are you trying to prove?' After we sank, they motored for an hour into driving rain, pulling an enormous anchor. Neither boatman suggested cutting the tether. They simply hunkered down and got on with the job they were hired to do: get the *waitpela* to Kaminabit. "You are crocodile men," I said when we made landfall, feeling guilty for their ordeal. They nodded and said nothing.

Nadya and I join Fraser and Tolly for breakfast. I go via the bush where I left my paddling shirt last night. But for a sodden, swollen chest pocket, the shirt is now dry. I dig out the pulpy remains of my Em Nau crackers out of the pocket. A detour off the Sepik could be a good idea. We need some time to think over our next move.

|| On our map, Chambri Lakes appear as one vast lake, some twenty kilometres long and ten wide, on the south side of the Middle Sepik. The lakes are only four metres deep and are unnavigable in some places during the dry season. Maybe this is when the lake transforms into several lakes. Packing just an overnight bag, we head off with Fraser and Tolly, their canoe clattering along a winding channel that gradually widens until it joins a great expanse of island-studded water. British adventurer Christina Dodwell paddled here in the 1980s and reported how the Chambri waterways were choked with *Salvinia molesta*, a fast-growing aquatic fern native to Brazil thought to have escaped from local aquariums and ornamental ponds. The fern can double in size every eleven days to form a thick carpet that smothers the water. Old clumps act as anchorage for grasses and reeds, creating floating islands that cannot be crossed. The effect on local communities was devastating. No longer able to get about readily or catch enough fish to trade with the inland tribes for sago, many Chambri were forced to leave their homes and head for the coast in search of work.

Fraser swings the canoe to left and right to avoid reed islands, but much of the lake appears free of Salvinia. A light breeze ruffles the reeds, and I think of mops of unruly hair on the head of a submerged green giant. Stunted trees sprout from the larger islands, their short branches making ideal roosts for rainbow bee-eaters. Out they dart, unperturbed by the noise of our outboard motor, snatching insects off the reed tops. Their beaks resemble curved knives, but they do not use them to skewer their prey. Instead, they return to their branch holding the doomed insect. When it wriggles, they bash it on the branch before swallowing it. Creatures of kaleidoscopic radiance, their black beaks and matching masks seem to mark them as aerial assassins. Terns, surprisingly, are their company, and white-throated cormorants, two species I associate with the coast. As the crow—or tern—flies, we are about 150 kilometres from the sea, but as the Sepik flows, we are much further.

Our first stop is Aibom, an Iatmul village known for producing earthenware pots. For ten minutes, we gaze at a woman sitting cross-legged under her house, patiently smoothing the clay sides of a portable stove. This object resembles an oversized eggcup but with a semi-circle cut out of one side. On the inside are three knobs that will support a small frying pan. Fishermen on a daylong excursion can put the stove in the canoe and cook sago or fish for lunch or burn grass to keep away mosquitoes. The stoves sell for K50 (Can$20) in Wewak, the woman tells us. As the *natnats* are plentiful under her house, we don't stick around. How can the woman concentrate with them milling around her head? We climb back in the canoe and head further south.

At our next stop, we come across an oddity. The only whites we have met since arriving in Papua a month ago are a pilot and his wife on Yuo Island and an old Kiwi pastor on Kairiru Island. When we pull in at Chambri village, we shake hands with an anthropologist and artist from Paris. Nicolas Garnier has been visiting this part of the Sepik for years, and his fascination for Chambri culture comes across strongly. He accompanies us to the *haus tambaran*. Most carvings we have seen along the Middle Sepik have represented ancestors, river gods, or crocodile men, but here there are cross-faunal liaisons: a man with a growling pig's head, another with a crocodile's tail. Do these mutant offspring belong to legend? Vincent in Kanganaman told of a woman who married a crocodile and gave birth to eagles. Or are these images emblematic of the tribe's close relationship with its surroundings?

Nicolas tells us the carvings are, in fact, totemic. The tribespeople *are* the creatures—especially the pig, crocodile, and eagle, but also the flying fox and rat. Totemism is important, he says, when it comes to delivering and understanding speeches in the *haus*. Rather than say things directly, speakers prefer to use metaphors. Thus, if a speaker tells a story about a pig—the pig running away, evading capture for a while, finally getting caught—then it is for the Pig Clan to consider the inferences. And it is just as important to understand what goes unsaid. Men sit in order of seniority. Junior clansmen are not expected to speak but must watch the Elders carefully during a debate. The Elders may say nothing and express their approval or disapproval only through the way they chew their betel nut: fast and agitated or slow and ruminative.

These insights point to sophistication I hadn't appreciated before. Since beginning our voyage on the Sepik, I have regarded village life as primitive, and it is technologically. Nicolas Garnier is not the first anthropologist to recognize a complexity in social interactions that might escape detection at first glance. Renowned American anthropologist Margaret Mead spent time here in the 1930s, researching interactions between men and women. She noticed that the women of the Tchambuli tribe (as she referred to the Chambri), unlike those of other tribes, had greater status. Despite a patrilineal system of land ownership and a custom of bride purchase, women provided for everyday needs and controlled the purse strings of the household. They did the fishing and bartered surplus fish for sago with inland tribes. They tended the gardens and made mosquito bags (plaited sago-shoot bed nets) to trade. On our journey so far, we have not encountered any "big women" with power and responsibility, with the possible exception of Mathilda in Korogo. Women generally play second fiddle to their men.

While Mead was training her lens on the Chambri, her husband, British anthropologist Gregory Bateson, was studying the neighbouring Iatmul tribe. He documented the practice of *naven*, a bizarre ritual involving cross-dressing, usually performed by the *wau* (uncle) to celebrate the first achievements of his *laua* (sister's child). Typically, the *wau* dressed up in filthy women's clothes that made him resemble a decrepit widow, dangled the remains of an old sago pancake from his nose, and limped around the village. On finding the *laua*, he would rub his buttocks on the child's leg before presenting him or her with a chicken. At times, an *iau* (aunt) or *tshaishi* (elder brother's wife) would practise *naven*. Wishing to honour a boy returning from a successful fishing expedition, for example, the woman dressed up as a man and chased him with a stick. He might seek refuge in the *haus tambaran*, but under these circumstances the woman had license to enter and beat him.

We check into a guest house run by an amiable, articulate man called Robert, and Nadya asks him about the role of women in Chambri today. Women still barter fish for sago, he says, but they also go to Maprik or Wewak to sell their catch—though the trip is hardly worth it. A motor-canoe to Pagwi costs K40, a bus to Maprik K15, and another to Wewak K15 (K5 extra for transporting the fish). At the market, a woman then has to pay K5 for her stall and pay again for somewhere to sleep. She may make K200 from sales, but, having bought salt, cooking oil, and medicine, and paid K55 or K70 to return, there is little cash left.

"Do women take the lead in Chambri, Robert?" Nadya asks.

He smiles. "Men and women here...have their different role to play."

Whether he means neither sex dominates or men enjoy privilege as they do in other Sepik villages is unclear.

In the afternoon, we walk beside the lake, pausing in front of one hut to watch a determined band of men heave heavy logs onto forked uprights to form the floor of a new hut. We stop at another to gaze at what at first seems like a small bear testing the bars of its wooden cage. The size of a large domestic cat, the spotted cuscus has blotchy brown and white fur, a face like a weasel's, and a prehensile tail. It is a difficult creature to see in the wild as it is nocturnal and lives in the treetops. Nadya and I beheld a relative in the jungle near Manokwari at the western end of Indonesian New Guinea in February. Our guide led us to the marsupial's favoured tree at midnight and spent twenty minutes making comical squelching sounds by sucking on the webbing between his index finger and thumb. We looked up into the tree expectantly. Two hours and five trees later—one with lianas hanging down aplenty—he told us to switch our flashlights on. Walking down one liana was a bewildered beast with pointed ears and a white belly. Finding three humans rather than an attractive mate sitting at the base of its tree, it realized its mistake, awkwardly about-turned, and headed back up to its nest. Common brushtail possum, we learned later. Unlike this possum, the spotted cuscus seems to have no ears and reminds me with its rounded features of a sloth. I had expected to find monkeys in the trees of New Guinea, but for some reason there are none.

Before we leave in the morning, Nicolas asks us if we have any medicine for diarrhea (a disadvantage to being a lingering anthropologist?), and we give him some Imodium capsules. We are back in Kaminabit by mid-afternoon.

It is time to say *lukim yu* to our crocodile men. Fittingly, the farewell dinner at Cyril's guest house is crocodile, and we take pictures of each other gnawing the fire-blackened steaks, which are gristly but not unappetizing. Nadya and I are sad to see our boatmen depart. Fraser and Tolly have made good, dependable, patient companions. We settle up, tipping them as generously as we can. Tolly confides to Nadya that they appreciated the gifts of betel nut en route. He also compliments her on her Tok Pisin. We haven't been speaking much since rejoining the river at Pagwi as most residents of the Middle Sepik know English, but Nadya has always had a good ear for foreign languages and understands more than she can say. Tolly waves goodbye with both arms.

"I could paddle to the sea with those guys," Nadya says as we watch their canoe yammering upriver in the fading light. "It felt like we weren't just their clients."

"I had my doubts about Fraser at the start."

"He was just quiet. Did you realize the drums we listened to in Yentchen were for your birthday?"

"What?"

"I told Tolly. He arranged it."

I look upriver again. What a splendid gift.

|| "So, Cyril, how is the Sepik east of here?" I ask the following morning. Breakfast is banana fritters and tea.

"It's quiet."

"Quiet?"

I would have thought that the further downstream you travel on a big river, the deeper and more navigable it becomes. Surely, the nearer the estuary you get, the larger the communities, the busier the boat traffic, and the greater the trade with coastal ports. But our map shows this is not the case. There are two villages, Timbunke and Tambanum, on the hundred-kilometre stretch from Kaminabit to Angoram and then just one, Marienberg, on the remaining fifty kilometres to the estuary. The busy part of the river is the section we just passed through, and it is busy because the paved road from Pagwi to Wewak allows villagers to take their produce to market and return with supplies. It means tourists can visit Korogo, Yentchen, Kanganaman, Palambei, and possibly Chambri, the cultural and artistic hub of the Sepik, and photograph crocodile men, witness skin-cutting ceremonies, and buy wood carvings. If we hire a motor-canoe to go east, it will be expensive, Cyril cautions. Gas in Pagwi is K20 a gallon. In Kaminabit, it is K30.

I ask him if he knows of anyone who could sell us two canoes, preferably adult ones that are not doubling as sieves, but he shakes his head. There are fewer dugouts on this stretch of the Sepik as it is mostly swampland. Not as many trees of the right size like in the Upper Sepik.

"Is there much to see between here and Angoram?" Nadya asks.

"No. It is more of same."

"How about after Angoram?"

"I have never been that far, but people say it is rough and dangerous. There are *raskols* and drunk men."

God, not *raskols* again.

"What can you tell us about Blackwater Lakes?" my wife asks, poring over the map.

I see she is running her finger along the Karawari, a tributary that joins the Sepik a little east of Kaminabit. The Karawari has a tributary of its own, the Korosameri, and this passes close to a pair of lakes.

"They are more interesting. Gongat tribe lives there. They worship gods with long nose like mosquito!"

"Is it possible to paddle there?"

"Yes, by shortcut through swampland. If you want, we can go together."

Nadya and I look at each other. Is our voyage destined, then, to end at a lake feeding the great river? With my heart set on paddling all the way to the Bismarck Sea, I am not happy with this, but, as

Nadya reminds me later, I should not be "absolutist." We did not begin our voyage at the source of the Sepik near Telefomin, and we have already skipped a stretch in the middle. We need not finish our journey at the sea.

10 NAUDUMBA

The Sepik catchment area encompasses some 78,000 km², and nowadays more than 400,000 people—more than 70,000 in the floodplain alone...During the rainy season, the river may swell in places to a width of 30–70 km for a period of five months. The depth of the lower reaches of the river may extend to 35 m, but sandbars quickly form in the shallower middle and upper reaches, ensnaring drifting trees and branches that can swamp or shatter canoes. Furthermore, thunderstorms can churn surprisingly high and erratic waves. Some stretches of the river flow between sun-baked mud banks that can rise several metres above the normal waterline, but other stretches spread into impenetrable marshes.

—ERIC K. SILVERMAN, "The Sepik River, Papua New Guinea: Nourishing Tradition and Modern Catastrophe"

"Welcome to *natnat* canal!"

Cyril kills the engine and steers the canoe toward a narrow gap in the riverbank. A horrified egret looks up, abandons its hunt for frogs among the cane stalks, and beats a hasty retreat, crying *ar-ar-ar*. We all duck our heads as the boat glides under a low branch and buries its nose in the tangle of hydrophytes, grasses, and river debris clogging the canal beyond. The sun disappears, and the temperature dips. Trees surround us suddenly, trunks submerged in water. Flies buzz around our heads. Cyril tips the outboard engine forward so the propeller is clear of the water, and Nick stands up in the bow. We have entered the swamps.

Nadya and I take the cue and pick up our paddles. I am pleased. For once, I can stand and paddle in a dugout without fear of losing balance and going for an involuntary swim. *Naudumba*—meaning "Sago Cluster," sago being Cyril's clan totem—is seven metres long, and her hull is twice the width of the canoes we used on the Upper Sepik. It has been made from one gigantic tree, likely kwila, and is roomy enough to accommodate two spoon-backed wicker chairs with armrests from the guest house. Sitting on them makes us feel a bit like patrol officers from the colonial era, but we have made it clear to our captain that we have no interest in being idle passengers over the next three or four days.

Once a driver for the fancy Karawari Lodge (US$812 a night for a single), then a guide with Trans-Niugini Tours aboard the river cruiser *Sepik Spirit* (US$3,680 for a single berth for four days), Cyril Tara has been acquainting high-end tourists with the Sepik and its waterways for three decades. Hiring him and his canoe, we understood last night, would be costly: K150 a day, plus gas. But this wasn't the tourist season, we countered. No one else was staying at his guest house. Did he have, perhaps, a *seken prais*? Laughing, he admitted that business would be slow until August. K75 a day would suffice. He seemed to understand, too, our desire to travel quietly and slowly, and I was jubilant to learn he had an old copy of Pratt and Beehler's *Birds of New Guinea* we could take along on our trip. Up front is Nick Tumas, wood carver, crocodile hunter, Seventh-Day Adventist, and Cyril's long-time friend. Both near fifty, these two are the oldest escorts we have hired.

After twenty minutes of weaving through trees, we break out into the sunshine once again and enter a floating meadow of waist-high reeds with spiky leaves. Water weeds cover the canal. Paddle through this, and we'll get snarled up for sure. Nick does not hesitate. His strokes are deliberate and powerful, and Nadya and I attempt to harmonize ours with his. It's slow-going, but I can appreciate the design of the bow on these dugouts now. If pointed like a Canadian Prospector, the bow would leave the foliage standing upright to brush against the paddlers. The Papuan shovel-nose bends the plants over so they are angled away from the canoe as it passes.

Dig and pull, dig and pull. The sweat begins to pour. Our sluggish pace delights the mosquitoes. Dig, pull, slap. Dig, pull, slap. I keep an eye out for ridged backs and narrow eyes. *Pukpuk* are supposed to hang out in the swamps during the rainy season, aren't they?

"Garter snake bird!"

"What?"

"There!" yells Cyril, pointing up. "In the tree."

An isolated dead tree pokes out of the meadow to our left, its branches resembling antlers. A black bird with a kinked neck, a beak like a dagger, and a white stripe decorating its face observes us unperturbed from the uppermost "horn." Like an egret, but smaller than the eastern great and more sinister looking. I would like to pull out the binoculars and bird book, but this is no time for contemplating the beauty of nature.

"I didn't know PNG had garter snakes," I say to Nadya.

"Maybe the bird eats them."

Dig, pull, slap. Cyril makes noisy *kark, kark* sounds—an attempt to send the bird packing—but it doesn't budge and seems to eye him with disdain.

We burst through another fringe of trees and join the Karawari River. Cyril drops the prop and swiftly fires up the outboard. Upstream we shoot, the rush of air blasting away the mozzies. I sit back in the wicker chair and rub saliva on the welts rising on my ankles and wrists. Thoughts of malaria drift across my mind. The atovaquone-proguanil combo we are taking daily had better be working its magic. A Swedish anthropologist who lived in the swamps of East Sepik Province in the 1980s contracted malaria five times and dengue fever twice.

We stop briefly at a flooded village called Mameri and then join the Korosameri (pronounced "Cross Mary") to Blackwater Lakes. Like Chambri, these are studded with floating islands. Does Cyril know why they are called black?

"Because of the mountains?" he speculates vaguely when I ask.

"Perhaps because the water is not moving?" Nadya suggests. "The Sepik is brown because it is constantly eating its banks."

Our destination is Govermas, a tiny village at the southern end of the largest lake. Cyril's friend Dominique Smari, a local guide, shows us around. He is a wiry, blithe man in his late thirties with two wives and thirteen kids. We watch two women stitch sago leaves to a wooden frame to make a roof for a new house (good for five to ten years, says Dominique) and three men turn an erima trunk into a canoe, a job that will take them three weeks to do from start to finish.

"He must chop very properly," Dominique remarks. One of the three men is straddling the trunk and swinging his axe exuberantly between his legs. "Or he cut something else off."

In addition to pumpkin and taro plants, betel nut and papaya trees, the village has lipstick trees and gaharu. Pinch a prickly pod of the lipstick tree and out spurts red paint that is good for decorating faces before a *sing-sing*. Dominique squirts some over Nadya's fingers, and she smears it on her lips and my nose. Gaharu we have not heard of, so Dominique brings a cross-section of the trunk to show us. The wood is orange and as dense and heavy as mahogany, the bark deeply furrowed. There are three sorts of gaharu, he says—queen, king, and *pukpuk*—and a kilogram sells for K600 at market. How is it used? He is not sure, but it is rare and much sought after for its aroma. It should, in fact, fetch K3,000 a kilo, he insists. Do we happen to know any international buyers? We shake our heads, having no idea what the wood is, but Nadya takes a photo and promises to make enquiries. Gaharu, we would later learn, is eaglewood or agarwood, the diseased and resinous heartwood of lign-aloes. From it comes essential oil used in perfumes and incense prized for centuries by Muslims, Hindus, and Buddhists. Agarwood is one of the most commercially valuable plant products in the world, a litre of the oil selling for as much as Can$70,000.

The people of Govermas are fond of pets. A month-old piglet Dominique calls Mateo follows him about. When he stops, he has to kick it away; otherwise, it suckles his toes ("He thinks I am his mother," he explains). Perched outside one hut are two white-bellied sea eagles, and, sitting in the window of another, a Blyth's hornbill, their wings clipped. Seeing them close up, we get a better sense of the sheer size of these birds. The eagles, Pratt and Beehler inform us, are between

White-bellied sea eagles with clipped wings.

69 and 79 centimetres tall and have 178 to 218-centimetre wingspans—roughly the dimensions of the American bald eagle.

New Guinea's only species of hornbill is even larger, standing between 76 and 91 centimetres. We gaze up at the solitary male for some minutes as he sits silently on his perch returning our gaze. With rufous neck, blue liner around his red eye, and horn-shaped beak, a Blyth's hornbill is like no other bird in the tropical forest. Sadly, the sea eagles and hornbill are captives for life, utterly dependent on the villagers for food. I hope that if we get to see any of PNG's regal canopy dancers—the Raggiana bird of paradise or its plumed clan—it is not under such circumstances.

"Do birds of paradise come around here?" I ask Dominique.

"Not to village," he replies. "Sometimes you can see at top of hill behind village."

As the heat of the afternoon is thick, and he knows of a waterfall where we might bathe, off we go. It is a short walk up a steep and increasingly overgrown trail that ends in a grassy clearing so hemmed in with trees that we get no view of the lakes. The clearing is home to the first bird we saw on arriving in New Guinea: a hooded butcher-bird, a bird very like an English magpie and just as raucous.

I walk around the clearing and peer into the wall of foliage enclosing it, wondering once again what it conceals. When I was growing up in England, my father taught my brother and me that a single tree or hedge could house a community. The most obvious residents are the birds, arriving and departing, but we should also look closely at the leaves—especially the undersides where insects hide—and into the crevices of the bark. Our primary interest was in butterfly and moth caterpillars. Look out for telltale semicircular bitemarks in the leaves and for their droppings, he'd say. I do this now at the edge of the clearing, lifting branches. It does not take long to find something: a plump green sausage the length and thickness of my middle finger, yellow stripes and blue spots decorating its sides and a horn arching from its rear like a tail. I have seen its kind before in England and Canada. Distant relative of the lime hawk-moth or tomato hornworm: similar size, similar horn, but different markings. The caterpillar sits asleep on the spine of the leaf it has clipped almost to a stub. I wonder what the moth will look like. When we were kids, Dad had us raise such caterpillars in jars so we would better understand a moth or butterfly's lifecycle and make the links between a leaf-gobbling sausage and its airborne, nectar-sipping counterpart.

There is no way to get to the waterfall through the tangle of trees and bushes, so we head back to Govermas. I hear the three canoe builders hacking away at the tree trunk as we approach and think about our continuing voyage on the Sepik and its waterways. It won't do to end it in the swamps or on an adjoining lake. Our journey would feel incomplete. I wish to return to the Sepik, merge again with its flow, and paddle to the sea. Cyril says the Lower Sepik is quiet, but he probably means that few tourists visit. Tourists don't visit the Upper Sepik either, and that added to its appeal. If Nadya doesn't want to paddle further east, maybe I can talk to the village big man when we return to Kaminabit, ask if he knows of a river-worthy canoe I could buy. Nadya could go with Cyril in his motor-canoe back to Pagwi and take the road to Wewak. We could meet there in a week or two's time.

We bathe in a creek close to the village and then join Dominique's family for a dinner of tilapia, tulip, coconut rice, and pumpkin. Linma, Dominique's oldest daughter, is a crocodile lady, the first we've encountered. She had her back carved last year, an opportunity granted to women as well as men in this tribe. Like the crocodile men we have met, she is not shy about showing us her decorated skin. Nadya and I gulp as she turns around and rolls up her shirt: there are at least a hundred ridges on her back, some protruding almost as far as nipples. She is a skinny, slight girl of about 5'4" who must have a high tolerance for pain. Partly in English, partly in Tok Pisin, she tells us about her initiation.

After a week spent coated in mud and sequestered in the *haus meri* (no men permitted to enter), she emerged the evening before the cutting ceremony and rubbed her back against a banana tree to make the skin supple. A *sing-sing* that lasted through the night kept her awake. She arose at five the next morning with the other novitiates and washed herself, and then had her skin cut. This lasted forty minutes. After the ceremony, women rubbed oil in the bleeding wounds and then mud, and Linma sat by a fire while the cuts dried. Over the following two weeks, the women fed her sago jelly and tulip and applied more oil and mud to her wounds until the skin became tight. Then they rubbed ashes from the fire into her skin to create welts. She cried as they did this, and her family had to hold her down so she didn't run away.

"Why did you go through this, Linma?" I ask. I expect her to say her family desired it. Her father, aunts, and uncles had paid K1,200 for the ceremony.

"*I laikim,*" she replies simply. I wanted it.

"If she don't have, she will not learn how to be a woman," her proud father adds. "She will fail to do her duty like look well after her kids."

Crocodile skin (left). Linma, Dominique's crocodile daughter, with Nadya (right).

Depending on the bride price, some or all of the money will return to Linma's family when she gets married.

|| "A white woman can't travel safely alone in this country!" Nadya replies. "You know that."

We are lying side by side under our mosquito net in a hut next to Dominique's. It is dawn, and the sun has found us, arrowing in through the sago slats of the wall. I find it remarkable how quickly the days begin and end in this country. The sun is suddenly bearing down each morning when we wake, and we are soon wiping our brows. In the afternoon, just as abruptly, it is an orange ball dipping behind the forest canopy, and we must dig in our bags for the headlamps. I have just made the mistake of suggesting that my wife and I part company for a while.

“What’s with making it to the coast anyway?” Nadya continues. “Cyril already told us there’s nothing to see between Kaminabit and Angoram. Beyond that, it’s mangrove swamps. Is this some kind of macho thing? Are you after bragging rights?”

“Our friends back home won’t care if we canoed the length of the Sepik or not, but I do want to see our voyage through...see it to its natural conclusion.”

I have this image in my head of us bursting from the jungle one fine morning on a makeshift raft and getting pounded by big waves, terns and cormorants our company, the sweet taste of salt water on our lips. If I am honest, I am probably guilty of trying to emulate the colonial explorers of the last century, aiming to achieve something bold and heroic like Ivan Champion or Jack Hides. I know this is a ridiculous ambition.

“You know, you might try asking me,” Nadya says tearfully. “The way you just state what you want to do, you sound like a dictator! We are in this together.”

We lie in silence. This is where I should reach for her hand and say sorry. Without my tenacious wife, I couldn’t have undertaken this venture. In a male-dominated, unpredictable, and dangerous country, she has been steadfast. At every village, she has taken on the role of an ambassador, chatting to adults and children, cheerily asking questions, making them feel at ease. I have never been sociable in that kind of endearing way. And she never complains about getting mucky or bathing in a muddy river, about the unrelenting heat, or the incessant mosquitoes. Instead of apologizing, I lie there quietly, peeved.

After breakfast, we paddle for two hours across the lakes, threading our way through a labyrinth of bushy islands and marooned trees, our destination a tiny hilltop village called Kaningara. The first thing we see is the corroded tin roof of a Catholic mission, dazzling under the morning sun. Polish Catholics built it in the 1970s, Cyril tells us, but have long since departed. Beaching the canoe, we climb a steep dirt path.

The mission is a cross-cultural hybrid with syncretic Christian and local iconography. The pillars supporting the roof are like those we have admired in spirit houses: carved with images of scowling tribal warriors, grinning, white-faced ancestors, and sinuous waves representing the river. An altar and lectern, both with legs fashioned similarly (one with a crocodile climbing up it), stand at one end of the church. Pictures of the risen Christ and Pope John Paul II are on the wall behind. To the right, a wooden statue of Christ on the cross shows the messiah's stricken body, but its angular face is that of a tribal warrior. A second statue of a winged, gowned angel is endowed similarly: frizzy hair, beard, Papuan facial features, muscular hands. A statuette of the Virgin Mary stands next to a *kundu* drum. Bench pews radiate from the altar. Without walls on three of its four sides, the church is full of light. I wonder if we are looking at an attempt by the vanished Polish fathers to bring the bible into the local context, or an effort since they left by the villagers to merge traditional and adopted faiths. Did this construction replace the traditional spirit house?

No. A few minutes later, we are with village Elders under a sago roof in a *haus tambaran*. Hanging from the rafters of the *haus* are cobwebby cane masks with jutting noses like insect proboscises.

"Why are their noses so long?" I feel like I am asking Bonny, the big man, a foolish question, given Cyril already mentioned this feature to us in Kaminabit. The Gongat tribe clearly worships the mosquito god.

Bonny regards me patiently from his seat at the centre. With his stooped back and whitened jowls, he seems ancient. Crocodile snout, not mosquito needle. Like the tribes of the Middle Sepik, the Gongat revere the *pukpuk*. Villagers dance at the skin-cutting ceremony, Bonny says, wearing grass skirts and the long-nosed cane masks (made of cane as wood is harder to come by in the lake region). He launches into a description of the now familiar initiation process. It seems that Kaningara is a special site for this, as a former prime minister was initiated here, as well as several tourists.

"And what did they hope to gain?" Nadya asks skeptically.

"Special power, wisdom," Bonny replies. "We are always ready to give them special power. We have extra power to give."

"And what happens if a novitiate dies during the ceremony?" she asks after a moment of reflection. "Is the body returned to the parents?"

No, no. They remove the head, peel off the skin, and decorate the skull. The body is buried under the floor so his spirit can enter the *haus*. The *haus* must pay the family a pig or money to compensate.

"It is very important the father fix all his problems before his son enter the *haus* to become crocodile," he adds. "If not, bad thing could happen to son."

I wonder what happens if a tourist expires while under the knife.

We give Bonny some kina for our visit, and he follows us squinting out into the sun. An Elder who exits behind him starts shouting. We turn and look at him in surprise. He is livid. Did we not give enough? It's not that, says Cyril, as the man walks in circles stamping the ground and yelling at the surrounding huts. He is angry because his clan members did not come to the *haus* to greet us.

"He feels ashamed."

We bid the Gongat big man farewell at his house. Painted on the door are the words "Lord Have Mercy."

After a lunch of sago pancakes, bananas, and *pawpaw*, we make our way back across Blackwater Lakes and join a river feeding into the Korosameri. Now running downstream and with the four of us paddling, we fly along, our destination the village of Mameri. We don't talk much, and as I paddle I find myself thinking about post-missionary Papua. While Christian fathers must have encouraged tribes to renounce their gods and follow Jesus, contemporary Papua exhibits an easy coexistence between the introduced religion and local beliefs. But there must be conflict too—times when beliefs clash—for example, regarding life after death and the destiny of the soul. If a corpse gets a Christian burial, the soul goes to heaven, a crocodile burial and the spirit sacralizes the *haus tambaran*. I recall our visit to the *haus tambaran* in Yentchen and Dennis's remark about the gods of the river: "We respect our god, but they are god with small 'g.'" Does Jesus reign supreme at times of doubt? There must be occasions where villagers follow the teachings of the bible and others where they turn to Indigenous practices. Now that the missionaries have gone home, I wonder if Papua has seen a resurgence in recent years of its ancient faith systems. In Kaningara, indeed the entire Middle Sepik region, induction into crocodilehood is a serious business, and graduates wear their "scales" with pride. Tourists come from far to witness the initiation ceremony, and, here in Kaningara, a few participate. The tradition is clearly empowering for the tribe, as Bonny indicated, helping it to maintain its identity. Nadya and I would probably need to spend a year here to determine how two quite different faiths cohabit, and how villagers resolve contradictions.

|| May 4, 2018: Mameri
How to go to the toilet:

1. Climb down ladder. Step onto overturned canoe. Walk along canoe, minding snoozing white duck with red wattles on face.
2. Step down from canoe into thigh-deep muddy water coated with film of gasoline.
3. Holding onto side of parked canoe containing 3 laulau and dead turtle covered in flies, walk under James's hut.
4. Let go of canoe, and walk from stilt leg to stilt leg, giving leaky drum of gasoline wide berth.
5. Now head for Vera's hut next door. She will point to lone shack twenty metres away.
6. Climb rickety steps of shack. Sweep aside tarp curtain and behold section of overturned canoe with hole in it.
7. Go about your business. Do not think about your return, wading through waters that you have just made muddier.

We spend the final night of our voyage into the Sepik swamps with James Mambu, another of Cyril's pals, a portly, affable man in his late thirties who makes a living as a *mossai* (cinnamon) trader. I sit with Cyril and Nadya in his spacious house, peering through a rent in the limbom flooring at the mucky water below. Forty minutes it took to go to the toilet this morning. I look over at our host, sitting cross-legged on the other side fishing for breakfast. His line trails through another slash in the floor. He jerks and pulls up a thrashing catfish. I wonder if the fish on the end is one of the ones I noticed earlier. Hearing splashes while I was on the throne, I turned to see writhing gray backs and flashing tails in the water below the latrine.

"Why does he live here?" I ask Cyril as James takes a knife to his catch. He has told us that the Korosameri floods Mameri six months of the year. "I mean, he has a garden downstream that doesn't flood, right?"

"Yes, but it is safer for him to stay here. It is important community stay together. If he live alone at his garden, bad spirit may come. Or *raskol*. He can also keep *mossai* here."

Piled against one wall are sacks of cinnamon awaiting transport to buyers in Indonesia. James buys the spice from nearby villages at K5 a kilo, he has told us, and sells it in Jayapura for K15.

"And in July and August, I bring visitor like you to stay and James make some money." We have just spent a night in one of his four guest rooms.

We watch as the gutted fish goes on the fire. James has dry firewood stacked on trays suspended beneath his house. I asked him last night while we were having tea where he gets his drinking water from, suspecting he scoops it up in a bucket from below. "From the sky," he insisted without elaborating. I looked outside for a rainwater tank but couldn't see one.

I sense a dark shape passing under us: a midget canoe containing a crooked figure. I hear knocking on the stilt legs. Neither James nor Cyril reacts. As she is paralyzed on one side of her body, James's sister uses a pole rather than a paddle to propel herself. Vera is a short woman, barely reaching Nadya's shoulder, with a boyish face and a broad smile. She rarely sees the likes of us, judging from the way she was staring at Nadya's hair and touching our skin last night at dinner.

"Kokoriam!" she calls out, greeting us in her tribal language before we see her head appear at the top of the ladder. She does not speak English or Tok Pisin.

Giggling mischievously, Vera limps over to her brother with some mysterious objects tucked under her withered right arm, which rests permanently against her stomach, the hand balled into a fist. James calls us over. One of the items is rattling like chainmail.

"Vera has some things she wants to give you."

She lays them on the table and stands back, grinning sheepishly. The first, made of sugar cane leaves woven together, resembles a fan but has fifteen-centimetre tassels. I pick it up and try wafting my face. Vera shakes her head, takes it from me, and waves it around her good leg.

"*Yimbunga*," she says. Not a fan. Mosquito swatter.

The item that rattles is a *bilum*, made not of natural fibres as is customary but of Job's tears (adlay millet seeds). Hundreds of them, sewn into hexagons. I look closely. The centimetre-long seeds look like apple pips, some chestnut in colour, others ochre. A pinhole goes through each so it can be strung together with the others. Even the long shoulder strap is made of Job's tears threaded on a string. I think of tiny train carriages. The bag is the work of an artisan with extraordinary dexterity and patience.

"Who made this?"

"Vera. She made all these things," James replies. "I sell them at the market."

Nadya and I look at him incredulously and then at Vera. She giggles.

The third gift is a necklace of Job's tears. At the end is a hollow, white crocodile tooth, the tip brown with decay. Vera picks the necklace up and points at me. She picks up the *bilum* and points at Nadya. In turn, we give her a hug, and she squeals with delight. I have not hugged a Papua New Guinean before. I ask her brother what we can give in return, knowing that we really have no way of reciprocating. Would it be insulting to offer her some money? No, he says. She would like that. She takes the kina and smiles.

|| Down the Korosameri we slide, Nick standing up front with a tall paddle, Nadya standing or sitting behind him with the short, me standing behind her with the other tall paddle, and Cyril sitting idle at the stern. It's like being back on the Upper Sepik, the current brisk when we catch it but *Naudumba* sluggish when we round a bend too close to the bank or sweep too wide in an arc. This long canoe could do with a rudder.

"Do you miss being aboard the *Sepik Spirit*?" I ask Cyril, remembering the fancy tourist boat he worked on.

"No. *Sepik Spirit* was very luxury, but Trans-Niugini did not pay me well," he replies. "They still call me sometime, and I do short contract."

Other tour companies call him too, he says, wanting him to come up with an itinerary for a river trip for a group of tourists and do a cost estimate. If they like what he proposes, they take him on as a local guide. Then he has to go to Wewak, meet the tourists off the plane, bring them to the Sepik. It is good money, but typically only lasts two or three days.

"Tourist always in rush. Never have much time. Sometime, they want to do everything in one day!"

"So how do you make a living when there are no tourists about?"

Three ways. He catches and smokes piranha, grows tobacco (a leaf sells for K1), and hunts *pukpuk*. Buyers come to Kaminabit once or twice a year for crocodile skins. The market for them might be as far away as Singapore.

Our pace has slackened again, and Nadya and I dig and pull with a little more vim. I hear Cyril chuckling behind me.

"Naddy is just sticking paddle in. No water is moving!"

I sigh. It's difficult to use the short paddle while standing. You have to deepen your stance and crouch over. Paddling while sitting in a basket chair is awkward too, as the armrests get in the way. This is the second time our guide has made such a remark. Nadya sits down, drops the paddle in the water, and gives it a shunt backwards.

"Well, I guess it's your turn then, Cyril."

The paddle floats down to the stern, and Cyril fishes it out. Parking his butt on the starboard gunnel, he starts digging the water feverishly. He probably wasn't expecting his clients to pitch in with the paddling, or, perhaps, in this macho culture, he wasn't expecting a woman to do so. His burst of effort lasts ten minutes. Chest heaving, he lays the paddle across the canoe in front of him and digs out his smokes. I grin and watch Nick. How effortless and graceful his strokes are by comparison. This man is capable of paddling for hours on end and seems never out of breath.

"Did I upset Naddy?" Cyril whispers.

"Yes," I reply, turning to him. "You hurt her feelings. And it's Nadya, not Naddy."

Lunch is at the confluence of the Korosameri and Karawari. James Mambu's garden is here, and we fall into the company of his brother and wife. While we hide from the sun under a palm awning and eat sago and papaya, Daniel, clearly a man in his prime, hacks out the innards of a tree, seemingly oblivious to the heat. The embryonic canoe is resting on a cradle unshielded from the sun, but he doesn't seem in the least bothered. He chops with his axe without pause, and sweat streams down his brow and chest. So chiselled is his body, if I saw him on the street back home, I'd wager he was a bodybuilder. His wife Susan is also athletic, although she has an anxious look on her face. She approaches Nadya tentatively. Her breasts hurt. Could Nadya inspect them? Does she have any medicine?

It is odd that the French anthropologist we met in Chambri is the only person to ask us for medicine since we arrived in the country. On our hikes into the interior of Indonesian Papua, villagers came to us with festering cuts on their hands and arms, toes that were inflamed. Keeping the wounds clean was evidently a challenge. Nadya dug out alcohol swabs, antiseptic cream, dressings, and painkillers. Go to the hospital, she advised, before it gets any worse. I expected similar entreaties on this side of the island, especially given that PNG is less developed and there are fewer hospitals or clinics. It is easy to imagine that Sepik tribesmen would drive axes into their feet while hollowing out tree trunks, women would run into trouble while giving birth at home, and snakes would bite kids who run around barefoot. And the population would surely fall prey to infectious tropical diseases like malaria, yaws, tuberculosis, gastroenteritis, typhoid, and hepatitis. However, we have only seen people who look fighting fit. Active, outdoor lives and simple diets of sago, fish, vegetables, and fruit must be responsible. I remember that Paul, the MAF pilot we met on Yuo, said that the unhealthiest Papuans live in towns. Post-war, urban Papua must now combat cardiovascular disease, diabetes, peptic ulcers, and cancer. A contributor to such illnesses would be the kind of food available, and I think of the *kai bars* in Vanimo and Wewak and their steel bins of deep-fried filets of fish and dough balls in batter, their sweating fries, jumbo sausages, and chilled sodas.

With cancer in mind, Nadya tells Susan to check her breasts for lumps. She spent the morning paddling her canoe, she tells us, so the problem may be muscular. Nadya says she also gets pain in her chest after a day of paddling. She suggests staying off the river for a while, and I get some Tylenol out of our medical kit. Women, we have heard, are more prone to ill health than men. They work harder, don't eat as well, and are less likely than men to go to the hospital when the need arises. And PNG has one the highest rates of domestic violence in the world. Three out of four women are raped or assaulted at some point in their lives. The closest hospital to this tributary of the Sepik—and one offering only basic health care—is in Wewak, a two-day paddle upriver followed by another day on the road. Patients who are seriously ill must fly to Port Moresby.

The scraps from our lunch go to Daniel's pet, a sea eagle with clipped wings hopping around our legs as a sparrow might under a campground picnic table back home. It saddens me to see it like this.

Our return to Kaminabit is by means of another reed- and debris-choked *natnat* corridor that sees us digging and hopping about like maniacs. We put our *yimbunga* to good use. The reeds fold back as *Naudumba*'s shovel nose ploughs through, Nick digging deep with his tall paddle. Nadya, reunited now with her short paddle, calls a halt after twenty frantic minutes so we can catch our breath. She snaps a picture of the sole witness to our exertions. Once again, a lone garter snake bird is looking down at us from a dead branch. Cyril squawks and flaps his arms, trying to scare it off. I stare at him, mystified. Not too fond of this fellow. A bad omen? When I ask him later, he looks at me quizzically.

"No, no. Snake bird is funny one. The one we don't want to see on river is palm cockatoo. We believe it is evil spirit."

As black as a raven and of similar size, the rare palm cockatoo has an erectile crest of black spikes and blood-red cheeks. The bill, one of the most powerful in the bird world, resembles a dinosaur claw. Nadya and I saw one or two in West Papua. Its screeches are as grating on the nerves as those of its snowy sibling, the sulphur-crested cockatoo.

It takes us forty-five minutes to emerge from the swamps. As before, Cyril drops the prop without delay. We lose our needling tormentors, the sudden rush of wind blowing them away and drying our cheeks. After a few minutes, we see huts ahead.

Naudumba nudges behind another motor-canoe, and Nick ties up. I look about for our waterlogged catamaran. Not where we left it. Climbing onto the riverbank, I walk upriver a bit. Sunk? Gobbled by the Sepik? There: the adult canoe, now separated from its partner. I slide down into the shallows and try and drag it out, but it weighs a ton and I can't get good footing in the mud. Each time I lift, the river tries to seize it. Sweating and gasping, I finally get the front third onto the bank. I run my hand down the inside of the hull and find a long crack where the clay plugs used to be. I pause for a moment and then let go. Down the mud ramp it slides, then it's gone. Destined for the river bottom or perhaps the Bismarck Sea. I look upriver and down, hand shielding my eyes from the sun. No sign of the baby canoe. Hopefully, it went to a little girl so she could go fishing.

11 TO THE SEA

When I first entered the jungle and let go of my margins of safety to become vulnerable to a place I didn't understand, it was terrifying. I had slowly learned, however, to live with that fear and uncertainty. Also, I realized that the physical journey was not the great accomplishment. The value of the trip lay in everyday encounters, and the destination gradually became a by-product of the journey. Again I reminded myself that it was my ability to understand the local people and adapt to their way of life that had allowed me to get this far.

—ERIC HANSEN, *Stranger in the Forest*

Mayflies. Thousands clouding over the river, ditching themselves in it, squirming, drowning. I reach down and scoop one up. Different from the brown fly with striped abdomen and veined wings common in Canada. This Papuan cousin is ghostly white, with globular, black eyes and a yellow thorax, the wings thin as tissue paper, the front pair edged in yellow. The two antenna-like tails wilt as the dying insect twitches in my hand. I flick it onto the half-submerged log I am sitting on, hoping to see it revive and fly away, but its wings stick to the wood and it clearly hasn't the energy to pry them off. I look again at the river and all these bright white dots thickening the air and think of confetti. Where are the fish? Why are the rainbow bee-eaters not feasting on such bounty? Where are the children? We've heard that kids here wade into the river, fish the flies out, and eat them. I wonder what has prompted the flies to emerge in such numbers today—

apart from the fact it is the first week of May. Maybe the rain last night.

It is late afternoon and sweltering. Good day to do laundry, and I have succeeded in getting through the pile beside me without giving our soap to the Sepik. I peel my shirt off the top of the pile and shake off the flies. It was blue when I bought it in Canada. It was blue-brown before I washed it today. It remains blue-brown. What did I expect? I look at the debris floating down the muddy river, then at my immersed legs. I can't see my toes. Can't even see my knees an inch below the surface. How blasé we are about clean water in Canada, sprinkling our lawns, washing our cars, filling our dishwashers, our laundry machines, our swimming pools, squandering gallons that are fit for drinking. Potable water: anytime, anywhere, at the twist of a faucet. I pick specs of dirt off my shirt and return it to the pile. Maybe, when it is dry, it won't stink quite as badly as it did.

A canoe approaches containing four women, including Nadya and Cyril's daughter Kalida. They are returning from a fishing trip in the swamps on the far side of the river. Two hours ago, they paddled over and vanished into the rushes. They are all grinning, so they must have had success. I see a heap of glistening silver bodies in the hull, most the size of my hand, but some bigger.

"Forty-five!" my wife cries jubilantly. "And I caught seven of them."

"Wow, how did you manage that?"

"With a bamboo stick and a fishing line and hook. The secret is knowing where the fish are. We paddled up little creeks to ponds, and the girls looked around for bubbles. A couple of places we stopped, there was nothing. Then we found a place where there were loads of fish."

"What did you use for bait?"

"Berries."

"Berries?" Guess piranha prefer those to mayflies.

"The girls have a special technique. They jerk with the wrist when they sense a fish is nibbling the berry."

"Aha. The *natnats* must have been happy to see you."

"Actually, not really. They were no worse than last night."

Getting back to Kaminabit has made me realize there were hardly any mosquitoes at the Blackwater villages. While eating dinner in Cyril's kitchen last night, despite having our shirt sleeves rolled down, collars turned up, and hats on, we were on the menu for a host of uninvited guests. With no light to see by except from our ailing headlamps, we proved easy prey. I asked Cyril why there were so many *natnats* in the Middle Sepik, aware it was probably a dumb tourist question. "Well, Tony," he would reply patiently, "as you know by now, it is swampy around here, and it is still the rainy season..."

"Well, Tony, there was once a sorcerer living in Palambei," he said, "who do many bad thing. He made some people fall sick, other people they got eaten by crocodile, and other ones fall in the river and drown. So the villagers decide to kill the sorcerer. They catch him, tie him with rope, and they burn him. But they cannot burn his stomach. So they tie it up and throw it in the river. Next day, a woman from the village went out fishing and saw it. 'What's that?' she says and paddles over and unties it. Out flew thousands of mosquitoes."

The sorcerer's revenge. Nadya asked Cyril if he minded living in a place where there are so many mosquitoes.

"*Natnats* are good!" he replied, surprised at her question. "They take bad blood away. I like him!"

After dinner, we asked Cyril if he would be willing to escort us downriver to Angoram, our casual enquiries along the riverbank about dugouts for sale having met with shaking heads. Nadya and I agree we have formed a pretty good relationship with Cyril that extends beyond the merely transactional. He is friendly, cheerful, and, we reckon, trustworthy. As a professional tour guide, he is used to satisfying the whims of *waitpela* and understands why we wish to paddle rather than motor down the Sepik. Like most Papua New Guinean men we have met, Cyril wanted to negotiate a good price.

"August, you know, is my golden month. Before that, I want to build a shower and repair the toilet and do many improvement to the guest house," he said, not committing himself.

The mayfly storm has abated. Kalida and her two pals slice open the piranha and dump the entrails in the river. I gather up my laundry and sniff it, wondering whether other women upriver are busy cleaning out fish.

In the evening, we strike a deal with our host. We will paddle with him to Angoram and pay the same daily tariff as we did for our excursion to Blackwater Lakes plus the fuel Cyril will need to motor back to Kaminabit. Nick will come along once again and so will Cyril's cousin Chris Tupma—for the sole reason he has a more powerful outboard engine. We accept this deal and pay Cyril a deposit. I dig out my final packet of Gudang Garam cigarettes and give them to him. His eyes widen.

"Why did you not give me this one before?"

"Because, Cyril, they are bad for your health," I say, clapping him on the back.

|| "These pancakes are awful. Who made them?" I holler through the kitchen door.

"The gecko made them!" Cyril hurls back. So there are geckos in PNG.

The new day is bright and promising. After breakfast, Nadya and I chuck our bags aboard "Sago Cluster" once again, and Nick and Chris heave Chris's 40 hp outboard onto the stern and screw it into place. Cyril marches up and down the riverbank, trying in frustration to get a signal on his phone. Before leaving, he wants to confirm that his friend from Israel is coming this summer. A villager using a cell phone to make a call or send a text is a rare sight in these parts. Reception is poor or nonexistent. The villagers who have cell phones only use them to listen to music or take photos. To make calls or send texts, they must get data, and that means a trip to town to buy K3, K5, or K10 coupons. Powering up is a further challenge as the only electricity comes from small solar panels. We only saw one cell phone on the Upper Sepik.

Edmund comes to see us off. I met this soft-spoken giant while buying soap in Kaminabit's only store yesterday. He claimed to be the policeman here, but I had my doubts. In his raggedy T-shirt, shorts, and flip-flops, he looked no different from anyone else: no uniform, no badge, no baton. We haven't met or even seen any police since arriving in the country, although there was a station in Wewak. Edmund told me Kaminabit was peaceful, but drunks could sometimes cause a rumpus.

"What do you do when that happens?" I asked. "Arrest the man and take him to town?"

"Oh no. With my friend, I take him into bush and beat him hard. After that, he sleep."

"What about sorcerers?"

"No sorcerer in this village. We kill all of them. Their heads are under *haus tambaran*."

We shove off mid-morning. I look over my shoulder as the huts recede. Our stay was pleasant; no one seemed surprised to see us. Like many villages of the Middle Sepik, Kaminabit must get visitors in the tourist season. Cyril's guest house and his kitchen are basic but better than most we've encountered. As he said, his latrine needs fixing. The unthinkable almost happened after breakfast as I hovered over the hole cut in the rotten bamboo floor. I heard a sharp snap under me, and suddenly my elbows were at floor level. Yelping, I heaved myself out of the hole I had enlarged. Another fifteen centimetres, and my feet would have been decorated. I remembered Nadya falling through the sieve-like floor of the guest hut in Waku on the Upper Sepik and then thought of *Slumdog Millionaire*, where the boy hero plunges into the ungodly pit below an outhouse in Mumbai and emerges tarred to the eyebrows.

Behind the latrine was an invisible bird whose call I recognized. It appeared to find my misadventures amusing. I thumb through Cyril's bird book. Kookaburra. So PNG, like Australia, is home to this chuckling kingfisher. I look up the "garter snake bird" we saw in the swamps but find no such bird listed in the index. It looked like a heron or egret, so I go to that section of the book. Not a heron or egret. With its snake-like neck, the bird is a cousin of the cormorant: an Australasian darter.

The pages of the book are dog-eared and warped from water damage. I assume Cyril got it from a tourist.

"I got it from our primary school many, many year ago," he says when I ask. "A woman from America donate it to the school long time before. Look inside front cover."

> *To the children of Kaminabit. Learn the names of your beautiful birds and protect them.*
>
> *NANCY HOPWOOD, USA, August 1951*

I suspect the children of Kaminabit already know the names of their birds, but in their own languages.

East of Kaminabit, the river seems sluggish. I recall the words of my Black brother from a Black mother in Green River: "In west Sepik, river is narrow and current is strong. You go fast," John Mariati had said. "In east Sepik, river is wide and water don't move. You paddle and sweat!" Maybe the river feels weighed down by the detritus of the rainy season, transported from its upper reaches. The current seems at times nonexistent, and *Naudumba* must plough through rafts of water hyacinth. In the past, like Salvinia, this invasive and attractive aquatic plant with its violet flowers and glossy leaves used to be a menace in the backwaters, choking canals and lakes and making fishing and transit difficult. Now there is less, Cyril says, but he is not sure why. I hoist a clump of it out of the river. The feathery brown roots collapse and wind themselves into a dripping wad that resembles bedraggled hair. This would certainly snarl up propellers.

It takes us three hours to reach Timbunke. An Irish priest called Father Michael Donovan lived in this village in the 1980s and early 1990s, "saving souls" and writing letters home, which he subsequently self-published. "The people here have a saying: a man can travel one hour after a meal of sago, but after a meal of sago and fish he can walk for a full day," he wrote on February 23, 1983. "My neighbour Philip Luki, who lives only twenty yards away from me killed thirty-one crocodiles yesterday and sold their skins to a European buyer," he observed on May 30, 1985. "Speaking about cows, one very respectable gentleman comes to Mass on Sundays with a cow's tail in his hand," he wrote on July 25, 1988. "He uses it to keep away the mosquitoes." And on February 25, 1989, "Last month we were returning from Wewak to Timbunke when we came across the unexpected," he reported phlegmatically. "We were held up by masked men and robbed of our personal belongings. We were about one hour out from Wewak when there was a tree across the road. Two men armed with an axe and bush knife surrounded the car. We ran off and gave them everything."

"How is the road to Wewak?" Nadya asks the only person we meet during our brief stop at Timbunke to stretch our legs and eat a lunch of smoked piranha and sago pancakes.

"Very bad," Matthew replies. "This place is not a good place to live."

He is a young man campaigning for change and intends to run for president of the Local Level Government (LLG) in the election in July. It's not just the road that's a problem, he tells us. Timbunke floods badly every year, and people lose their homes. And it has no market. The villagers must spend K100 in travel costs to get their vegetables to market in Maprik. Then there is the serving president. He is a greedy man, keeping funds for himself instead of using them to improve the lives of the people. In this country, most people are poor. Only corrupt politicians have money. These things are not acceptable. Something must be done.

This is the first time a Papuan has spoken to us about the political system, or given us a sense of a governance structure separate from the tribal model. We have been travelling in a kind of Sepik bubble.

"Is LLG politics at the village level?" I ask.

"No, there are wards below LLG. Each ward elects a councillor to serve in LLG, and this has about twenty councillors who are elected every five years."

"What's above the LLG?"

"Provincial government—here, East Sepik Province—then national."

"So how good are your chances of getting elected?" Nadya asks.

"Many people know me. The problem is you need lot of money if you want to be big man in politic! If you want people vote for you, you must pay them."

As we paddle away from Timbunke, Cyril tells us that tourists used to visit the village, but now few do. There is little for them to see. The mission fathers put a stop to crocodile initiations, not only in Timbunke but also in many other villages in the Middle Sepik, including Kaminabit. This is the reason Cyril couldn't enter the *haus tambaran* in Gongat: no scars. To get in, he had to pay a fee, a bushel of betel nuts.

Another casualty of rising waters is Tambanum, an hour's paddle from Timbunke and our final destination for the day. The rainy season here was so severe eight years ago that the houses in the upper half of the village were washed away or reduced to piles of sticks. During one ferocious storm, waves rolled through the village and the water turned dark. Once a village with 130 houses, Tambanum now has seventy-seven. The *haus tambaran* vanished. Suddenly destitute, many villagers had to pack up their remaining belongings and start over on firmer land. Tambanum is less a village now than a string of huts on either side of the Sepik. For some villagers, their downstream gardens have become their new homesteads.

We are in the company once again of the Iatmul tribe. Margaret Mead and Gregory Bateson lived in Tambanum for six months in 1938, conducting fieldwork and taking photographs. Mead described the villagers in her journal as "gay, irresponsible, vigorous people, always either laughing or screaming with rage." I think back to the Iatmul we met in Korogo and find "gay" and "vigorous" about right for Mathilda and Collis. There is no sign of the stilt-less house the two anthropologists built on the riverbank, with its uneven cement foundations plugged with river clay, and I wonder if it was a casualty of floods. If the house was all they had hoped it would be, it must have been quite a landmark. In a letter dated June 24, 1938, Mead wrote,

> *There must be room for people to gather without breaking or spoiling or pilfering anything. There must be a place in which to do medicine which has a wall dividing the audience from the operating theater; there must be blank surfaces on which children can put their papers to draw...there must be ways of dividing visitors into informants and mere looklooks...There must be small trade ready at any moment to buy a fish or a coconut brought by a daring three-year-old.*

After their time at Chambri, Mead and Bateson clearly had a sense of what to expect in their interactions with the Iatmul.

According to our guidebook, it is easy to find the only guest house in Tambanum. Look out for the hut with a big smiley face above the entrance. As we wander among the huts, I find myself searching for the banal yellow ideogram we are accustomed to in the West. How out of place that would be here. A sturdy-looking hut, larger than the others, comes into view. It is covered in wavy patterns representing the river. The character grinning at us from the gable is by no means generic. The face emerges from the zigzagging waves. The wide mouth with its rounded teeth is a slit window; the pupils of the eyes are two dark portholes. Untrimmed palm leaves serve as bushy eyebrows and a beard.

"Good spirit smiles on house and passerby," Rocky Cambai, the bushy bearded owner, declares proudly, leading us up the ladder to the entrance. His guest house, with its extra fortifying piles, survived the flood of 2010.

Perhaps contemplation of this disembodied head prompts Nadya to ask Cyril about the practice of headhunting. Some Westerners believe it still happens in PNG, she tells him.

"There is no headhunting now," he replies, laughing. "It ended in 1930s. Missionary priests told tribes they must stop fighting and taking head. They say it is not will of God. But some still fight about land right. Now land is registered. There is also marriage between different tribes so less fight."

"Have the villagers kept the skulls of their enemies?" Nadya asks.

We know some heads were buried under the columns of a *haus tambaran* to endow it with sacred power. The Karawari tribes of the eastern Sepik liked to put them in the mouths of the wooden crocodiles they carved. These they would consult before setting off on a hunt or going to war.

"No. Police confiscate skull." He remembers policemen touring the villages collecting skulls when he was a kid. "The power transfer to the police."

"After chopping off the heads, what did the warriors do with the bodies?" I ask, suspecting I know the answer.

"Eat him!" Cyril cries, baring his teeth.

The most notorious case of headhunting and cannibalism in New Guinea involving a Westerner concerned Michael Rockefeller (third son of Nelson Rockefeller) who, in 1961, was collecting tribal art in the southern Asmat region of West Papua. He vanished after his dugout canoe capsized offshore. According to his companion, a Dutch anthropologist called René Wassing who stayed with the canoe and survived, Michael tried to swim to land, a distance of some nineteen kilometres. He was never seen again and was presumed drowned. An investigation into his disappearance sponsored by the Rockefeller family revealed he had made it to shore only to be speared, decapitated, and eaten by Asmat warriors who sought heads to propitiate their gods, prove their sexual prowess, and take revenge. Subsequent investigative journalism supposes the killing and consuming of Rockefeller was a reprisal for a raid on an Asmat village three years earlier by Dutch officers and police that left five Asmat dead. The patrol's mission had been to put a stop to headhunting.

Traditionally the home of renowned wood carvers who inlay their masks with cowrie shells, Tambanum is supposed to be famous for its tribal art. Maybe we are here at the wrong time of year. There are no masks on display in the new *haus tambaran* when we visit late afternoon. No finely crafted *garamut* drums either. There are only two men sitting on a berth, looking at their laps and crunching betel nut. They nod when we greet them, and I shake hands with one. Neither seems inclined to chat, so Nadya and I don't ask about the art. This spirit house seems to have lost its spirit.

|| East of Tambanum, the Sepik looks more like a lake than a river. The far bank is distant, and the many water hyacinth blooms seem anchored. No trees lean over the water, spilling lianas and casting shadows. Only a ragged, broken line of *tiktik* canes fringes the river. The new day is sunless and still. Clouds resembling heaps of dirty laundry lean against one another. We'll likely get rain later. I realize what I see now will be my memory of this stretch of the Sepik: broad, bloated, lethargic, slaty, unremarkable. But how was it last month? How will it be next? It occurs to me that, this time next

year, the river may not even flow here. It may have found an alternative path to the sea. Angraman, a Middle Sepik village near Tambanum, used to be on the banks of the river, Cyril told us last night, but no longer is. Just like Tipas. What a profound difference that must make to villagers' lives. I think of the Saint John River back home in Fredericton. During the spring melt, it always floods, submerging the bankside walking trails and perhaps a stretch of the road; people living too close get water in their basements. The inconvenience generally lasts two or three weeks. The river never sweeps houses away or alters its course.

My shipmates are quiet this morning. Bowman Nick, dipping his paddle into the river soundlessly, sets the pace. Nadya follows his lead. Behind me, Chris steers in the stern, and Cyril, who must be through his Gudang Garams, sits beside him smoking local tobacco in a rolled-up newspaper.

For the first time, I feel at peace paddling standing up in a dugout canoe. My body has adapted to heaving a heavy Papuan paddle forward and back. Resisting the impulse to lean over and dig deep into the water, I find I can now paddle effectively without losing my balance. I have learned how important it is to switch sides frequently to avoid backache. I have also come to appreciate the damage a tropical sun, reflected off water, can have on fair skin—my cracked bottom lip, burnt ears, and peeling ankles bear testament to that. Nadya also seems more comfortable these days, better able to handle the relentless heat that suffocated her before. Her breathing is now deliberate and controlled and in harmony with her paddle strokes. Every half an hour, she puts her paddle down and—regardless of what everyone else is doing—takes a break, rolling her shoulders and drinking slowly from her water bottle.

Nick stops paddling and points upriver. Three tall masts like skeletal plants pierce the clouds. Telecommunication towers? No. One is nodding forward over the river with a long brown cylinder suspended beneath. We edge closer. Now we hear the churning of diesel engines, the echoey thump of wood on wood, and the bleeping sound of a reversing vehicle. I can see two barges moored to the riverbank, a black tugboat roped to one.

“Log Pond,” Cyril announces flatly.

We are back with Global, the timber company from Malaysia. The nearest barge, marked *Shun Chang*, is stacked high with logs and sits low in the water. The hull of the other, yet to be loaded by the cranes, rears up from the river. Chris angles *Naudumba* toward Kunduanum, the village adjacent, and I ask Cyril what he thinks of this foreign presence.

“They are stealing *our* land! They are destroying *our* forest!” he erupts. “What will next generation use to make canoe? What? They will have no kwila for make house. Only Malaysian man and our government get rich! Money not go to people of Sepik. There is no good benefit for community.”

I recall John Youpa, Global’s disgruntled payroll officer in Tipas, being just as bitter. When a timber company comes, it must pay royalties to the landowners for the right to extract resources, he told us. Global did this, but the royalties, once divided among the tribes, amounted to little. As for the government, it gets revenue in taxes from the company and, as a result, has a strong interest in maintaining a good relationship. It turns a blind eye to human rights violations and abuse of the environment. The foreign logging company soon gains a foothold in the country, and as years pass the tribes begin to feel like tenants. The company starts to behave like it is the landowner. John told how Global, through promising to build roads, schools, medical clinics, and water tanks, adopted a strategy used by missionary churches. The tribes recognize the benefits and come to regard them as essential for the development of their villages, but some of these benefits never materialize. Even if they do, at what cost?

Kunduanum is like any other village we have seen on the banks of the Sepik except that it borders a wasteland. Global employees living here have a two-minute commute to work from their thatch huts sheltered by coconut palms to a dirt wharf littered with betel nut husks, plastic bags, and beer cans. I ask Cyril if we can visit Log Pond. He sees no reason why not, given there is no perimeter fence or guard. Nadya is reluctant to go.

A path leads to a poorly built plank shelter that is probably the site office and a shed with a heap of empty Warrior Dark Rum bottles

Deforestation.

and flattened SP Lager Beer cans underneath. The sign in front says, "No selling alcohol, drinking alcohol, drunkard at Log Pond Area. Merry Christmas and Happy New Year." No one seems to be in either building. We continue to the edge of the work zone and watch towering yellow log loaders with mechanical hands seize logs in twos and threes and carry them over to the operating crane. Once the barge has been loaded, the tugboat tows it downriver to a freighter anchored offshore. Global started shipping logs from this spot five years ago, Cyril tells us. The timber leaves the country without being processed.

Engine exhaust and sawdust fill the air. We cover our mouths and noses and watch two Papuan labourers wearing ball caps and flip-flops attach thick steel cables to a log. They scuttle away as the crane takes up the slack, and the log lifts from the ground and swings in their direction.

"Let's get out of here," Nadya says.

We return to the canoe and paddle on, giving the barges a wide berth. For the first time on our voyage, we see gasoline on the surface of the river and wedges of foam resembling miniature icebergs.

“This water make children sick,” Cyril remarks miserably. “Fish people catch are thin ones, no good to eat.”

I recall watching a documentary about the damage caused by a Malaysian timber company operating near Vanimo in Sandaun Province. It described how the state had bullied customary landowners into signing agreements forfeiting their rights to the trees on their land, rights that were subsequently sold to Malaysian interests. A community health worker talked about the rise in cases of cholera and diarrhea in the area. Villagers had no choice but to drink from and wash in the river below the logging site, water contaminated with waste oil and diesel. The Malaysian workers and their families, by contrast, took from the water tanks they had built for themselves.

“Can’t the tribes do anything about this?” Nadya asks.

“If complain, company send policeman to get you!”

Nadya slaps a foam-berg with her paddle in disgust. It breaks into smaller pieces, but the filmy bubbles remain.

“I will organize people in Sepik area,” Cyril hisses. “There will be civil war!”

|| Foam-bergs sail down the river with us for the first twenty minutes of our two-hour paddle to Krinjambi, another village not on our map. Arriving there is like arriving in one of the Upper Sepik villages. Pandemonium. Bare children fly about in all directions, yelling. We make for a bamboo shelter as we did in Oum Number 1, and kids form a tight ring around us several deep, shoving each other and giggling. Behind them, their seniors leer at us. It is good to be in the shade. The clouds have shoved off, and the sun is blazing again.

“The children are so happy to see you!” exclaims Cyril, following close behind us. He shakes hands with some of the Elders and tells them our story. “Green River,” I hear, “*stopim* Pagwi” and “*kanu bagarap*.” Nadya sits on a bench, prods some stomachs, and says, “This your sister?” and “How old are you, mister?” I join her, remove my cap, and wipe the sweat from my brow. The act provokes a gasp from the crowd, so I return the cap quickly to my head. I look around. Many pairs of eyes are trained on me. Maybe they haven’t seen hair quite like mine before. So I sweep the cap off again, this time in an extravagant arc. Back on my head it goes, but backwards. Gales of laughter. Off it comes, gets a twirl, and then back on, this time sideways. Some of the mothers crack a grin.

After twenty minutes of hobnobbing with the crowd, we go for a walk along the riverbank. In Oum Number 1, we saw sago harvested, the cutting open of the fat-trunked palm, the pounding of its innards with an adz. In numerous villages, we have seen sago flour turned into pancakes. What we haven't seen is the step in between harvesting and cooking: sago rinsing. Now we watch a teenage girl standing in front of a waist-height wooden trough on wooden legs, tilted at a sixty-degree angle. In the middle of the trough is a sieve made of coarse cloth. She takes handfuls of the stringy sago pith and, adding water scooped up from the river, presses it against the sieve. Out spurts milky fluid on the other side. This trickles down to the end of the trough and into a canoe. There, the starch separates from the water and settles on the bottom. The girl scoops the water out of the canoe. What's left resembles sludgy blancmange, stiff enough for her to peel off the hull, fold, and stuff in a sack. It will gradually harden in the sack and become the crumbly, tofu-like cake we have seen in people's kitchens on the Sepik. I wonder whether eating this sago, rinsed in the river, will make the villagers sick, given the industrial activity going on upstream.

We spend the night in Kundiman, a tiny flooded village on a tributary of the Sepik. Chris's powerful outboard engine propels us there in twenty minutes. The soil seems good here as papaya, banana, water apple, coconut, and betel nut palms are all heavy with fruit, and the people look in fine health. Kundiman stands on reclaimed land, Cyril tells us. The Yuat River carved a new path through the jungle a few years ago, leaving behind nutrient-rich silt. I hadn't considered that floods might be constructive.

"The river gives, and the river takes away," Nadya remarks as we swing our bags up the ladder of the guest house and admire the orchard from the verandah.

At dusk, we unroll our sleeping mats and hang our mozzie net. Through the floor, we hear Cyril's voice booming. "*Peles bilong ol*

Canada...*Ol baim kanu long* Green River..." Everyone has clearly gathered around him.

"He's doing it again," I say.

"Telling our story?"

"Yup. What are his motives, do you think?"

"Probably three things: genuine interest, social capital, and economic gain. He likes it that we are not whistle-stop tourists on a day package. We are here to travel slowly on his river and learn. We ask questions, and we show interest in tribal life. He is also building his reputation, no doubt. He speaks English and knows people from other countries. The villagers come to see him as smart, well connected, and influential. This might be important when it comes time for Kalida to get married. And, given foreign visitors pay the village big man, not Cyril, for their night's stay, it may be in leaner times that Cyril can ask a favour of the Chief."

While I don't like being made more of a spectacle than we already are, I recognize Cyril's spiels help remove suspicion and make us feel more welcome at a village. I remember what Nicolas Garnier said to us in Chambri: Storytelling has power in PNG. Good speakers get to sit near the big man in a *haus tambaran*.

|| What took us twenty minutes yesterday takes us an hour this morning. The difference makes all the difference. Without the clattering engine and travelling now at jogging speed, we can train our binoculars on the covey of eclectus parrots squabbling high in the canopy, we can appreciate the funnel designs of the Kundiman fish traps sprouting at intervals from the riverbank, and we can hear the distinctive two-syllable shrieks of the helmeted friarbird—*wa-wow! wa-wow!* We even get a whiff of the yellow flowers on a vine cascading from a low-hanging branch. A White Saun and two cattle egrets pad around one of the bamboo traps and peer into it with interest. Bee-eaters perform aerial acrobatics alongside the canoe, pleased with the flies we disturb when paddling close to shore. One bee-eater, a flash of colours, skewers a longicorn beetle with whip antennae as it takes to the air.

“The friarbird is timekeeper,” Cyril says as the two-syllable shriek ruptures the silence once again. “He wake fisherman up in morning and tell him, ‘Get up now! Get up! It is time to go fishing!’”

A little later, he points to a stand of towering trees with wide girths, the big men of the rainforest. “See those? Very good for make canoe. Erima tree canoe can last four or five year, but best is nar wood canoe. This can last twenty year.”

Paddling down the Yuat reminds me of paddling down the Dio, the narrow tributary that began our trip, the jungle, buzzing with sounds and activity, leaning over the water. I am almost sad to see *Naudumba* merge with the mother river. I dig out our map.

Veering from left to right and almost doubling back on itself, the Sepik looks particularly intestinal as it approaches Angoram. It appears to be putting off the inevitable: its melting into the sea. Bits resembling snipped hosepipe have broken off the body of the river and become bent lakes. We can either stick with the highway or cut through the swamps to Kambaramba (so many villages beginning with the letter “K” around here) and join an equally wide parallel route to Angoram. Cyril opts for the latter. The shortcut was once a river, he assures us, so the going should be fine.

The hyacinth-carpeted channel we enter is no wider than the one we took to Blackwater Lakes. It is hard to believe this was ever a river. We stab holes in the carpet with our paddles and try to sweep the plants aside, but the feathery roots coil around the blades. Every third stroke, we must stop and scrape them off. We labour for twenty minutes, everyone taking a turn with the paddles, and make little headway. It doesn’t help we are six in the canoe. A man called Dixon, needing a ride to Angoram, joined us in Kundiman. *Naudumba* now sits a little lower in the water. We begin to sweat and slap. *Natnats* cloud around our heads. It must be here and not at Palambei that the unsuspecting fisherwoman opened the sack containing the sorcerer’s stomach. Shirt off, breathing hard, Dixon is in front of me, doing a stint with the short paddle. At least two hundred mosquitoes prickle his back. He seems unconcerned until I mention it to him, and then he begins to dance around like a lunatic, flapping his arms and making the canoe rock. Nadya tells him to turn around so she can brush him down with the *yimbunga*. Perhaps each of us should be carrying a cow's tail like Father Donovan's parishioner.

After another twenty-five minutes, we arrive at a dead end: a solitary house and a wall of tangled, impenetrable reeds. A girl is standing in front of the house, hands at her sides, untroubled by flies. Chests heaving, we wipe our faces and stare at her stupidly. She sticks her arm out, pointing at the corridor *Naudumba* has just cut, a corridor that is quickly disappearing. We must go back the way we have come. She makes a T with her hands. But make a hard right. We have missed a junction. How to get back? There is no space to turn the canoe. Stern first. Now the real toil begins. Digging with paddles will not be enough. We must climb out onto the water plants and the waterlogged logs and, gripping the gunwales, shove and yank. We submerge to our knees, to our waists, throw our stomachs over the side of the canoe and kick when we cannot get footing. Cyril shouts instructions. Water flies everywhere. Happily, the turn is not far away. We overshoot it, and then steer *Naudumba*'s bow down a reedy cut that cannot possibly be an exit from the swamps. But, after ten more minutes of tugging and hustling and cussing and swatting, out we spill onto the Sepik secondary road. Chris drops the prop.

Half an hour later, we are in Kambaramba, where it is market day. For the first time since joining the Sepik, we find some bread for sale. What a treat. But it seems out of place, and, dehydrated, we have a tough time digesting it in the midday heat. Equally challenging are the smoked sago sausages. We know the jelly sausages wrapped in banana leaves, but these ones resemble frankfurters and have the consistency of licorice. As we sprawl flaked out under a tree, I ask Cyril about our chances of finding a canoe in Angoram and paddling to the sea.

"You cannot do!" he replies. "I told you before. It is too dangerous. You can take PMV bus to Wewak or go to airport."

"We don't want to go to Wewak or fly anywhere. We want to finish our journey on the Sepik."

In the afternoon, we paddle the remaining twenty kilometres to Angoram. The river is wide and featureless, and our pace lethargic.

Cyril Tara, Nick Tumas, and Naudumba.

Cyril smokes and sighs. He is itchy to get home and wants to switch on the engine. No way, I say, when he suggests it. Nadya and I want to savour our final moments on the Middle Sepik. He shrugs and continues crunching the banana shoots and *laulau* he got from the market. He must eat these, he says, to neutralize the acid from betel nut. A lifetime of chewing betel has made his teeth sensitive. Maybe the water apple helps strip some of the red stain from his teeth as well. Nick is the only Papuan on board with white teeth. Being a Seventh-Day Adventist, he is not allowed to drink, smoke, swear, womanize, dance, or chew betel nut, he told us last night. Sounds every bit as strict as the Revival Church Clifford told us about in Oum Number 1.

"So what do you do for fun?"

"Fish and carve masks!" he replied with a broad, pearly-toothed smile.

And a master craftsman he is. He carved the metre-tall wooden head of a Sepik warrior that guards the entrance to Cyril's guest house, and he has turned the prow of *Naudumba* into a river deity with horns and flared nostrils.

Established by the German colonial administration in 1913, Angoram is the administrative centre for the Middle and Lower Sepik and home to about two thousand people. A road links it to Wewak, and there's a small airport. We round a bend in the river, and the first signs of the largest village on the Sepik are ahead: tin roofs and a cellphone tower resembling a fairground helter-skelter. Christina Dodwell, the intrepid Englishwoman who paddled a dugout alone down the Sepik in the 1980s, ended her voyage here. The villagers brought her gifts of watermelons, sugar cane, *pawpaws*, and a fly swatter, and yelled out "Sepik *meri!*" Angoram is on the north side of the river, but we pull in next to huts and open shelters on the south where Cyril has *tambu*.

A lot of people are milling about or sitting on bamboo berths beside sacks of vegetables, bulging *bilums*, and plastic jerry cans of water. One man with a young family sits cross-legged beside a stack of portable clay hearths of the sort we saw in Aibom on Chambri Lake. Several pigs are chasing about under the berths and thrusting their snouts into open bags before being kicked away. Our captain stands up and bellows "Ambima!" as we make landfall, Dixon securing *Naudumba* before disappearing in the crowd. A bald man with a white beard and hair sprouting from his ears descends the ladder of his hut and approaches. Cyril shakes his hand warmly and tells him our river story. Ambima listens carefully and nods, then shakes his head and mutters something.

"What did he say?" Nadya asks.

"He says he is too old to go with you."

"Go where?"

"To Lubia."

"Where's that?"

"On the coast," Nick says, joining us.

"Ah."

"But his son Wally can take you in his boat. Lubia is where the road start. You can ride in betel nut truck from there to Madang. He say you must wait here with the others. They want to go to Madang too."

"*Long wanem taim im go*?" Nadya asks Ambima. What time does it leave?

"*Faiv klok, no sikis.*"

"This man is councillor," Nick whispers. "You are in good hands."

Nadya and I get our bags and take Cyril aside to settle up. What will we do once we reach Madang? he asks, folding the kina notes and tucking them inside his shirt. Our visas are almost up, we tell him. It is time for us to leave PNG.

"If you come back, you must go to Highlands," Cyril says, handing me a scrap of paper with a name and a phone number on it. "I have a good friend living in Mount Hagen. He can help you."

We shake his hand, thank Nick and Chris, and wish them a safe return. It will take them four hours to get back to Kaminabit, three of which will be in the dark, a dubious prospect as their only source of light will be Cyril's cell phone.

Wally and his boat do not appear at five o'clock or six. Nor at seven or eight. At nine, Ambima rescues us from the pigs, which are definitely hungry, and takes us to Wally's place to lodge for the night.

|| The Lower Sepik is a largely uninhabited wilderness, and we enter it in the dark twenty-seven hours after saying *lukim yu* to Cyril and his crew. The fibreglass launch we are in has an engine, but it is not in use. Together with eleven other silent passengers and their *bilums*, bags, and clay hearths, Nadya and I will drift downstream. Ben (not Wally), a hulk of a man who speaks no English, is our captain. Why are we going at night? Why must we keep quiet?

Propped against Nadya, I assume we will drift in and out of sleep as the boat drifts along, jolted awake when we hit submerged logs, until the sun rises. But this isn't what happens. Just after midnight, I become aware we are no longer moving. Ben taps our shoulders. Leaving our bags on the boat under a tarp, we must disembark, climb the ladder of a hut, and stretch out on the floor to sleep. We have no idea who owns the house, but we are in the village of Bim apparently. It is a tricky night without our mosquito bed net.

Ben rouses us at 5:30 a.m. Time to get back into the boat. On goes the engine. Everyone gets settled. Nothing happens. 6 a.m. 6:10. 6:20.

"What's happening?" I ask no one in particular, not knowing how to say this in Tok Pisin.

"Ben hear engine start down river," the man with the clay hearths whispers. "Maybe *raskol*."

Nadya rummages through her bag for our binoculars, and we take turns trying to make out what's ahead.

Suddenly, Ben engages the throttle, and the boat charges out across the river. We huddle down, lean forward, and peer through the thin light of dawn for another boat. Nothing. I look around at the other passengers and try to make out their faces. A girl of about twenty-five with her short hair screwed into tight knots seems angry; another of about the same age in a "Skel Rice" T-shirt, bleary-eyed and blinking, seems scared. I realize after a few minutes that our boat is sprinting for an island midriver. I look up at our skipper, standing at the stern. The way he is squinting at the south bank suggests the threat will come from there. Get to the far side of the island, and all will be well. More tense minutes pass, the engine roaring and shaking. Could pirates have got wind of two *waitpela* on the Lower Sepik? Egrets fishing near the island flee, crying out in alarm. The boat arcs around the tip of the island and begins tracking the north bank. Ben stands up straight, returning his weight to his heels, but does not retard the throttle. Maybe this stretch of the river is always a sticking point for passenger traffic. Another five minutes pass. Our skipper eases back the throttle.

Our final day on the Sepik is cloudless and fine. I expect the river to get ever wider as we approach the sea, but, in the Land of the Unexpected, I am not so surprised when exactly the opposite happens. Ben knows a shortcut to the estuarine village of Watam. Mid-morning, the engine barely ticking over, we find ourselves in an eerie green tunnel, weaving around towering, fat-trunked sago palms. We must duck our heads and keep our elbows tucked in to avoid the snagging thorns on the fronds that arch over us. We know now that a sago palm takes ten years to reach its full height of twelve to fifteen metres, so these would appear ready for harvest. As we swing from left to right, the song Wally's kids taught Nadya the night before last comes into my head:

Mister Lunchtime,
Where's my sago?
In the basket
Waiting for
My hungry stomach.

After a brief stop in Watam for a breakfast of donuts for me and steamed clams for Nadya, we cross a tranquil lake skirted by mangroves. At the far end, the wind picks up, and the mangroves thin out to straggly lines, waves washing about their spidery legs. The water deepens, and we are suddenly at sea. The swell lifts and lowers the boat, and terns hover over our heads, screeching. I take a deep breath and smile at Nadya, and she smiles back. This is not quite how we imagined arriving at the Bismarck Sea, but I feel relieved and happy. I look over my shoulder at the forest receding behind us and realize I can't see the gap from which we emerged. It is almost as if the jungle has closed ranks behind us.

Ben gradually turns the boat to the south, and we track a coastline flecked with coconut palms. In the distance, blurred by haze, a volcano rears out of the sea, white cloud mopping its furrowed crown. This is Manam Island, our guidebook says, home to six thousand people until the volcano erupted in 2004. Only two thousand returned, the rest finding new homes on the mainland. Displaced by natural calamity. I think of the Sepik and flooding.

Our captain steers for shore before we reach Manam. Suddenly, we are humping our gear up an inclined beach and getting bitten by sand flies (a nice change from *natnats*). Lubia, it appears, is a turnaround for trucks shipping betel nuts to Madang, and Ben tells us we can get a ride. How long will it take to reach Madang? He doesn't know. Six hours? No. Eight or nine hours. No, the man with the clay hearths says, it will take two days because a bridge has collapsed near the town. After a couple of hours, our Isuzu Reward is ready to depart. Butts on sixty-kilogram sacks of nuts, handkerchiefs pressed to our mouths as the wheels churn dust and sand, we resign ourselves to getting to Madang whenever we do. Feeling relieved but sad, I take Cyril's note out of my pocket and look at the name scribbled on it: "Paul Riss. Mt. Hagen. tel. 7455 6178."

12 VIEWS FROM ABOVE

> *Papua New Guinea's Defence Force has deployed 440 troops to stop landowner violence and unrest in the country's highlands. The soldiers will go to the Southern Highlands capital of Mendi and to the neighbouring Hela Province, site of the PNG Liquified Natural Gas project. On June 14 in Mendi, angry supporters of a candidate in last year's contentious national elections set alight an Air Niugini Dash 8 aircraft at the airport and burned down court buildings...On June 20, in Hela Province, landowners set fire to equipment and blocked roads in Angore, an area leading to the PNG LNG project, operated by ExxonMobil.*
>
> —*ABC NEWS*, June 22, 2018

The battered PMV we have chartered rattles away from Mount Hagen International Airport and heads east along a rutted highway. I thought on our first day back in Papua New Guinea we'd shake hands with Paul Riss at the airport and head west into "Hagen," as the locals call the town thirteen clicks away. There, we'd have dinner, get to know each other, and plan our treks. But Paul says Hagen is "*nogut.*" Too many men hanging about and causing trouble. I reach down and try to prevent the eight plastic bags of groceries at my feet from spilling their contents. We just made a stop at a supermarket called Tininga and bought canned meat and fish, cooking oil, rice, instant noodles, sugar, Em Nau crackers, and tea: supplies for our first expedition.

Wishing for a different view of the country, Nadya and I have returned to PNG to explore the Highlands, in particular Hela Province. Tari, one of the principal towns, is home to the Huli tribe, whose warriors wear elaborate boat-shaped wigs fantastically decorated with parrot feathers, cuscus fur, and everlasting daisies. In the ranges nearby, we might witness the outlandish courtship display rituals of the blue bird of paradise or King of Saxony bird of paradise. That plan has gone out the window. Tari is close to ExxonMobile's LNG (liquefied natural gas) installation, where violence has just erupted. Plan B is to trek into the mountains of Jiwaka Province, which Paul assures us is also inhabited by birds of paradise, although he has no idea what sort.

I look at Cyril's buddy sitting beside me. He hardly seems suited to the high altitude hikes I proposed to him by email from Australia last month. A couple of the peaks are over four thousand metres. A smoker in his fifties, calves wormy with varicose veins, Paul certainly doesn't have the chiselled physique of a Sepik tribesman. Sitting next to Nadya is Jo Golomb, another guide who is about Paul's age and also on the stocky side. Both are fluent in English. We met the pair less than two hours ago, and now we are on our way in dwindling light to Kimil, a village where Jo has relatives. I look out the window at a road roller pressing flat sizzling asphalt and plastic buckets lying in puddles of tar. Three men with bush knives and *bilums* amble barefoot along the side of the road, one ejecting a plume of betel nut spittle. How different from the tidy, sterile suburbs of Cairns, where we stayed while waiting for our Papuan visas. Written on the torn upholstery over my head are the words, *"Plis nokem spietim buai lo windo"* (Please don't spit betel nut out the window).

After a night in Kimil, we walk two hours up a dirt road to Kowi, Jo's home village. People dash from their houses along the way and seize our hands. Two women hug Nadya around the waist and refuse to let her go. How come Nadya and I are causing a stir like on the Upper Sepik? Mount Hagen, the largest town in the region and a centre for Highlands tourism, is only twenty kilometres away. Tourists go there to organize climbs up Mount Giluwe, PNG's second-tallest mountain; they go for the "Mount Hagen Show," an annual tribal *sing-sing*.

"When did white people last come here?"

Paul thinks for a moment. "Twenty-five years ago?"

An Australian logging company set up shop, he says, and we see the rusted shells of industrial saws mounted on crumbling iron girders. A buckled sign says, "Sawmil."

In Kowi, a bride price ceremony is in progress when we arrive. The bridegroom and his *tambu* have brought pigs from their village, and the bride's family has slaughtered and roasted them with taro in a *mumu*. Nadya and I saw a ground oven like this in the highlands of West Papua. It is made by putting fire-heated stones in a pit lined with banana leaves, placing the food on top in layers, and then covering this with more banana leaves and wads of grass. The food takes two or three hours to cook. The sides of pork lie hissing on a banana-leaf mat beside a heap of sweating taro roots that look like translucent purple potatoes. A man in sweatpants and a tuque slices open the pigs and hacks off their trotters. Another holds up an eyeless, charred head for us to see. Women then carry the food to a communal area in front of the huts, and everyone sits in a circle around it, guests on one side, hosts on the other. Paul waves us over to the Kowian side. I wonder if we are intruding, but no one seems to object to our presence.

The father of the bride, a man of about sixty with white smudges in his beard, steps forward. He is well dressed: shirt with collar, sweater, slacks with creases, sneakers. I look around and realize that practically everyone else is in smart clothes as well: two women are wearing striped dresses with pleated sleeves, a young man is in a faux leather jacket and has wraparound sunglasses perched on his ball cap, and a toddler is in a fleece jumpsuit with hood. Many of the villagers are wearing coats. It could be that the villagers have dressed for the occasion, but those we met on our walk here didn't look so different. The huts are also superior to those we saw in the Sepik: plank frames, plank fences, florescent tube lights, and tidy vegetable plots with cassava, coffee, taro, sugar cane, and tanket plants. A few of the huts have corrugated tin or plastic roofs.

"Abraham say the visitors have not brought enough," Paul whispers in my ear. The father, I see, has a wad of bills in his hand.

"How much have they brought?"

“Only five pigs and K2,000. The bride price is ten pigs and K10,000.”

This, I recall, was the going rate to purchase a wife in Kubkain on the Sepik. Taxi boatman Gerry was soon to get married. He had managed to raise K6,000 by himself, he informed us, and he expected his family to make up the balance. No pigs there. Instead, he had to supplement with eighteen kina shells.

“Why is bride price so expensive?” Nadya asks.

“Everyone who helped raise the girl must get some money. Her mother, father, aunts, uncles, and cousins. The aunt and uncle often do a lot. They teach the girl many thing. They must be paid well.”

“Is bride price a good thing? Can the girl choose who she marries?”

“Yes, she can choose, but her father must say it is okay. He wants good match, a boy from family who can pay right price. It is also good for couple because bride price makes marriage big thing. The boy and girl usually stay together.”

Bride price makes me think of dowries and English nobility and the opening scenes of *King Lear* when the king entices his daughters' suitors by offering lands and fortunes. Dowries are the reverse of bride price, the bride's family transferring wealth to the groom's, but the idea of a transactional marriage is similar and surely raises ethical questions. The bride price is so high in PNG the suitor cannot possibly afford it. He must turn to members of his family for loans and becomes indebted to them—presumably for years unless he lands himself a high-paying job in town. Perhaps more concerning is the bride's status after wedlock. As she has been bought by her husband, is she now his “property” to do with as he pleases? Nadya and I already know the rate of domestic violence against women in this country is among the highest in the world.

Three men from the visiting clan get to their feet. It is clear from the serious expressions on their faces and their conciliatory gestures that they are making assurances to the father. I assume one of the three is the bridegroom.

“Will there be trouble?” I ask.

“No,” Paul says, eavesdropping. “They are promising to bring rest of pigs and money in August when they sell their coffee.”

Some Kowi women begin ululating, and everyone smiles. Before setting about the feast, the home crowd must formerly welcome the guests. They do so by walking by them in single file, reaching down and shaking their hands. The visitors do not rise to their feet. It would appear they must remain deferent on this delicate occasion. The PMV driver who gave us a lift from the airport yesterday is in the file.

"He is same *wantok*," Paul tells me when I point him out. "You must participate in family and in your village. If you don't, when big problem rise and you are away, people will say when you come later, 'What are you doing here? Where were you yesterday?' You can become enemy. Jacob can be driving his car today and making money, but instead he is here welcoming other clan."

This is the bright side of bride price. It is a way of confirming relationships and forging new ones, a way of remaining embedded in and valued by your community. It is good for *wantok*.

|| The dirt path behind the village is steep, fissured, and slippery. For every two steps we take up, we slide down one step. The Highlands region has seen a lot of rain lately. At times, we have to leave the path where it has been too deeply quarried by the rain and hack a way through the bush. Wiry roots looping across the path make us trip, and a Papuan equivalent of the Australian "wait-a-while," a vine-like palm with long tendrils bearing hooks, tears at our sleeves and ears. Jo cuts me a walking stick with his bush knife. It feels odd wearing hiking boots and lugging a sack up a mountain after spending months in flip-flops on a river or near the sea.

Our party is large, far larger than I wished for. Pausing for breath, I count eighteen villagers walking with us, many of them teenagers and children, chatting merrily.

"Where are all these people going, Paul?"

"To Homa Tapia...Like us," he replies, panting.

"They left at exactly the same time that we left."

"They heard we were going and want to come with us."

I sigh. I thought it was clear to Paul what our mission was. Four people can walk into the wilds without causing great disturbance, especially if their aim is to spot birds, but not twenty-two. And what happens when we stop to eat? I see none of our companions has brought supplies—not even empty water bottles to refill at streams. We have provisioned for four people on a trek lasting four or five days. I should probably have guessed in Kowi that we'd have company when Paul and Jo introduced us to their teenage sons, Richard and Jonas, and two students, Jonathan and Thomas, studying tourism and hospitality in Mount Hagen. None of them lived there. Nadya has allowed Thomas to shoulder her backpack. I sense our guides find it a bit odd I have not given up mine.

The path threads through bamboo and banana trees and then enters a pandanus grove. With their tubular stilt legs and bushy crowns, the pandanus trees strike me as oddities of the forest. Some look like they could uproot and wander off, and I think of triffids. I remember pandanus from the highlands of West Papua, where they bore fruit resembling cobs of corn but blood red in colour and the length and thickness of my calf. The West Papuans harvest them for oil and, at birdwatching hides for tourists, suspend them as bait above bird of paradise display grounds. The pandanus here are of a different variety. They have the same knobbly buttress roots but globular, studded fruit like durians that Paul tells me can be cooked and eaten and taste like coconut.

As we gain height, I chat with Paul about the recent trouble in Southern Highlands and Hela provinces. The newspapers in Australia had reported an escalation: smoke billowing from a smashed passenger jet, the burnt-out shells of vehicles, and men in tribal headdresses brandishing assault rifles. Commencing operation in 2014, ExxonMobil's K19 billion liquefied natural gas project, the largest resource extraction venture in PNG, was supposed to bring unprecedented wealth to the nation, generate thousands of jobs, induce an increase in government spending, and improve living standards. A report published in April 2018 by Jubilee Australia Research Centre, a body that investigates corporate behaviour overseas, revealed the venture had not lived up to its promises. Predicted to double in size between 2014 and 2018, the economy had, in fact, only grown by 10 per cent and all of this in the resource sector. Household incomes were supposed to rise by 84 per cent and employment by 42 per cent; instead, both had fallen, the former by 6 per cent, the latter by 27 per cent. Government spending on health, infrastructure, education, and law and order was expected to rise by 85 per cent; instead it had dropped by 32 per cent. According to the report, one reason for the shortfalls was the exceptionally low taxes ExxonMobil paid: for 2016, K3.2 million, one-thousandth of the share it expected in sales of LNG for that year. Another reason, according to Paul, is corruption in the national government.

"The landowner accuse government of making false promise, not paying them royalty from profit made by company. Government promised to pay landowner by installment based on company profit, but they don't do this. Government says it must repay loan to develop LNG site, but landowner say money just go into 'Waigani swamp.'"

"What's that?"

"Waigani is where Parliament is located in Port Moresby. So now the landowner are very angry. They burn LNG machine and dug up road to Tari. In Mendi, they attack state property, courthouse, provincial governor's house, and Air Niugini plane. The police cannot stop because there are too many protestor and they have gun."

"Where did they get those from?"

"Irian Jaya across the border. They paid for them by selling cannabis. Or, sometimes, corrupt police sell them gun from their armoury."

I think of the landowners exploited by foreign mining and logging companies and let down by their government. Will violence flare up on the Sepik if the Frieda gold mine goes ahead or Global continues to ravage the forest and defile the river? I remember the foam-bergs of industrial effluent downstream of Log Pond and Cyril's talk of kids getting sick from eating contaminated fish. Would there be civil war like he said?

After two hours of sweat and slog, we emerge from the trees onto a grassy saddle beside a cellular tower with rusty legs. It looks incongruously out of place. Our view ahead is of thickly forested mountains, white cloud blurring the more distant ones. Given how sheer the sides of the mountains are, I am surprised I am not seeing bare rock, crags, or turrets. Just tiers of trees, standing tall, reaching for the sun. Nadya tries but fails to get a signal on our phone.

Down we go now: another greasy, vertiginous path with tripwires and muddy chutes. I follow close behind Jonathan and a Homa Tapian lad about his age, stepping where they step. At times, Simon hangs back and chops steps into the mud with his bush knife so I don't slip on my ass. I still lose control in places and only avoid catastrophe by stabbing my stick into the ground with both hands and spinning around to face uphill to arrest my slide. My feet double in size and weight. I must stop and pry off mud pancakes. Jonathan and Simon wait patiently. I see they are walking with little effort, their flip-flops tucked into the back of their pants, mud squirting between their toes. I think of Fice and his chums from Green River Christian Secondary walking just as breezily through the swamps to Waku. As we go, my compadres educate me about the forest.

"This is watercress," Jonathan says, plucking stalks from a stream and folding them into his mouth. It sounds like *water caress*.

"Fern is for *mumu*," offers Simon, fondling a massive herringbone frond arching over the path. "It keep heat in."

"See this white blood?" Jonathan slices the head off a plant with his bush knife. A bubble of liquid weeps from the cut stalk. "We put it on boil to heal."

Jo, when he catches up with us, also has something to show me: a rhinoceros beetle the size of a plum. It is a hornless female, shiny and metallic like it has just been polished. It hisses and nods its head in his grasp, its legs motoring futilely. Before I can say something appreciative, Jo has deftly pinched off her legs and flicked them away. He sticks the beetle, hissing furiously, in his jacket pocket and smiles.

"I will eat him later."

The gradient eases, and we emerge from the trees. We are on a narrow ridge now, with steep drop-offs to either side, an unlikely place for a clearing and half a dozen huts. An old lady sits on the dirt in front of the nearest, peeling coffee beans and staring at us. She tells Jo she is lucky to be alive. Two weeks ago, her home almost disappeared into the valley. She didn't use to live two feet from the cliff. *Bikpela ren i pundaun.* Heavy rains. Nadya and I peer over the edge. A huge crescent of exposed earth stretches along the side, the roots of trees sprouting from it like tufts of hair. Far below, we can make out the shattered remains of trees, an arboreal train crash.

Deeper into the forest we go, gaining altitude. Hours pass. The trail is marked by goopy puddles and slashed leaves, but in places the forest has reclaimed it. Nadya and I wait and let the bush knives do their work. At a ring of empty huts circling another clearing, we stop to eat. Nadya peels the lid off a can and uses it to scoop corned beef onto crackers for our guides and their sons. I remind Paul that we cannot feed everyone, and he nods, saying, "They will look after themselves." But then I see Jo and Jonas dividing what Nadya gives them in half and passing it to the others. I look away, feeling guilty. Jo smiles at me. He has white teeth, I notice. He is not keeping up his energy by chewing betel nut as most men do. He must belong to one of the more ascetic Christian denominations. Perhaps he will take the beetle from his pocket and put it on a cracker. No. It remains, pulsing, in his pocket.

The final hour of our trek is up a long incline. We are still under a green dome, but I sense that now more forest is below us than above. Our pace is slow, and I see, looking over my shoulder, that our party is down from twenty-two to eleven. I guess not everyone was bound for Homa Tapia after all. I look up at the trees and through them, down at the bushes brushing our feet as we climb. No signs of animal or bird life. Maybe we are still making too much noise. I had this idea in Canada that a tropical rainforest would be humming with life: poisonous snakes unwinding from branches, glittering frogs burping from saturated epiphytes, fat-bodied spiders creeping out from under decaying logs, bird-wing butterflies flapping through the shades, fruit-nibbling possums shaking the branches, bandicoots scampering across the paths. But it's not like this. There seems as much life as in our little woodland park back home in Fredericton.

"Waik! Waik! Waik!"

Nadya and I freeze. A bird about the size of our common grackle streaks through the trees below us, a flash of white and yellow. It settles on a branch and shrieks again, dipping its head before shooting off.

"Raggiana?" I whisper.

The Raggiana bird of paradise is the bird most associated with Papua New Guinea. It adorns the national flag and, pictured with a tribal spear and a *kundu* drum, is the national emblem.

"Maybe," Nadya whispers back. "But aren't the plumes of the Raggiana maroon?"

Paul comes up behind us. I ask if he saw the bird.

"I heard it. Don't worry. Tomorrow, we will get up very early. Peter knows the tree."

|| "Krerk!"

6 a.m. Eight of us are standing under the display tree, looking up and squinting as the first rays of sunlight stab through the forest canopy. Nadya and I take turns scouring the leaves with our binoculars, wishing a splash of light to form into plumes of fiery feathers.

"Krerk!"

We look at Peter, inquiringly. Up there, up there, his bony finger keeps indicating. He is a gaunt, unassuming man of about forty who lives with his wife and six-year-old son in the highest hut in a string of them bordering the trail. Yes, we were welcome to stay, he said when Paul rapped on his door last night (Paul was *tambu*), but we would need to hike back to the nearest stream, as he had no running water. He insisted Nadya and I take the family bed for the night, a bamboo tray draped with a threadbare mosquito net.

"Krerk!"

"When the male say 'krerk,'" Jo whispers, "he is telling there is danger."

I look at him. This morning he is wearing a T-shirt with "Greetings from PNG" on the front in blue and red letters. Below are colourful images of a flowering hibiscus, a parrot in flight, a palm tree, and a smouldering volcano, and, under these, the words "Land of Natural Beauty."

"I wish I can catch that bird and kill him!" Jo says cheerfully, no longer bothering to whisper. "Then you can see him very well."

The sun gathers strength. Light slithers down the tree trunks and settles on us. We massage our stiff necks and squat down. Not a murmur, not a squeak from above. I see that one of the Homa

Tapians accompanying us has a slingshot for shooting birds in his back pocket.

We scramble back to Peter's house and, rubbing our eyes, breakfast on sweet potato fritters his wife Sarah has roasted. Should we pack our bags and march on to Maikmol, the next village on our trek? After yesterday's eight-hour uphill trudge and this morning's predawn early bird, none of us feels especially lively. The view of the province from Peter's place is magnificent. At this altitude—three thousand metres ASL or thereabouts—we can now behold the Bismarck Range to the north, the spine of Papua New Guinea that, at its eastern extreme, divides Jiwaka and Madang provinces. The country's tallest and third-tallest peaks, Mount Wilhelm and Mount Herbert, respectively, are somewhere on the hazy horizon.

"This land need development!" Jo cries, sweeping his arm extravagantly from left to right.

His *tambu* own much of the land we can see, he claims. If he were governor of the province, he would build roads through the forest so the villagers could transport their coffee to market and tourists could come to see the birds of paradise. He tells us that his brother ran for office fifteen years ago. Jo raised K200,000 for his campaign by selling land to Digicel for a cellular tower.

"Why did your brother need so much money?" I ask.

He looks at me like I'm naive.

"To pay for vote. Highlanders buy vote. That is the way here! We must give K10,000 to each ward or people don't vote for us."

"What happened? Did your brother win?"

Jo fishes the rhinoceros beetle out of his coat pocket and tosses it onto the hot coals. Remarkably, it is still alive. It jerks, flips onto its back, and tries in vain to spread its wings.

"His opponent bribe people in election office to open ballot box and change vote. Five hundred vote go to opponent. So we belt up election manager and go to court to demand recount. But opponent burn ballot box! So we burn down his village and a school. I was arrested by police and put in prison for two month, but my brother bail me out."

One problem, he tells us, is that rich men often run for office. They buy votes to win the election. Then, when they are elected and get funding for public projects like building roads or hospitals or schools, the money disappears. They get even richer. Another problem is that two candidates may have the same resources, but the people will only vote for the one belonging to their tribe. To vote for the other, even though he might be more dependable and honest, is considered an act of treason.

Thus, *wantok*, intended to benefit the community at large, impedes the political process. This reminds me of what Paul said about the Waigani swamp, swallowing revenue from natural gas extraction. Governance at the national level would appear similarly compromised. I recall the jaded police officer we met while travelling on the road from Lubia, near the mouth of the Sepik, to Madang the month before last. He was manning a makeshift shelter called "Transit Point" next to a river where the bridge had collapsed. The betel nut truck giving us a ride could go no further. No motorized vehicles could.

"When did the bridge collapse?" I asked him.

"Five months ago."

"When will it be repaired?"

"We don't know."

The only way to cross was on foot by means of a jerry-rigged bamboo catwalk. On the other side you could then catch a PMV to town. All the PMVs had gone for the day by the time we arrived, so we spent a night on the floor of the policeman's shelter and walked across the river the following morning, a young man charging us a kina each to do so. I wondered at the time what the rate was for farmers crossing fifty times or more with sacks of betel nut or copra on their backs, trying desperately to get their produce to market.

"The government don't concern about life of small people," the officer said before we parted. "The politicians are millionaires, but the village people have nothing."

Shaking his head, Jo retrieves the ash-coated beetle from the coals, peels away the wing cases as one might the shell of an egg, and bites into the abdomen.

"We don't vote for good men. We vote for corrupt one."

In his book on PNG, Papuan historian John Dademo Waiko speaks of the inherent tension between customary practices in Papuan society and the corruption that has infiltrated the country through modernization. In order to gain and maintain status and power in their communities, big men accept gifts, and, in due course, reward the givers. Politicians and public servants nowadays emulate this practice to amass wealth and secure alliances: they accept bribes from transnational corporations and ignore the social and environmental damage their operations incur. It occurs to me that receiving gifts from foreigners may well have been endorsed in the colonial era when Christian missionaries, wishing their dark-skinned understudies to see the light, handed out iron tools, glass beads, and tobacco.

Nadya asks Paul his opinion on building more roads and cell phone towers. He thinks for a while before answering.

"Modernize bring many good thing. Now tribesman can travel fast by PMV or aeroplane. Before, they stay put because they believe enemies or bad spirit live in next valley. When road is build, we know there is some people living on other side. In old time, where cloud and earth meet, that was end of world! There is no one else living here. Digicel come here in year 2000. It is very good. Before, we make fire or cut white leaf and put them in line to say to village on next mountain, 'You must come.' But we are losing way of our ancestor. Before we wear Chinese clothe we buy in Hagen, we wear bark from tree and tanket leaf and cap made with vine and feather. Our people have *sing-sing* to celebrate marriage. Now we only have *sing-sing* for visiting politician or tourist because they bring money, and they pay us. No pay, no dress! This is very sad thing. My son have nothing, no traditional gears."

I look at my mud-crusted boots and then at the forest, stretching away uninterrupted for miles. I know that, as well as for the birds and bandicoots, I came to PNG to see tanket-leaf tunics, feather headdresses, and dugout canoes. I had wanted to appreciate the gulf that separates my sanitized urban life in Canada from the raw unpredictability of a developing tropical country, where sealed roads, cell phones, and internal flights were few. I remember watching a documentary in Fredericton from the 1960s showing European expeditioners in jungle shorts encountering naked Asmat warriors with bones through their septums and human skulls dangling from their necks. What we have encountered in our six weeks here is a kind of frontier nation, thrust down the developmental road by colonial intruders last century and struggling to find its way since they withdrew. In PNG towns, there are banks and buses, streetlights and supermarkets, but the villages we visited had no electricity, no running water, no reliable means of communication, no hospitals, no police, ill-maintained roads, and the odd low-wattage solar panel. Even though the country is rich in natural resources (oil, gold, copper, timber, liquefied gas) and corporations have accessed those resources for decades, the majority of Papuans have not prospered.

That said, I will return to Canada with images of a tribal life that is robust and enduring. The men and women we met on the Sepik were lean, fit, cheerful, practical, self-reliant, and fiercely proud. They lived on the banks of a river that was bountiful in fish, and they could grow a range of fruits and vegetables in gardens that satisfied their daily needs and yielded produce for sale. Though their villages were often far from market, these people were also resourceful, exchanging their fish with inland tribes for sago. They had achieved, in fact, what Sean Dorney, Papua New Guinea correspondent for ABC News in the 1980s, called "subsistence affluence," a wealth derived from a deep understanding of the land and how to work it. The lives of the river dwellers were certainly simple, but I will not remember them as impoverished. They were vulnerable—at risk of losing everything when the Sepik flooded or when a hostile tribe or *raskols* struck—but, as it seems here for the Highlanders, a strong sense of community and a tradition of obligation, captured in the word "*wantok*," clearly made them resilient.

In the evening, we gather around the fire and eat with our hosts, sharing our food as we did on the Sepik. Peter brings taro, *kaukau*, and *shako* leaf tops from his garden, and we dig noodles and tinned fish out of our packs. Sarah prods the potatoes with a stick, turning them, and they sweat and blacken. Finally, they are done. We crack them open but have to wait to take a bite—the steam pouring out scalds our lips. So we wait and listen to the dark forest thrumming below us, to a million nocturnal creatures beginning their day.

Nadya asks Paul if he is from around here. He was born in Kiram near Mendi in Southern Highlands Province, he replies, but had to move away when an enemy tribe attacked and burnt the village down. Now he lives in Pasulim, his wife's village, not far from Kiram.

"It is good because I have baby girl, and my wife sister help with baby."

"How many kids do you have?" I ask.

"Two. Richard and now Rachel. I use to have second son, but he die last year. I was away from home when it happen. He fall from pandanus tree and hit his head. My wife tell me later he was dizzy for while but continue his work. But she call me crying at 4 a.m. next morning. Tyron stop breathing, she tell me. I must come home. So I rush back to village, but I am too late."

"Sorry to hear that. What a terrible accident."

"Not accident. It was sorcery."

A classmate, jealous of Tyron because he was the son of a tour guide and had money, cast a spell on him, Paul explains. His *tambu* urged him to take revenge, seize the sorcerer, and burn him.

No one says anything for a while, and we listen to a curious jabbering sound coming from the forest.

Richard interrupts the silence. "We no longer believe in witchcraft and these kind of thing, but when someone die without being sick for long time, we believe it is sorcery."

Just like on the Sepik. We are Christians, but sometimes we are not.

I think of the sorcery tales we heard in the lowland villages and on Yuo Island. It seems that, despite Christianity, sorcery violence persists in twenty-first century PNG. Women in particular still get branded as witches and are tortured—the accusers pressing fire-heated bush knives to their arms and breasts or raping them with red-hot pokers. This is a sordid practice, but I wonder, too, if it is a symptom of a traditional way of life asserting itself, a way for men to maintain their power over women.

"So did you take revenge for your son?" I ask Paul before we go to bed.

"No. If I kill the boy, I have to pay money to his family."

|| "Waik! Waik!"

5:45 a.m. A cry shatters the silence. Four of us are sitting under the courtship display tree, holding our breath. No Peter, no sons of guides, no Homa Tapian with a slingshot. This time, hopefully, we are invisible from above. Yesterday, Nadya described to Jo the sort of bird hides they have in West Papua. And, with the help of a local lad with a machete, they made one out of sticks and palm leaves. Now we squint through saucer-size portholes punched in the roof.

"Waik! Waik! Waik-waik-waik!"

A male lesser bird of paradise drops through the canopy to its lek, a branch at a forty-five-degree angle some fifteen metres over our heads. Throwing his maroon wings forward and fluffing up his yellow-and-white tail plumes, he shrieks and spins in circles, announcing himself to the world. Two more males drop through the canopy and settle on a branch to one side. Their plumes and colours are not as full or radiant: these are probably juniors, here to learn a trick or two. The lead male begins his dance, shimmying up and down the branch, flicking his wings forward and back, and shrieking in volleys.

"Waik! Waik! Waik, waik, waik, waik!"

He pauses, rubs his beak on the branch, and looks about. Just a warm-up, it would seem. His plumes wilt and curl beneath him into a quarter-moon. He waits. I train our binoculars on the bird. Yellow crown. Green throat, but black where it meets the beak. Maroon chest. Two whip-like wires trailing down the body, bordering the deflated plumes.

The ladies arrive, four of them, alighting suddenly on branches above the performer. If they weren't staring with such obvious interest at the main act, you could believe they belonged to a different species entirely. Without plumes or wires and slighter in build, they have dark brown heads and cream breasts. They tilt their heads and look down critically, uttering not a word. Showtime. The male responds by erecting his plumes and throwing out his wings once again. He

Lesser bird of paradise.

lets loose another string of shrieks, the cries so shrill they slice through the forest. He goes through his dance routine, hopping up, hopping down his branch, tipping himself forward, fluffing up his feathers, and nodding his head encouragingly. Again and again, he performs his moves, pausing now and then to rub his beak on the branch. Finally, the boldest female joins him. What features does she wish for in a mate? Plumes of exceptional lustre? A dancer who knows his steps? Great vocal cords? His outstretched wings throw a shadow over her.

It is only when the show ends that I realize it lasted forty minutes. I look at Nadya and Jo and can tell by the expression on their faces that, like me, they have been under a spell. An American nature writer once reported how an unexpected encounter with a weasel at close quarters stopped her in her tracks. So mesmerizing was the moment, she felt like the world around her had vanished. Until now, I thought that was an exaggeration. I know it is not unusual for male birds anywhere to pump up their feathers and perform when courting females, but the astonishing thing about birds of paradise is that the males seem designed for the job. The ancillary plumes serve no other purpose. I recall the erectile ruff of the magnificent bird of paradise, the flaring skirt of the western parotia, two forest glade dancers we observed in West Papua. The sole function of the tail wires of the twelve-wired bird of paradise that we saw in the forests near Jayapura is to tickle the face of the female during the mating ritual. In fact, so demonstrative are the male members of this esoteric avian family in plumage, voice, and courtship act that they would seem to have no fear of predators—except, perhaps, human beings.

|| A short, bald man comes barrelling toward us as we hike the path to Maikmol later in the morning. We move to the side to let him pass, but he slows to a trot and then doubles over in front of us, chest heaving. He takes a deep breath and introduces himself. His name is David, and he is the village pastor. He has come to tell us that we must go no further. I look him up and down. His T-shirt is two sizes

too big for him, his pants ripped off at the knee, and his flip-flops too small for his feet.

"*Stopim hia*?" Nadya says, looking at Paul, unsure whether she understood the man correctly. "*Wanem*?" Danger ahead? A landslide?

Another burst of Tok Pisin from the breathless pastor.

"We must wait because...village...not ready," Paul translates haltingly. Nadya and I are not the only ones taken by surprise. "Now he wants us to pray."

Pastor David takes a big gulp of air, wipes his brow, and looks heavenward. He then dips his head, presses his palms together, and closes his eyes. Jo and his son are quick to follow suit, putting their hands together. Paul and Richard do the same. Nadya and I survey the circle of bowed heads, look at each other, shrug, and bow our heads. Last time we prayed was when Jeffrey Waino rallied his kids at Green River Christian Secondary before dismissing them for Easter break.

"Papa God, *tenkyu tru*...special *taim*...strong *pawa*...*amamas*..."

The pastor delivers his prayer at a breakneck pace. It appears he is thanking God for something important. Why speak so fast? Maybe he was taught to say his prayers like this by missionaries. The prayer lasts three minutes and ends as abruptly as it began. David looks up and smiles beatifically. We must wait ten minutes before continuing, he implores.

We hear Maikmol before we see it: a rousing chorus of voices in song. A couple more bends of the trail, and we are there. A wooden arch, threaded luxuriantly with purple flowers, marks the entrance. Fifty villagers, young and old, splattered head-to-foot in white paint, stand beneath it. Prompted by the pastor, we halt some distance away. I can't make out the words they are singing, but there is no mistaking the fervour. A warrior, armed with a bow and arrow, parts from the crowd and sprints toward us. He is wearing a skirt of leaves, a feather headdress, and sunglasses. Hard on his heels is another with a red-and-white face, bracken in his hair, and a spear. Nadya and I take a step back as the pair approach. They skid to a halt two metres from us, and, scowling and hissing, lunge with their weapons. Two women are following behind, making the kind of shrill cries we heard at the

Welcome to Maikmol!

bride price ceremony in Kowi. One has a parrot-feather coronet and is waving a bunch of marigolds over her head. The warriors retreat, yelling and shaking their weapons. Pastor David giggles.

A boy of about seven steps forward and holds up a sign saying, "Welcome to Maikmol and Kavali Memorial Zoo." The singing subsides. Taking this as a signal to enter the village, Nadya and I move again, merge with the crowd, and pass tentatively under the arch. As soon as we do, the warriors seize me under the arms, and, before I can protest, hoist me into the air. Several sturdy women do the same with Nadya. They carry us—backpacks and all—down a flight of mud steps into the village square and set us down. Two elderly women put flower garlands around our necks. Taking our hands, they lead us to a bench, and the villagers squat on the ground in front. We sit down and girls bring pineapples and bushels of peanuts and pile them at our feet. Another old lady presses a cassowary-feather *bilum* into Nadya's hands and hugs her.

I smile self-consciously, shake hands, clap people on the back, and return hugs. I have no idea how to respond appropriately and yet feel I need to find a way. These people have gone to great trouble to prepare for our arrival. How they knew we were coming, I have no idea. No one seems to have a cell phone. Maybe their Homa Tapian neighbours living on the next ridge lined up white leaves in a clearing or sent a runner. I guess I should have learned by now how to let go, ride with the moment. After all, our arrivals at the villages of the Upper Sepik were often just as lively. It occurs to me that Nadya and I haven't really been in control of our fate since crossing the border into PNG. I had thought that buying a canoe would have given us control, the freedom to go and stop where we pleased. Nothing of the sort. For the foreign visitor, liberty to roam alone simply isn't an option. Even Papuans, given that all land is owned by one tribe or another, can't wander where they wish. We have come to realize not only that our safety depends on the people taking charge but that we learn more because they do. And yet I still cannot get used to being "carried" along like this. Being looked after makes me feel like a tourist.

Joseph, the village big man, rises and launches into a speech. He is about the age and build of Peter in Homa Tapia, same lean physique, same keen eyes. Paul translates. The people of Maikmol have been waiting for many years for visitors from another country to come... they even built a zoo to show them the wonders of the forest...they put animals and birds in cages, and they waited patiently...but no one came...the animals and birds died, or they escaped...Now, finally, two visitors from Canada have come. When they return, they will tell their countrymen about Maikmol. More visitors will come! Today is just the start...

Joseph retreats. I look around the circle of painted faces and wonder, not for the first time, what Papua New Guineans make of us. Their initial reaction to our sudden appearances is generally guardedness, even suspicion. Why are we here? What do we want? The Elders of the tribe may remember the Aussie *kiaps* striding through on their patrols or the Christian missionaries building their churches and proselytizing. But over four decades have passed since the country gained its independence, and most white settlers have gone home. About fifty thousand were living here just before 1975; now the number is two-fifths of that. I had wondered if our arrival with our backpacks, boots, and binoculars, our fancy clothes and ready cash, might induce envy and resentment. In the last century, many Papuans were so astounded at the provisions and equipment of visiting Europeans that "cargo cults" emerged. The cults believed the *waitpela* had somehow intercepted cargo that rightfully belonged to Papuans, gifts sent to them by their ancestors from the spirit world. Cult leaders bid their followers cease work, destroy their gardens, and build airstrips and docks. Soon the ancestors, piloting great planes and ships, would bring them the wealth that was their due. That idea would seem to belong to the past as not once have Papuans solicited us for gifts.

I look at Jo and Paul. Jo is grinning, clearly enjoying the occasion; Paul's face is expressionless. It is time for one of the visitors from Canada to say a few words. It would be nice to crack open a box of ball caps or flip-flops and pass them around to express our gratitude. Then I think, maybe not. That would smack too much of being a privileged tourist, a patronizing colonizer even. Nevertheless, I feel guilty turning up empty-handed at this village. At least on the Sepik, we had Gudang Garams to share with the men. I get to my feet and ask Paul to translate.

"It is a great honour to visit your village today..."

After a lunch of pineapple and peanuts, Joseph and some villagers take us an hour down the mountain to see their zoo and get water from the nearest source. Dazzling blue Ulysses butterflies the size of my hand glide between flowers with orange blooms the villagers have planted to line the way. The zoo is four tumbledown bamboo cages that look like they were constructed years ago, and a functioning one containing an angry adolescent cassowary. The bird goes berserk when we approach, thrashing the bars with its wings and stabbing its beak through the holes. Nadya suggests to our hosts that many visitors would likely prefer to see the wonders of the forest in the forest. Might the villagers build hides rather than cages? Remembering our time in the West Papuan highlands, she tells them about a lodge where tourists watched birds of paradise and bower birds from hides. Local villagers owned the lodge, and some, including the Chief, worked there. Promising not to hunt the birds for their feathers, the villagers got a slice of the proceeds. A community development model of birdwatching. Joseph nods thoughtfully as Paul translates. We donate money to the Maikmol villagers' project.

Near the cages, water gurgles out from under a rock and collects in a muddy pool. As I wash my face and refill our bottles, I wonder if the source of the mighty Sepik begins similarly. I imagine trekking northwest through these mountains and, after many days, exhausted and exhilarated, locating it. I imagine following its descent, seeing it widen and deepen, and, eventually, hearing the echoey *chok-chok* of a man hollowing out a tree trunk to make a canoe.

|| A month and a half later, after two further hikes in the Highlands, the last an ascent of Mount Wilhelm, and several bird of paradise forays in Milne Bay Province, Nadya and I head for Port Moresby, the capital. On our final evening in PNG, we get an unexpected text message and a phone number to call.

"My white brother from a white mother!"

John Mariati, the bear-like electrician we met in Vanimo and got to know at Green River.

"Ah, my Black brother from a Black mother! How are you?"

"When I have *buai,* I am well. Now I have plenty *buai.*"

Shame this mellow character couldn't have paddled a stretch of the Sepik with us. I can picture him sitting in the stern, chewing his betel nut dreamily and apologizing for being a sinner. He would have been a reassuring presence and witty company. With Jeffrey Waino, the Green River school principal, John will stick in our memory as a source of inspiration for our voyage. Funny that John's uncle in Tipas was probably the scariest Papuan we encountered.

"So you give tasty biscuit to *pukpuk* and make good friend?"

"We didn't see many *pukpuk,* John. They were hiding in the swamps."

"Too bad, too bad."

I want to tell him it was just as well there were few crocodiles as Councillor Tobius, the big man of Imombi, gobbled up all my pineapple creams, but the call cuts out.

"Take care, my friend," I text. "Remember us to your *tambu.*"

ACKNOWLEDGEMENTS

Tenkyu tru to the people of the mighty Sepik and its waterways, without whose guidance and generosity Nadya and I would not have been able or permitted to canoe from Green River to the Bismarck Sea. *Tenkyu tru* in particular to Jeffrey Waino and John Mariati for helping to launch our voyage, to Fraser and Tolly for patiently shadowing our pontoon raft on the Middle Sepik, and to Cyril Tara and Nick Tumas for taking us to the Blackwater Lakes and to Angoram.

Tenkyu to the villagers who gave up their time to paddle with us, namely Fice, Alex, Tom, and Kingston from Green River Christian Secondary School, Estley and Bilicus from Tipas, Jeffrey and Melwin from Imombi, Anton and Nicodemus from Iniock, and Jamesy and Lee Matthew from Oum Number 1. *Tenkyu* to the Papuans who connected us with others or arranged our stays, especially Yuli in Jayapura, Dorothy in Vanimo, Rayut in Mockwai, John Youpa and Jobby Molnobi in Tipas, Councillor Tobius in Imombi, David in Iniock, Walter and Clifford in Oum Number 1, Gerry and Israel in Ambunti, Robert and Catherine on Yuo Island, Leo Singut and Peter in Pagwi, Mathilda and Collis in Korogo, and Dominique Smari in Govermas. The two guides who led our treks in the Highlands were Paul Riss and Jo Golomb. *Tenkyu tru* to them for keeping us safe and introducing us to the Highland clans and the lesser bird of paradise.

A special thanks goes to my wife Nadya Ladouceur, whose ability to turn strangers into friends made our voyage on the Sepik not only feasible but immensely rewarding. I thank her, too, for devoting hours to reading and rereading the manuscript for this memoir and helping me improve it.

I am also indebted to Mark Anthony Jarman and Khurram Khurshid, two expert editors, for their hours of labour and thoughtful feedback.

I thank Professor Emeritus Bob Cockburn for his research tips, and I thank anthropologist Nicolas Garnier for educating me on Papuan customs and beliefs.

I would like to thank Steve and Barbara Pierce, the only people Nadya and I could find in New Brunswick who had been to PNG, for their sage advice.

I would like to thank the hard-working staff at University of Alberta Press, in particular Michelle Lobkowicz for her enduring faith that a promising manuscript could become a published memoir and to Alan Brownoff for his exceptional graphic work turning a book into a work of art. I wish to thank editor Kirsten Craven for her painstaking attention to details during the copy-editing process.

I am indebted to Arts New Brunswick for its generous creation grant and to travel writer Adam Shoalts for permitting me to use an excerpt from his travel book as an epigraph for my own.

I am grateful to John Ball in Fredericton, New Brunswick, for his unwavering support and friendship. I thank inveterate travellers Ros and Alan Calder in Australia for treating Nadya and me like family. And I thank our own family in England, Norah Robinson-Smith and Patrick Wright, David Robinson-Smith and Samantha Cunningham, and Pauline and Ian Pentland, for their unfaltering encouragement and love.

GLOSSARY

PREDOMINANTLY TOK PISIN

amamas: joy/good wishes
apinun: good afternoon
bagarap: broken
bai: will/shall
baim: buy
bandee: an initiate
big man: village Chief
bikpela: big
bilas: gem
bilong: belong
bilum: shoulder bag
brata: brother
buai: betel nut
em: him
faiv: five
garamut: tree-trunk drum
gat: get
gen: again
gude: hello
gut: good
gutpela: a good fellow
Hamas long?: How much?
hariap: hurry
hat/hotpela: hot
haus: house
haus boi: men's house
haus meri: women's house
haus tambaran: spirit house
hia: here
i: he
iau: aunt
kai: food
kai bar: fast food restaurant
kamap: come
kango: leafy green vegetable
kanu: dugout canoe
kar: car
katim: cut
kaukau: sweet potato
kiap: patrol officer
kisim: take
klok: clock
kokoriam: hello
kumbek: come back
kumin: enter
kundu: hourglass-shaped drum
laikim: like
laua: sister's child
laulau: water apple
liklik: a little
lip: leaf
lo: through
long: to
lukim: look

lukim yu: see you later
luluai: village big man
mi: me
mossai: cinnamon
mumu: earth oven
natnat: mosquito
nau: now
nem: name
nogut: bad
nokem: don't
nuis: new
ol: they
orait: alright
pawa: power
pawpaw: papaya
pay-back: compensation
peles: place
plis: please
prais: price
pukpuk: crocodile
pundaun: fall
raskol: bandit
ren: rain
saksak: sago
saun: egret
seken: lower
sikis: six
sing-sing: festival
skul: school
sori: excuse me
spietim: spit
stopim: stop
sutman: hunter
taim: time
tambu: family relations
tenkyu tru: thank you kindly
tiktik: wild sugar cane
tinpis: tinned fish
tok: talk
Tok Pisin: Pidgin English
tot: pig
trabel: trouble
tshaishi: elder brother's wife
tu: two
tude: today
tumaro: tomorrow
tumas: too
tumbuan: body mask
tumbuna: ancestors
waitman: white man
waitmeri: white woman
waitpela: white person
wan: one
wanem: what
wantaim: with
wantok: clan, kin
was-was: wash
wau: uncle
wawe: eagle
wetim: wait
windo: window
yimbunga: mosquito swat
yu: you
Yu stap gut?: How are you?

FURTHER READING

Allen, Benedict. *Into the Crocodile Nest: A Journey inside New Guinea.* Basingstoke: Pan Macmillan, 1987.

Bateson, Gregory. *Naven.* Redwood City, CA: Stanford University Press, 1958.

Champion, Ivan F. *Across New Guinea from the Fly to the Sepik.* London: Constable & Company, 1966.

Connell, John. *Papua New Guinea: The Struggle for Development.* London: Routledge, 1997.

Connolly, Bob, and Robin Anderson. *First Contact: New Guinea's Highlanders Encounter the Outside World.* New York: Viking, 1987.

Dodwell, Christina. *Travels in Papua New Guinea.* Oxford: Oxford Illustrated, 1983.

Donovan, Michael. *Called from the Fields: The Life of a Missionary in Papua New Guinea.* Self-published, 2018.

Dorney, Sean. *Papua New Guinea: People, Politics, and History since 1975.* Sydney: Random House Australia, 2000.

Douglas, Mary, ed. *Witchcraft Confessions and Accusations.* Abingdon, UK: Routledge, 1970.

Espey, David. "Childhood and Travel Literature." In *Travel Culture: Essays on What Makes Us Go,* edited by Carol Tragnor Williams, 51–58. Westport, MA: Praeger, 1998.

Flanagan, Paul, and Luke Fletcher. *Double or Nothing: The Broken Economic Promises of PNG LNG.* Jubilee Australia Research Centre, Sydney, April 2018.

Flannery, Tim. *Throwim Way Leg: Tree-Kangaroos, Possums, and Penis Gourds.* New York: Grove Press, 2000.

Gewertz, Deborah B. *Sepik River Societies: A Historical Ethnography of the Chambri and Their Neighbors*. New Haven: Yale University Press, 1983.

Hansen, Eric. *Stranger in the Forest: On Foot across Borneo*. New York: Vintage, 2000.

Hides, Jack G. *Through Wildest Papua*. London: Blackie & Son, 1935.

Hurley, Frank. *Pearls and Savages*. New York: G.P. Putnam's Sons, 1924.

Knauft, Bruce M. *Exchanging the Past: A Rainforest World of Before & After*. Chicago: University of Chicago Press, 2002.

Kulick, Don. *A Death in the Forest: How a Language and a Way of Life Came to an End in Papua New Guinea*. Chapel Hill, NC: Algonquin Books, 2019.

Liddle, Kay. *Into the Heart of Papua New Guinea: A Pioneering Mission Adventure*. Auckland: Kay Liddle Trust, 2012.

Lonely Planet. *Papua New Guinea*. London: Lonely Planet, 2016.

Marriot, Edward. *The Lost Tribe: A Harrowing Passage into New Guinea's Heart of Darkness*. New York: Henry Holt, 1997.

Mead, Margaret. *Letters from the Field 1925–1975*. New York: Harper & Row, 1979.

Mead, Margaret. *Sex and Temperament in Three Primitive Societies*. New York: William Morrow, 1935.

Pratt, Thane K., and Bruce M. Beehler. *Birds of New Guinea*. 2nd ed. Princeton Field Guides. Princeton: Princeton University Press, 2015.

Robin, Robert W. "Missionaries in Contemporary Melanesia: Crossroads of Cultural Change." *Journal de Société des Océanistes* 36, no. 69 (1980): 261–278.

Rowley, Charles. *The New Guinea Villager: The Impact of Colonial Rule on Primitive Society and Economy*. New York: Frederick A. Praeger, 1966.

Salak, Kira. *Four Corners: A Journey into the Heart of New Guinea*. New York: National Geographic, 2004.

Schieffelin, Edward I., and Robert Crittenden. *Like People You See in a Dream: First Contact in Six Papuan Societies*. Stanford, CA: Stanford University Press, 1991.

Wagner, Herwig, and Hermann Reich, eds. *The Lutheran Church in Papua New Guinea: The First Hundred Years, 1886–1986*. Adelaide, Australia: Lutheran Publishing House, 1986.

Waiko, John Dademo. *A Short History of Papua New Guinea*. Oxford: Oxford University Press, 1993.

Wetherall, David. *Reluctant Mission: The Anglican Church in Papua New Guinea, 1891–1942*. St. Lucia, Australia: University of Queensland Press, 1977.

Milton Keynes UK
Ingram Content Group UK Ltd.
UKHW040855030724
444933UK00004B/121